Inside Political Campaigns

INSIDE

POLITICAL

CAMPAIGNS

Chronicles—and Lessons—
from the Trenches

EDITED BY

James R. Bowers
Stephen Daniels

LYNNE
RIENNER
PUBLISHERS

BOULDER
LONDON

Published in the United States of America in 2011 by
Lynne Rienner Publishers, Inc.
1800 30th Street, Boulder, Colorado 80301
www.rienner.com

and in the United Kingdom by
Lynne Rienner Publishers, Inc.
3 Henrietta Street, Covent Garden, London WC2E 8LU

Library of Congress Cataloging-in-Publication Data
Bowers, James R.
  Inside political campaigns : chronicles—and lessons—from the trenches /
James R. Bowers and Stephen Daniels.
      p. cm.
  Includes bibliographical references and index.
  ISBN 978-1-58826-755-9 (hardcover : alk. paper)
  ISBN 978-1-58826-779-5 (pbk. : alk. paper)
  1. Political campaigns—United States. 2. Elections—United States.
I. Daniels, Stephen, 1951–   II. Title.
  JK2281.B69   2011
  324.70973—dc22

                                                    2010049164

British Cataloguing in Publication Data
A Cataloguing in Publication record for this book
is available from the British Library.

Printed and bound in the United States of America

The paper used in this publication meets the requirements
of the American National Standard for Permanence of
Paper for Printed Library Materials Z39.48-1992.

5 4 3 2 1

Contents

Preface

Inside Political Campaigns has two simple yet significant purposes: (1) to introduce students and other readers to the varied facets of election campaigns and inform them about how campaigns function in the real world of politics, and (2) to motivate readers toward a greater degree of civic engagement. We reached these goals by having our contributors, who are political scientists and undergraduate political science students, chronicle their direct, active participation in election campaigns. The roles and activities in which our contributors have engaged are many, ranging from volunteer, fund-raiser, research staffer, and campaign manager to candidate. Equally extensive are the types of campaigns in which they have been engaged, including mayoral, city council, state legislative, gubernatorial, congressional, and presidential campaigns. In telling their stories, our contributors vividly bring campaigns to life. Some are stories of victory, and others are stories of defeat. In one form or another, most major aspects of campaigning are covered within this collection.

Through these chronicles, *Inside Political Campaigns* blends the discipline of political science with the practice and art of applied politics. The book is written in the tradition of Richard Fenno's classic methodology of "poking and soaking." But where Fenno remained the detached observer, our book includes poking and soaking by participants. Because it showcases the firsthand experiences of participant political scientists, it is highly instructive about the "dos and don'ts" of campaigning and running for office. (To facilitate the productive use of these chronicles as a learning experience, Chapter 1 discusses ten lessons we believe you should look for as you read. In addition, each chapter begins with a note on the type of campaign presented and a reminder of the lessons to look for.)

This is an action book. Our contributors tell the stories of their campaign experiences in their purest and rawest form. Their chronicles, however, do more than tell good stories—and they are very good stories. They also are accounts prepared by people trained to look at campaigns and elections analytically and critically. In telling their stories, the authors don't mince words, and they are often their own harshest critics. Again, these are stories of both victory and defeat. The unvarnished accounts demystify campaigns and elections by speaking simply and directly, creating a sense that the reader has joined the campaign. In using this innovative approach, we want to do what a traditional textbook cannot—evoke the drama and action of campaigns through the authors' own accounts of their experiences, while still providing important insights and lessons. We encourage readers to enjoy the stories because their engagement is the key to seeing our contributors' insights.

As much as *Inside Political Campaigns* is about action, it is also about advocacy. We see a need to rethink how we and our fellow political scientists study and teach campaigns and elections. The book is part of an evolving argument that a fuller and more complete understanding of these subjects requires us to be more than just Wednesday morning quarterbacks analyzing the tapes of the Tuesday election games. Although core theories such as classic voting behavior and research strategies such as quantitative studies of incumbency or campaign finance are important—even necessary—they are not enough. A fuller and more complete understanding requires actually being there. This suggests a field approach that includes direct participation in teaching and learning and draws upon the qualitative techniques of the ethnographer and the participant observer in research.

Inside Political Campaigns reflects a fundamental belief that the best way to teach about elections and campaigns is to participate in elections and campaigns. We and our contributors are advocating for a science of "practicing what we teach." The study and teaching of campaigns and elections, more so than most other areas in political science, are open to a science of this kind. Our most forceful and intentional advocacy, however, is targeted at our readers. In offering these stories, we want to challenge you, whoever you are—student or worker, Democrat or Republican, liberal or conservative, Libertarian or Green— to get more involved and strive for a greater degree of civic engagement. We challenge you to find the motivation to participate in election campaigns, to go beyond your civic responsibility of voting. However, we also want you to be prepared for what is to come when you do participate. We want you involved, but with your eyes wide open. After you read *Inside Political Campaigns,* we believe you will indeed be prepared to join in.

—*James R. Bowers*
Stephen Daniels

Acknowledgments

One theme found both directly and indirectly in many of the chronicles in this book is the role that chance and opportunity play in campaigns. That *Inside Political Campaigns* ever became a book reflects that same theme. Though we are the editors of record and responsible for the materials presented in the forthcoming pages, Leanne Anderson, our original editor at Lynne Rienner Publishers, deserves credit for the initial idea for the book.

Throughout the project and until her departure, Leanne was a valuable partner. She provided names of potential contributors, many of whom were ultimately invited to join this project. At every step of the way, she proved herself to be an "author's editor," a distinction that anyone who has published in this discipline knows is truly a rarity. Thank you, Leanne!

The departure of an editor at any point before a project is finished can be disturbing and disruptive. Fortunately, that was not the case here. When Leanne departed, Lynne Rienner's excellent staff stepped in to fill her shoes, and we extend our appreciation to them. Claire Vlcek soothed our jittery nerves upon Leanne's departure and helped to maintain Leanne's original vision for this book. Jessica Gribble became our editor once the manuscript was submitted. Jessica ably guided us through the review and revision stages of *Inside Political Campaigns*. Jessica also became a new mother during the time she worked with us. We wish her and her baby daughter nothing but the best. Shena Redmond was our senior project editor, guiding *Inside Political Campaigns* through the production stage, and the book is a better text because of her.

We also extend sincere thanks and appreciation to Lin Mocejunas, who provided irreplaceable and expert secretarial assistance throughout the entire project. She has been a valuable contributor and partner to one of us (Bowers) for twenty-two years, assisting in all of his written projects, including the two books we (Bowers and Daniels) have coauthored.

We are also indebted to our contributors. Anyone who has ever edited a text of original works by scholars or practitioners has at some point in the project screamed (often to his or her publisher), "Never again!" Not so here with *Inside Political Campaigns.* It has been a truly collaborative project, not just between the two editors, but among us and our contributors. From the original long-distance brainstorming sessions about the themes for their contributions, to their responsiveness to our editorial suggestions and revisions, to the nearly four-hour panel and discussion at the 2009 Midwest Political Science Association Meeting, to the collegial friendships that have developed, there has never been an ego in sight. So we thank you. To work with you again (and we hope the opportunity does arise) would indeed be an honor and a pleasure.

Last, we wish to acknowledge the external reviewers for *Inside Political Campaigns,* both those who commented on the original idea and those who read the manuscript. It is a better book because of your feedback, whether we were able to fully implement your recommendations or not.

Inside Political Campaigns

1

Ten Lessons to Look for in Campaign Chronicles

James R. Bowers and Stephen Daniels

Given the fact that you're reading *Inside Political Campaigns,* there's a good chance that you're taking a college political science course on campaigns and elections and your professor has assigned this book as one of the required texts. You may be wondering why. More to the point, you may be asking yourself: "What lessons am I likely to learn from reading *Inside Political Campaigns*?" A great deal, we hope. There are many lessons to be learned from these campaign chronicles ranging from the serious to the absurd. We will discuss some of the specific lessons we want you to look for shortly, but first we want to tell you a bit more about the campaign chronicles that follow.

The campaign chronicles are our and our contributors' firsthand accounts of their own involvement and participation in election campaigns. All of us are political scientists much like your own professor, with the exception of two undergraduate political science students. When you read these chronicles, you will see various kinds of campaign functions through a participant's own eyes. You'll vicariously experience what it's like to be inside many different kinds of campaigns—from presidential to congressional, gubernatorial to mayoral, state legislative to city council, and even a local race for district attorney. The contributors show you how their respective campaigns handled (not always successfully) the kinds of challenges that all campaigns face (and traditional textbooks often discuss): the perils of challenging incumbents, the nuances of fund-raising in presidential campaigns, the effective use of free or earned media, the importance of opposition and candidate research, the nightmares of ballot access and campaigning for third-party candidates, the ways to motivate campaign volunteers (including when the candidate is your own father), the use of negative campaigning, and the importance of planning and strategy. Through these chronicles you will also come to appreciate the idea that despite the differences among the various kinds of elections, there are certain universal truths.

1

We want you to read these campaign chronicles closely and with an eye for detail. They are self-critical stories of defeat as well as victory. In fact, the authors write a lot about losing—the lessons learned from it, how to avoid it, and why you can still lose even when you run well. If you are a political science major or any student sitting in a course on campaigns and elections, you are there because first and foremost you are interested in politics, whether it's because you want to be directly involved in it or want to simply enjoy it as you would any other spectator sport. And don't let the discipline fool you. Politics and campaigns, although important, are sports and they are fun. We actually enjoy this stuff! We appreciate and want to encourage your interest. We understand that you're more inclined to be a political animal than a budding young political scientist. You want real action. You want something you can apply to the "real world"—and in its own way *Inside Political Campaigns* is about political action.

So again the question can be asked: What lessons will you learn by reading *Inside Political Campaigns*? No doubt you will draw some of your own lessons from the chronicles. We're pretty certain that your professor will also point out a number of lessons. Most likely those lessons relate to the larger body of political science or applied literature to which you've been exposed in class. They may also reflect your professor's own experiences if he or she has been active in campaigns. Between the lessons you uncover and those your professor points out, you will have a much better understanding of and appreciation for campaigns after reading *Inside Political Campaigns* than before.

Nevertheless, we'd be remiss in our duty if we didn't take time to preview some key lessons we believe you should look for while reading these campaign chronicles. We've picked ten. Although there is a rough order in these lessons and some are more conducive to a campaign's success than others, you shouldn't regard them as a model that will help predict outcomes or guarantee success. They are simply what they are—ten lessons to consider.

Our purpose in previewing these ten lessons is to help you see the campaign chronicles as more than just the good stories that they are. We want you to also appreciate the chronicles as a series of case studies done by participant observers—participants who are trained to look at campaigns and elections analytically and critically. They are political scientists, and even though they are writing in a distinctly nonacademic way, they do not leave their critical eye behind. Nor should you. Each story makes a useful point or set of points with regard to campaigns. With this in mind, we want you to look at these chronicles collectively and see what you can draw from their deep descriptions of campaigns. But don't go looking for some grand or "unified theory" of campaigns from them. We and our contributors are not sure such a theory can ever exist in a meaningful and useful form. Instead, we want you looking for important patterns, common contextual factors, and shared characteristics that together contribute to a fuller understanding of campaigns.

Lesson 1: *All* Campaigns Are Basically Local Affairs

Some ideas seem trite, a few so much so that we no longer take them seriously. Our first lesson may appear to be such a one, but it is deeply and fundamentally true. The late speaker of the US House of Representatives, Thomas "Tip" O'Neill, regularly proclaimed a lesson learned from his father: "All politics is local." The same can be said about campaigns and elections, and this lesson is evident in each of the campaign chronicles. Vladimir Gutman's "Funding Hillary's 2008 Presidential Campaign" (Chapter 4), for instance, drives this point home through its examination of the decentralized nature of fund-raising even in a presidential campaign. It shows the overwhelming importance of state fund-raising organizations for bringing in the dollars and how those organizations rely on even more decentralized and local networks and contacts. It doesn't get much more local than his description of the problems in getting a Chicago alderman to pay up for a block of tickets to a major Clinton fund-raiser the alderman bought for some of his constituents.

The chronicles about running for Congress by Tari Renner and Richard J. Hardy (Chapters 5 and 9, respectively) also underscore the importance of the local. The Renner campaign's allegation concerning the incumbent congressman's real place of residence reflects the importance of localism and how "of their districts" members of the House are expected to be. Similarly, Hardy's use of his former and current students in key campaign positions and as volunteers highlights another aspect of localism in congressional campaigns—in staffing. And Hardy's chronicle reflects still another aspect of localism for campaign staffing—that ties can be personal ones as well—in the death of Maria Bartlett, a volunteer, in a car accident as she was returning from a campaign errand. This tragic accident will underscore the idea that campaigns are local in terms of emotional space and the intimacy that develops among those involved in a campaign.

Bottom line: All politics is local. Ignore this old cliché at your own peril.

Lesson 2: The Rules and Procedures Under Which Campaigns Operate Matter

Almost everything of consequence in politics takes place within some institutional setting or set of rules—and they matter. There's an old saying in legislative politics that goes something like this: "If you let me control the procedures, I'll beat you on substance every time." Within reason, the same can be said about campaigns and elections. The rules and procedures under which they operate affect everything from ballot access to fund-raising to the number of terms an officeholder may serve and more. Michael Munger's chronicle of running for governor of North Carolina as the Libertarian Party candidate (Chapter 11) is a perfect example. Munger reveals that North Carolina makes it almost impossible for third parties to get their candidates on the ballot. Add to this the rules for candidate debates that only invite "serious candidates," and you can see the effects procedures and rules have on third-party candidates.

Stephen Daniels's "Long-Term Strategy in Local Elections" (Chapter 3) gives another perspective on such "threshold rules"—the rules that govern access to a place on the ballot. Munger's challenge was to get over the high hurdles set in North Carolina to gain his place on the ballot. Similarly, you will read how Daniels's citizen group—the Community Advocates—used threshold rules to keep things off the ballot. Daniels notes that before the Advocates were formed, he successfully used the rule on the appropriate date for filing a referendum request to keep an issue off the ballot. The Advocates successfully used signature requirements to keep another referendum issue off the ballot but failed in a second attempt when that issue reappeared a year later; they and their allies did manage to defeat that issue at the polls. In addition, the Advocates used the rules on the form and wording of a referendum question to force the incumbent mayor to withdraw his "strong mayor" referendum.

In Chapter 12, Aaron Wicks's chronicle of multicandidate mayoral primaries shows that government rules are not the only ones that matter. Endorsements by the major political parties are essential for candidates and their campaigns, and each party—even at the local level—will have its own rules and procedures for determining who will be endorsed and receive the party's support. Wicks's story clarifies the importance of party rules. In Rochester, New York, where his story takes place, Democrats use a weighted vote rule at the county convention in determining who will be the party's designated candidate. It means that not all votes cast are equal. Consequently, a candidate receiving the largest raw vote total can actually lose the designation or nomination because his or her opponent had the greatest weighted vote total. This practice is similar to how the Electoral College operates in presidential elections. As Al Gore found out in the 2000 election, winning the popular vote doesn't win you the presidency. You have to win a clear majority of electoral votes, which are in effect weighted.

Gutman's "Funding Hillary 2008 Presidential Campaign" provides a different kind of example (see Chapter 4). He highlights how the federal campaign finance rules under which candidates for president operate, particularly the individual and corporate limits on contributions, structure fund-raising. Equally important, he explains the importance of loopholes, or what the rules don't say. Gutman's candid discussion of the widespread practice of "bundling"—a foreseeable, yet allowable, way around the federal campaign finance limits—provides a powerful example of the importance of loopholes and how they too can structure campaign fund-raising.

Bottom line: Rules and procedures matter—and they're not necessarily fair.

Lesson 3: Planning, Organization, and Strategy Matter

We selected Chapman Rackaway's and Stephen Daniels's chronicles as Chapters 2 and 3 because both superbly summarize most elements of the chronicles that follow them. Rackaway ties up in a nicely wrapped package how planning and organization are essential to any campaign's success. Planning and organization affect every element of a campaign, from developing walking lists to fund-raising to executing a media strategy. For excellent examples of their nitty-gritty importance, you will only need to look at Gutman's and Kevin Anderson's chapters. In Chapter 4, Gutman explains how the Hillary Clinton campaign organized donors in tiers and worked out the mechanics of phone calling for donations. But perhaps his best illustration of the importance of organization and planning for fund-raising is his description of how the campaign put together and executed a major fund-raising event in Chicago. In Chapter 6, Anderson explains the organization of Bill Clinton's research department in the 1992 presidential campaign. It was divided into two main parts: Opposition Research, which looked for information on the candidate's opponents, and the Arkansas Record, which looked for information to defend the candidate's record as governor. Anderson worked in the latter, and he describes not only how that part of the research department fit into the larger campaign but also how its daily work was organized.

Good planning and organizing can't guarantee a win, but the odds of losing are dramatically increased without them. On this note, we suggest a corollary to Lesson 3: Even well-planned and well-run campaigns lose. One thing you should notice in reading these memoirs is that the candidates involved lost as often as they won. In three chronicles—Hardy (Chapter 9), Renner (Chapter 5), and James R. Bowers (Chapter 10)—in which the candidates are all political scientists, each one loses. Nonetheless, all three campaigns were well planned, well organized, and well run. Why is this so? As Daniels shows in Chapter 3, campaigns play out in a given political context that almost always favors one candidate over another. Renner and Hardy were running against incumbents. Bowers had to contend with quasi-incumbency and race-based politics. All that good planning, organizing, and strategy can do is allow you to maximize the management of political circumstances to the best of your or your candidate's advantage. Daniels also reminds us that planning and organization will not suffice if the campaign lacks a strategy with a clear goal. Good strategy includes a well-communicated narrative that gives voters reasons to vote for candidate Smith rather than candidate Jones. Elections are about the politics of ideas, and the battle can extend beyond a single election. Contemporary grassroots conservatives understand this, as did their movement predecessors. In the 1990s, Newt Gingrich knew it as well. And the Community Advocates in Downers Grove, Illinois, applied this lesson on the local level effectively between 2004 and 2009 to return good government to their town.

Bottom line: Plan well and have a good strategy too!

Lesson 4: Campaigns Are About Taking Advantage of Opportunities

Although it is true that planning, organization, and strategy matter, contingency is ever present. As the once ubiquitous bumper sticker said: "S&*% happens!" Planning, organization, and strategy help a campaign react successfully when the unforeseen event leaves what the bumper sticker refers to. But contingency works in the other direction as well in creating opportunities. Much of what goes on in a campaign involves taking advantage of the opportunities presented to you or that you create.

Several of the campaign chronicles in this book address opportunities surrounding candidates' decisions to run. At the beginning of Chapter 12, Wicks explains how a split within a party can make the party vulnerable to an insurgent candidate like the mayoral candidate for whom he worked. In his chronicle of volunteering in a state legislative campaign (Chapter 7), Michael Smith reveals his own political ambitions and how Missouri's term limits for state legislators served those ambitions. He knew well in advance that the seat he coveted would indeed become empty by a certain date and that he could plan accordingly. Jordan McNamara's chronicle of his father's campaign for district attorney (Chapter 8) presents a similar use of opportunities. McNamara's father became Oneida district attorney by taking advantage of the opportunity created by District Attorney Michael Arcuri's election to Congress and accepting the appointment to finish Arcuri's term. That allowed him to campaign as the incumbent.

In a slight variation on this theme, you will discover in Chapter 10 how Bowers's opponent, Lovely Warren, won a seat on city council when Democratic Party leaders and the mayor "created" an opportunity for her to do so by presenting the current council member from that district with an offer that was too good for him to refuse: Take a well-paying job in City Hall or be faced with a possible three-way primary. Likewise, the "Draft Hardy for Congress" movement discussed in Chapter 9 can be seen as a created opportunity that inclined Hardy to run.

Other chronicles point to other uses of opportunities. In Chapter 5, Renner reveals how a candidate can react when his or her opponent gets caught up in a scandal. There you will learn how the incumbent congressman's engagement to the daughter of a notorious Latin American dictator gave the Renner campaign opportunities to raise much-needed cash and to gain free media attention. Another example is Daniels's explanation of how the Advocates used the "mistakes" of the incumbent mayor to organize a viable opposition and eventually to help defeat him.

Bottom line: "Chance favors the prepared mind" (Louis Pasteur).

Lesson 5: Incumbency, Like Inertia, Is Hard to Overcome

Context matters, and some contextual factors *really* matter. Some might think of campaigns and elections as contests in which each candidate has an equal chance of winning. Although that is true in theory, reality is often quite different. As many of the campaign chronicles make clear, factors such as money or the partisan distribution of the electorate can affect a candidate's chances and may even tilt an election in favor of one candidate over another. Among such factors, incumbency is perhaps the most important in tilting the scales. This lesson squares with the political science literature on the incumbency advantage, and the chronicles provide unique insights into the various ways incumbency conveys advantage.

Incumbency is nearly impossible for challengers to overcome. Renner couldn't overcome his incumbent Republican opponent despite the controversy surrounding the latter's engagement to a notorious dictator's daughter (see Chapter 5). Hardy wasn't able to beat his incumbent Democratic opponent either (see Chapter 9). Yet the Hardy chronicle also suggests that a challenger can at least come close to beating an incumbent.

Bowers's situation was a bit different (see Chapter 10). As you will see, his opponent was a "quasi-incumbent," having been appointed to the City Council only a few months before the primary. Her appointment was intended to bestow the trappings of incumbency upon her. This status, added to other factors such as the role racial politics played in the campaign, increased the nearly insurmountable odds against Bowers winning. His plight underscores the importance of incumbency, even if it is only a quasi-incumbency. It is enough to convey advantage, which motivates politicians, political parties, and campaign strategists to use appointments to tilt the electoral scales. In Chapter 8, McNamara's story reinforces this lesson. As his chronicle makes clear, it didn't hurt his father's electoral chances that he was appointed to fill the office vacated by his predecessor's election to Congress.

Clearly, incumbency is difficult to overcome—at least in a single election. But with perseverance and a good strategy, it may be possible, as Daniels indicates in Chapter 3. Here you will read about the stunning defeat of Downers Grove's two-term and seemingly invincible mayor by a candidate backed by Daniels's citizen group, the Community Advocates.

Bottom line: Inertia describes much in politics, and incumbents are the embodiment of this fact of political life.

Lesson 6: Money Matters, and It Matters Most for Challengers

As Lesson 5 attests, it's very hard for challengers to beat incumbents. But why is it so hard? Money—or the lack of it—is a key part of the answer. To campaign effectively, to be competitive, and to be taken seriously as a candidate by opinion makers, particularly the media, candidates for major office need money and effective fund-raising machines. For Hillary Clinton in 2008, this was particularly true given the fund-raising juggernaut the Obama campaign turned out to be (see Chapter 4). The Obama campaign raised more money than Clinton, and she was left loaning her own campaign millions of dollars as her own credibility as a candidate began to wane.

The lack of money also negatively affected both Hardy's and Renner's campaigns for Congress against their incumbent rivals. Renner was able to ride a short-lived fund-raising bonanza because of the scandal and controversy surrounding his opponent's engagement to the dictator's daughter (see Chapter 5). The bonanza, though, was never enough to overcome the incumbent's greater name recognition, fund-raising prowess, and the Republican-leaning nature of the congressional district in which he was running. Hardy came closer than Renner to defeating his opponent. But raising only one-third as much money as his opponent was one factor that kept him from crossing the finish line as a winner (see Chapter 9).

In Chapter 3, Daniels takes the same lesson down to the local level. The fund-raising skills of the incumbent mayor were significant enough to deter all challengers in his first reelection race: No one could afford to challenge him. More importantly, the mayor's strategy illustrates all too well why incumbency and money can work synergistically to stymie challengers. Incumbents can and do provide favors that benefit those willing and able to contribute to a campaign fund. As the story shows, the mayor's fund-raising apparatus systemically solicited money from businesses, including those that received some kind of benefit from the village government. Challengers can only promise what incumbents have already delivered.

Of course, it isn't the money itself that matters. It is what money buys— paid staff, political consultants, polling, media, and so on. "The Importance of Planning" (Chapter 2) is a good reminder of this. Rackaway points out that in his first campaign as a college intern, staff made many mistakes because the campaign had no resources and therefore could not effectively plan or run as the candidate may have wished. Renner's story in Chapter 5 will further highlight the problem for a campaign when it has insufficient funds to purchase media for the purpose of responding to a negative attack. The Renner camp had exhausted its campaign funds when the incumbent's campaign undertook a media blitz charging that Renner was soft on drugs and favored their legalization. Without the ability to respond with a media buy of its own, the Renner campaign was left employing a free media strategy at the last debate, centering on a "planned blow-up" by Renner to offset the damage of a negative attack.

Bottom line: "*Money, money, money, money. It makes the world go round!*" (*"Money,"* Cabaret). And the political world is no different.

Lesson 7: Campaigns Need Both Earned and Paid Media to Get Out Their Message

It is a truism that any campaign that hopes to be successful has to have a good paid media plan that defines its candidate positively and the opponent negatively. Again, a campaign needs to engage the battle of ideas with a clear, persuasive narrative, such as the Bowers campaign's extensive use of direct mail to define both its candidate and the opponent (see Chapter 10). The Bowers chronicle underscores the need for a structured message that (1) establishes the positives of the favored candidate, (2) undertakes an aggressive comparison of the candidate to the opponent defining the latter in negative terms, and (3) closes the media campaign with a restated positive on the campaign's candidate. Daniels (Chapter 3) shows that interest groups need such plans too.

A good paid media strategy alone, however, is insufficient. To get the message out, campaigns must also earn a certain level of free media. Few campaigns have enough money to buy all the media exposure they need. Free media can fill the gap and provide other benefits as well. Free media can sometimes be better than paid media because it does not come across as fake, self-serving, or simply purchased. It can help in putting the candidate in a positive light while showing the opponent in a negative light. It is much more powerful if a perceived neutral source delivers the message.

But free media cannot be controlled and shaped the way paid media can. The Renner chronicle about media, money, and mud illustrates both sides of free media (see Chapter 5). The media feeding frenzy centering on the incumbent Republican's engagement allowed Renner to have a short-term fund-raising bonanza of his own. It increased his profile and increased his challenger's negatives. The negative earned media for his opponent was, however, a mixed blessing for Renner. The scandal became the only topic most reporters wanted to talk about, thereby hindering Renner's effort to get out his own message.

Campaigns attract free media in other ways than spreading allegations about an opponent. There are, of course, the ubiquitous press releases, as well as events such as rallies; speeches; town hall meetings; and visits to schools, factories, and other places. Events are—or at least should be—carefully planned to convey the right message about the candidate in addition to simply getting exposure. In Chapter 4, Gutman's description of a major fund-raising event provides an excellent example of a planned event as a media opportunity. He describes in detail the planning of the fund-raiser that, among other things, required a room crowded with supporters. A crowded room says a candidate has a lot of energetic supporters, and that, in turn, could attract contributions. Without a crowded room, Gutman notes, a candidate like Clinton would look weak and unpopular, which would deter contributions. Because it was possible that the number of attendees might be less than expected, the staff used a room that could be split into smaller rooms. In other words, if too few attendees appeared to ensure the right image, then the staff could shrink the room to create a more positive image.

Gutman's chronicle also demonstrates how intense the concern over the staging of an event can be because of the media coverage. Free media is useful only if it sends the right message. As Gutman illustrates, even something as seemingly straightforward as where to host a fund-raiser can send the wrong message if a campaign is not careful.

Bottom line: Invisible candidates lose, and media is the key to visibility.

Lesson 8: Minor Parties and Minor Candidates Get Minor Attention

There is another form of "incumbency" that is important in framing the context for campaigns—the incumbency of the two major parties. Just as the privileged position of an incumbent derives from the inertia of the political system, so does the privileged position of the two major parties. In fact, the latter is even more important because it basically defines that inertia. Members of the major parties occupy almost all key policymaking positions, and they make the rules for the political system. Not surprisingly, those who write the rules tend to write them in a way that protects their privileged position. This means that independents, party insurgents, and minor or third-party candidates are at a distinct disadvantage.

Two chronicles—by Munger (Chapter 11) and Wicks (Chapter 12)—illustrate this disadvantaged position. Munger ran as a third-party candidate, and Wicks was a second-tier candidate in a primary with two main competitors. Either way, the outcome is likely to be the same—the candidate gets minor attention and loses. Though Munger in his North Carolina gubernatorial campaign as the Libertarian Party candidate got more media and voter attention than many third-party candidates do, he still suffered in comparison to the Republican and Democratic candidates. For instance, you will read how his minor-party status meant that he wasn't invited to all the gubernatorial debates. In addition, given the structural barriers protecting two-party electoral domination and the low probability that a third-party candidate could win, Munger couldn't attract sufficient financial backing. As a result, he didn't have the resources to effectively increase his visibility. Ultimately, his campaign had no choice but to focus on the goal of drawing enough electoral attention to keep the Libertarian Party on the North Carolina ballot as a legally recognized political party—in other words, keeping the dream alive.

Wicks's chronicle presents a different dilemma: His candidate for mayor was virtually ignored by the media or treated as an afterthought. Even though Wicks's candidate had a strong resume, the two other candidates were seen as the serious contenders by the media because they had more compelling narratives in the local political environment. Wicks's candidate was a twenty-year incumbent city councilman, a long-serving chair of the council's Finance Committee, and the first openly gay elected official in New York State. None of this, however, was a match for the drama unfolding between the other two mayoral contenders. As Wicks points out, one candidate—a black city council member—was the onetime heir apparent who eventually fell out of favor with the retiring mayor, the first African American mayor in Rochester, New York. This candidate also was a staff to and the protégé of a powerful New York state assemblyman, who was widely recognized as the real political boss of Rochester politics. The second candidate was a six-foot-six former police chief with an "aw-shucks" Huck Finn persona who came into the mayoral race after months of speculation he would run and a "staged draft" to convince him to do so. Widely popular and perceived to be more independent and reform-minded than the first candidate, you will read how this cop-turned-candidate rode into the race like Marshal Matt Dillon wearing Ronald Reagan's Teflon coating. As Wicks explains, with this narrative unfolding, his mayoral candidate never had a chance, despite being probably the most talented and qualified of the three. The narrative of the contest between the other two was just too strong, and Tim Mains became an "also-ran."

  Bottom line: The two major parties and their candidates play in the major leagues; everyone else plays in the minors.

Lesson 9: Campaigning Is a Contact Sport, Sometimes Played Dirty

In Chapter 3, Daniels notes that civic pride and good citizenship don't move elections. Self-interest does—people will pursue their interests through a wide variety of rough-and-tumble means. Not all of them are openly discussed in polite company. Call it what you will—negative campaigning, aggressive campaigning, or comparative campaigning—all campaigns do it. Be prepared to respond to it and to do it. Campaigns, after all, are about winning.

  The most obvious example of the rougher side of campaigns is, for lack of a better word, mudslinging. Sometimes mud is slung out in the open as part of a campaign's paid media strategy, as in Chapter 5, in which the incumbent's campaign accused Renner in campaign commercials of wanting to legalize drugs. Renner's own use of the incumbent's engagement to the dictator's daughter can also be seen as illustrating this lesson. Smith's description in his chronicle about using his candidate's opponent's check-kiting conviction against him (see Chapter 7) or Daniels's description of the use of the mayor's campaign fund-raising and spending record (see Chapter 3) provide additional examples. Or for another example (in Chapter 10), take any of the direct mail pieces Bowers describes sending out against his opponent in his 2007 campaign for city council.

However, you will also learn that at times mud is slung below the radar (and below the belt), through the rumor mill, anonymous phone calls, and mailings. Increasingly, mud is now slung anonymously on blogs and websites. In Chapter 10, Bowers shows how supporters of his opponent spread unfounded rumors through African American churches and media blogs. In reading this account, you may even find yourself a bit taken aback at how these off-the-radar attacks portrayed him.

Whether out in the open or off the radar, mudslinging is used for one purpose and one purpose only: to push your campaign narrative and win the battle of ideas by driving up your opponent's negatives among voters. It's part of the contact sport of campaigning. Beyond the few restrictions imposed by the law—and they are few—there are no formal rules for this sport, but there are pragmatic judgments that may impose some limits. Like any contact sport, what kind of hit you make on your opponent matters. Is it a "clean hit" or a "dirty hit"? Does it involve "clean mud" or "dirty mud"? Dirty hits may backfire and hurt you rather than your opponent.

How does a campaign or a candidate distinguish between the two? Unscrupulous candidates, campaign managers, and campaign strategists probably won't. Nonetheless, there is a line that can be drawn. The late Republican strategist Lee Atwater, who orchestrated George H. W. Bush's 1988 election as president, had a simple rule: Is it a fact? If so, it is fair game and can be used. Clearly, it is not a perfect rule, and it is one with which some may not be comfortable. But it's a workable one that allows for the maximum use of information. Does the Atwater rule mean any negative fact can be used against your opponent? That is a matter of judgment, requiring you to balance the relevance of the fact for the campaign and the likely downside or collateral damage. Something may be factually true and in the public record and still backfire.

So mud is a part of campaigns—whether Atwater's rule is followed or not. Though it may be best left unsaid in polite company or in a room full of naïve campaign reformers who want us to follow the advice of the "better angels" in us, mudslinging is a part of the fun of campaigns. It's done because, if it is done well, it works. That's why almost every campaign today tries to employ some kind of rapid-response team. Anderson's chronicle in Chapter 6 about his time on the 1992 Clinton presidential campaign research staff provides a wonderful example. During that campaign, Anderson worked in the Arkansas Record section of the research department. As noted earlier, this part of the campaign was responsible for knowing not only Governor Clinton's government record in Little Rock but also the skeletons in his closet.

Bottom line: It's not about how you play the game—winning really is the only thing.

Lesson 10: Being Prepared to Lose Is Easier Than Being Prepared to Win

This lesson isn't directly addressed in the chronicles you're about to read, but all involved in campaigns in any capacity, especially candidates, need to learn it. The basic lesson here is that despite the emotional turmoil losing can inflict on candidates and their supporters, it is always easier than winning, at least for a candidate running for office for the first time. "No, winning is what counts. It hurts more to lose," you may counter. But think about it. Losing, for first-time candidates, leaves them in no worse position than they were before. They're still who they were before the election began. Yes, there's a letdown, even an anxiousness as they go through the adrenaline withdrawal that comes with the end of the campaign. But most get over it and go back to being professors, accountants, nurses, husbands, mothers, or whatever they were before the campaign began. In short, their lives go back to normal. And they learn a lot along the way, lessons that can be applied in their next campaign.

Now look at winning. Sure, winning is great. It's exhilarating. There's a big election night party and victory speeches. Supporters cheer and cry tears of joy. Candidates hug and are hugged by everyone in sight and are told this win is the start of a great future in politics. But the next day, maybe even late on election night, the hangover kicks in—and that hangover is called governing. At some point shortly after their victory, exuberant candidates are hit and hit hard with a new reality. They now have to govern, and governing and campaigning aren't the same things (despite contemporary politicians trying to make them seem so). Many victorious candidates end up feeling like Robert Redford's character in the classic campaign movie *The Candidate*. His character was recruited to run for a US Senate seat because he was young, idealistic, and photogenic. His handlers felt they could manage and direct him. He wasn't supposed to win. But then his campaign catches on, and he beats the incumbent senator. At the end of the movie, Redford's character is seen sitting in a hotel room with a loud and happy crowd of supporters around him. Over the crowd's noise, he yells out to his campaign manager: "Marvin . . . What do we do now?"

As the movie's ending suggests, it's harder to be prepared for winning. Whether they are willing to admit it or not, candidates elected for the first time to office are generally ignorant about the position they have just won and are not really prepared to govern. Why? Part of the answer is that first-time candidates for any office don't really know the institution to which they have just been elected. Every elected office, be it the executive, legislative, or judicial branch, has its own culture, its own rhythm, its own rituals that need to be learned and internalized in order to be effective. Ideally, "newbies" should learn these things beforehand. But campaigns aren't conducted to learn about the office for which candidates are running. They're organized to win. Any learning about governing is likely to come after winning. The best that can be expected from those newly elected to an office is that they come to their position with a willingness to learn and, hopefully, some parallel experiences that facilitate learning.

A certain degree of ignorance about governing might explain why so many first-time candidates are willing to take the plunge and actually run. They simply don't know what they're in for if they win. It may also help explain, in part, why an officeholder who has left a particular office rarely seeks to run for it again at some later time. Admittedly, a professional politician never wants to look back. Progressive ambition points toward the next bigger and better prize, not that which has already been won. It's the politician's version of "been there, done that." But amateur or citizen politicians also seldom go back to an office they have left. Why? Having served in an office and left it, they know the perils of governing from it. For them, firsthand knowledge of the office may keep them from actually being prepared to win.

Finally, Daniels's story in Chapter 3 provides a related yet sobering message about governing. He explains that the mayor the Community Advocates help to defeat initially won his office and then ran unopposed in his first reelection campaign because of a superior, long-term political strategy. Despite his campaign successes, the mayor proved to be utterly incapable of governing. The mayor's shortcomings were substantial enough to more than cancel out the benefits of his political strategy and eventually led to his stunning defeat at the polls in his second reelection race. This is a reminder that campaigns are indeed about winning elections and not about governing. Success with one does not guarantee success with the other.

Bottom line: "Marvin . . . What do *we do now?"*

Marvin, the campaign manager, never answered this question for the candidate and then senator-elect. However, we can give you an answer as to what we want you to do now: Read, learn, and try to have some fun along the way. Look for and learn the lessons we have noted here, but also look for other lessons as well—lessons the authors of the chronicles suggest and lessons you find on your own.

PART 1
Planning and Strategy

2

The Importance of Planning

Chapman Rackaway

Type of campaign: Various

Role of author: Campaign planner, strategist, campaign manager

Lessons to look for:
- Planning, organization, and strategy matter.
- The "5P Rule": Prior Planning Prevents Poor Performance.
- Planning affects all parts and phases of a campaign: fund-raising, media, opposition research, and relationships within a campaign.
- A good campaigner goes through the same planning process as a good coach.

There's a gospel song titled "It Wasn't Raining When Noah Built the Ark." I've always thought that the song was actually written about my career as a political consultant. If there is any lesson that I learned on the job, it is to plan ahead. If there's any lesson that I can offer from my own political adventures, it is to plan before you act. In politics, as in acting, improvisation is only for the most naturally talented. And if you think you're talented enough to improvise, you're probably not. I didn't realize how much planning I needed to do until it was too late.

I started out in politics by volunteering for some local campaigns my freshman year of college. Like anyone, I suppose, I didn't know what I was doing. I assumed that I would go out and tell the world what I believed about my candidate and that somehow that would be enough. When I was just a cog in the wheel, I did just fine. I was able to deliver yard signs and attend rallies, but I didn't expect that two years later I'd be the communications director for a congressional campaign. Maybe it was the rapid rise up the organizational ranks of a campaign, or maybe it was my own overconfidence, but I was terribly unprepared. And the campaign paid for it. Why? Because I had yet to learn the importance to all campaigns of the "5P Rule."

The 5P Rule stands for Prior Planning Prevents Poor Performance. The 5P Rule applies to almost anything in life, but it's especially true in campaigns. If you look at successful campaigns, you never see the elements of success publicly other than, perhaps at the end of it all, winning. Most successful campaigns, as well as the competitive losing ones, have done an extensive amount of preparation that isn't detectable by the naked eye. No news reports get written about one candidate's direct mail pieces going out earlier than another's or one candidate's more aggressive door-to-door approach. But winning, or the possibility of winning, first takes hold with the five Ps. So you must first learn and understand the rule. That is what the rest of my chapter is about. It begins with the story of how I learned the 5P Rule: the hard way.

A Baptism by Fire

My real campaign education and how to prepare for running one came when I was in college. I was thrust prematurely into leadership in the congressional campaign of Douglas Lee, who in 1992 was running in the Nineteenth Congressional District of Illinois. I was originally brought on to Lee's campaign when my initial college-required political science internship fell apart. I was supposed to be doing very low-level local organizational work for Illinois senator Alan Dixon's reelection campaign. Dixon was, at the time, Illinois's junior US senator, the incumbent, and a moderate, so his renomination and reelection seemed safe. I had no idea when I took the Dixon campaign internship that I wouldn't have it for long. Dixon lost a three-way primary fight and when he lost his Senate seat, I lost my internship. I landed on my feet as a plain-Jane volunteer intern for the Lee campaign. I was quickly promoted to campaign communications coordinator, however, and from there it was baptism by fire. I went from being a cog in a wheel to being one of the busted spokes.

Lee was a first-time candidate, a moderate Republican running for a congressional seat in a district that had been redrawn so as to combine two Democratic seats into one. Lee hoped that the two Democratic incumbents, Congressmen Glenn Poshard and Terry Bruce, would beat each other up so badly during their primary that he could emerge as the winner in November. The Lee campaign also had a challenger in the primary, though he campaigned very little. We squeaked by in the primary but got killed in the general election. What we lacked, across the board, was experience. Lee was a good man, and I was proud to campaign for him. I just wish I wouldn't have had to learn on the job so I could have served his campaign better.

You might ask yourself why I was promoted from intern to a senior campaign staffer so quickly. Was I a gifted politico who adapted to the demands of the job so swiftly that I rose meteorically through the ranks? No. I wish. The reason I got the job and the title was much simpler: There was nobody else around.

There are plenty of opportunities to be a high-level official on a local campaign, and most of those opportunities exist because there are ever-fewer people who are willing to get involved than you might think. If you're the kind of person, like me, who does not automatically reject requests for help on a project, you'll find that you can rise through the ranks in a dramatic fashion, even in a few days. You can move up the structure quickly just by showing up. Therein lies the problem, particularly as it relates to a lack of experience, organization, and planning.

Unlike bureaucracies, corporations, or colleges for that matter, campaign organizations have no set structure. In a local or low-level campaign, you're making it up as you go along. If you have no experience, you're really designing a structure haphazardly. The Lee campaign was definitely guilty of that random approach to organizing. We had no full-time paid staff. We had a campaign manager, the candidate, the candidate's wife, and me. Except for the campaign manager, none of us had ever led a campaign before.

The campaign manager and candidate handled strategy. As a result, the candidate was torn between the administrative tasks the campaign needed and the campaigning activities that should have been the sole focus of our candidate. We should have been able to get enough people into the campaign to let the candidate do nothing but be the public face of our efforts. But with only four people on board, we all took on jobs that were beyond the time we had available, and often our skill set. In my case, I was downright naïve. When the people whose example you need to follow have no idea what they're doing, there's nobody to teach you those things. That was my situation as well. There was no one in the Lee campaign to learn from.

When I signed on to the campaign, I had no idea what a campaign plan was or why it was such a massive mistake not to have one. I just thought, "We need to get moving, right now." So I started handling the day-to-day operations of a campaign without a vision of why we were doing those things or how they all fit together to make a case for our candidate. Lee was a first-timer himself, so he was just as uncertain as the rest of us. Our campaign manager quit halfway through the campaign, so I never got to ask him about our massive mistake. Lee and his wife took over the management of the campaign, and that's when whatever momentum we had started to evaporate.

I let the enthusiasm of the campaign and the rush to just do something carry me along. If a friend asks you to run their campaign, the energy of the moment may inspire you to schedule press conferences and public appearances. Wait! Don't do it immediately. Don't just jump in. Plan things out. A football team doesn't show up without its playbook. A good campaign plan is a prerequisite for any competitive campaign. We didn't have one, and it killed us. For example, our campaign needed money. Every campaign does, but we had nothing. At the time, an effective challenger campaign should have been able to raise a quarter of a million dollars. But I didn't take the time to look at Federal Election Commission (FEC) reports to benchmark my fund-raising goals against other current and previous campaigns. We didn't even have a budget. We'd scramble around and raise enough money to pay for a direct mail piece or newspaper ad. We couldn't raise enough money for ads on television. But even the things we did pay for, we paid for up against deadline, and we just barely made those bills. We never once had enough money ahead of time to commit to things. I went in without any idea of how much money we needed and no sense of steady fund-raising on a schedule. I didn't prepare, and that lack of preparation led to my own poor performance.

We cut corners everywhere. When you're in a hotly contested election, primary or general, you absolutely can't cut corners. For instance, the two-color brochures we used looked amateurish, but we didn't have money for a real four-color brochure. Black-and-white photos done in-house weren't very attractive. Our materials would have looked bad in a college student government campaign, let alone a contest for US Congress. Had I developed a fund-raising plan, scheduled brochure production, and followed through, we could have looked like a professional organization. I wasn't prepared, and so I failed. Instead of carrying momentum forward, we became a joke.

A campaign ought to prepare outreach for selected voters. I didn't prepare for what neighborhoods we would canvass, what households would receive direct mail pieces, and what messages should be directed to those voters. First you have to know who your voters are. The number of people in the district, which ones are registered, what party those voters identify with, and their ages and socioeconomic status all offer valuable insights that a campaign needs. Breaking down the precinct subdivisions within the district, especially with maps, helps even more. You can't convince people to vote for you if don't know who they are. In the Lee campaign, we did little to none of this. We should have taken the time to prepare a voter analysis of our district. Preparation would have allowed us to know what communities were our base, what places to stay away from, and where we could pick up the undecided. Once again our lack of preparation led to haphazard and ineffective campaigning.

When I organized my first door-to-door activities for the campaign, I started with neighborhoods close to campaign headquarters. I was thinking about the convenience of our canvassers, but I'd missed an important consideration: that the neighborhood we were in strongly identified with the other party. Our canvassers got frustrated, we didn't have much success, and our opponent reaped the benefits. Had I any clue about the importance of planning ahead back then, I would have known that there were better neighborhoods in which to spend our time. We should have started with our party's loyalists to get canvassers comfortable and then move on to evenly split precincts where we had the opportunity to pick up the maximum number of votes. Haphazard actions led to a whole lot of wasted energy.

A well-planned campaign also knows its candidate and the opponent. Not the Lee campaign, though. We never did any opposition research. We had nothing to compare our candidate to when we needed to tell the electorate why our candidate was better than our opponent. Knowing the voting records, political positions, and personal traits of your candidate and your opponent guides your strategy in planning a campaign. A well-planned campaign also knows electoral history. One of the best predictors for a candidate, especially one challenging an incumbent, is the performance of previous candidates in the district.

Not learning electoral history was a mistake I corrected in later campaigns. Working on a state representative campaign in the late 1990s, I gathered data on previous challengers in our race. When I dug into the numbers, I saw that some candidates had come close and some hadn't. I immediately contacted the more successful candidates and started getting any information I could. Those candidates had one thing in common: Every one of them campaigned as a moderate, pointing out the extreme voting record of the incumbent. My strategy was made for me. We followed that very game plan, building our message on a consistent record of voting that became contrary to the district's interests, and we won by five points.

After the Lee campaign, my haphazard fund-raising was replaced by careful analysis of FEC data. Previous successful campaigns provided fund-raising benchmarks for my own campaigns, which encouraged me to set monthly fund-raising goals and organize events well in advance of when we needed money. Like Scarlett O'Hara in *Gone with the Wind,* we were never going to be hungry again. I learned how to spread out fund-raising events to provide a steady flow of money into the campaign, ensuring bills were paid and, most importantly, not burning my candidate out on fund-raising. When you're in a panic to raise a lot of money in a short amount of time, the effort becomes exhausting. Ironically, I learned over the course of a lot of campaigns that it's best to have fund-raising be an everyday part of the campaign duties. It's better to do an hour a night than a day every month.

I embarrassed the Lee campaign, too, due to my lack of preparation. I didn't do it intentionally. The National Rifle Association (NRA) is an interest group that normally contributes to members of my candidate's party. Lee asked me if I thought the group would give us money, and I didn't even think about it. When your campaign has raised $2,000 total, the chance to raise up to $5,000 with a single check is just too much of a temptation not to take. I made the call without looking up the fact that Congressman Poshard had a 100 percent voting record with the NRA and was a regular beneficiary of its donations. To this day, I can still remember the sting of the NRA's legislative liaison's laughter in my ears when I asked him for the NRA's support for Lee. If I had researched the group's donation history, I could have avoided that embarrassment. But when you're inexperienced and desperate, you don't think. You just react.

And the mistakes kept piling up. I had no business being in campaign leadership, other than being willing to take on the responsibility. All the necessary skills a campaign operative needs, I lacked. So I had to learn on the job, which

I did. But that on-the-job training probably kept some very good people from being able to hold elective office. Most especially, I could have helped Douglas Lee better. I'll never be able to apologize enough to the campaign for my lack of preparation and organization. Nevertheless, that campaign was my introduction to the importance of the 5P Rule.

Planning Is My Mantra

As my story from the Lee campaign shows, nothing is more damaging to a competitive campaign than jumping in without a plan. Don't believe me? Watch a football game for this lesson. Pay attention to either the head coach or the offensive coordinator, whoever calls the plays in from the sideline. If you don't know football, look for the guy with the massive sheet of laminated paper in his hand. That's your campaign teacher for the day.

Those laminated sheets the coach or coordinator holds are crib sheets from the team's playbook. Each play resembles an activity in a political campaign, and the coaches don't pick those plays randomly. Play selections get made as part of a deliberate process in which the coaches have examined their own strengths and weaknesses, as well as those of the other team. By doing significant planning ahead of time, the coaches do two things: (1) maximize the effectiveness of their team's abilities and (2) allow themselves to react intelligently to game scenarios they didn't plan for. By the end of this process, the teams know exactly what plays they're going to call at what points in the game. For example, a team on third down and short would normally run the ball, unless the team's preparation suggests that the opposing defense has a stout run defense. Then passing plays would be called for.

Why all this talk of football? Because a good campaigner will go through the same planning process as a good coach. A campaign manager and other high-level campaign staffers are a bit like a football coach and his or her coordinators. They figure out what plays to call, adjust strategy, and motivate the personnel to execute plays as well as possible. Every campaign manager/coach needs to have a playbook and a game plan. Campaigners who think they can just walk in and start a campaign are setting themselves up for failure. I know, because I did it that way in the Lee campaign. I had no game plan, and I tried to make it up on my own. I failed.

Campaigns need a ridiculous amount of attention and focus. So as soon as the decision to run is made, it's time to step back a moment. That can be very hard to do. There's an adrenaline rush you get from committing to a run for office. And the worry that opponents might be ahead of you in any aspect of campaigning can impel you to jump into campaign work without planning. I did it myself—I joined the campaign in April with a July primary. We were under the gun, and I immediately started making fund-raising calls, planning events, talking with county party officials. Instead, I should have taken a few days to plan.

Ever since the Lee campaign, planning has been my mantra. It reminds me of the unintended damage my inexperience did to their campaign. My lack of planning sabotaged that first campaign in countless ways. The multiple demands for the same time would lead to bad decisions on where to send the candidate. Sometimes, we'd miss an event entirely. It's a miracle that we even won the primary. We were not so lucky in the general election. When we faced real competition, we collapsed. It's unfortunate that my on-the-job training came at the expense of our campaign. Through the failures, I learned how to plan for events, but more importantly, deadlines. I committed to not making the same mistakes again.

I now make a point, whenever I agree to work on a campaign, of not doing anything public with the campaign for two weeks. Any campaign that brings me on has to commit to roughly two weeks of preparation, and I encourage my students to do exactly the same when they go to work on a campaign. Those two weeks let us write a campaign plan, do our research, and get ready to attack.

Planning and the Media

Campaigns do many complex things. Campaign advertisements, whether in the form of direct mail pieces sent to voters' mailboxes or broadcast ads on television, can be the most complex of all. Like everything else, they must be planned. And direct mail was another one of my failures of (no) planning and learning how to be a successful campaign operative and manager.

Direct mail is the ninja of a campaign: silent, sneaky, and deadly. The biggest advantage of direct mail is that you can get a message to a targeted subset of the population without the opposition getting wind of it. When you run an ad on television, everyone can see it. When the message goes to only specific mailboxes, your opponent may have no idea what you're doing or saying, at least not at first. If the opposition doesn't know what you're saying, they have no way to counter your message. Plus, if you have done your homework and can identify certain characteristics about the voters in your district, you can tailor the message to different people. Voters over age fifty-five can get a senior-friendly message, and people with specific interests can get messages that resonate with them. So even though many first-time campaigners write off direct mail, there's no campaign that should go without the straight-to-mailbox effort.

Direct mail is also a lot cheaper than television. Since we had to do everything in the Lee campaign on the cheap, we went with direct mail. It was one of the smarter ideas we had. Too bad, then, that we didn't do it right. Direct mail pieces might seem simple, but they require plenty of advance work. Photographs have to be taken. Text must be laid out. The size of the piece must be chosen, as well as the color scheme: a four-color piece looks much better than anything else. Paper stock has to be selected. The target population of voters has to be chosen. Once all those decisions are made, you send proofs to a printer, who will make a print-ready copy to edit. Then an exhaustive check of spelling, accuracy, and visual appeal has to be done. After the edit, the proofs have to go back to the printer for production. Already, you've invested about ten days. Then the mailing database has to be collected, although that's easier today than it was in the early 1990s. Finally, the pieces have to be bulk-mailed, and the postal service has its own built-in lag time. Total time from collecting the materials to a direct mail piece arriving in mailboxes can be as long as a month.

In the Lee campaign, we learned about planning direct mail the hard way. To close our campaign, we decided to send out five thousand postcards promoting our candidacy to targeted Republican primary voters. Our piece was a good one, using an effective layout to emphasize the strengths of our candidate. It looked good, but it was ineffective because it arrived at voters' mailboxes two days after the primary. Why? Because I didn't get times from printers or research the post office's delivery schedule. I didn't prepare. Adding to the frustration was the fact that our primary opponent didn't do any publicity at all, so having that piece out in time would have likely made our victory even stronger and positioned us better for the general campaign. All that time and money were wasted because of my inexperience and our poor planning. We won the primary, but by less than five points. We could have lost. Had we been a few points behind, we would have looked at the direct mail failure as the reason we lost. We got lucky, but we shouldn't have. The failure showed we weren't ready for prime time.

Planning and Opposition Research

The Lee campaign had a golden opportunity, and we blew it because of a lack of research and preparation. Remember, we didn't do any opposition research on our opponent, Congressman Glenn Poshard. We should have. Poshard had finished a Ph.D. at Southern Illinois University a few years before. We had heard rumors that Poshard had plagiarized part of his dissertation, but we never sought proof. I had no idea how to do that kind of investigation; none of us did. Had we known what we were doing and had the time to do our research in 1992, we could have found the same information that was uncovered in 2007, that Poshard had in fact plagiarized significant portions of his dissertation. Fraud is something that voters ought to know about—we had an obligation to inform the public about the ethical problems of their congressman, and we were derelict in our duty. A little research would have helped in any number of ways.

Research is a vital part of planning. I worked for a campaign that didn't have the money to poll, but we did hear from many constituents that our incumbent opponent voted against a Pledge of Allegiance bill they supported. The bill was largely symbolic, but it would have allowed the Pledge of Allegiance to be said at the beginning of school days. Knowing we had an issue that people, especially Republicans, were passionate about, we distributed a direct mail piece on the Pledge of Allegiance. A two-thousand-piece run was enough to increase our support 5 percent. All thanks to preparation.

There is always the possibility that the candidate will not want to attack his or her opponent. In future campaigns I never again missed opportunities like the one with Glenn Poshard. If I could get out verifiable information that called our opponent's voting record or professional behavior into question, I would do it. However, some candidates for whom I worked refused to go down that road despite the costs of not doing so. One candidate for office was absolutely opposed to anything other than boosting his own name recognition and positives. When I managed his campaign for state representative, he made it very clear to me that he did not want to engage in any comparisons with the opponent. We built a campaign that focused on who the candidate was, but that was only half the battle. Our opponent made questionable claims about her own experience and fitness for office—and we never challenged her. To this day, I don't know if she deserved credit for the successful community activities she claimed. We heard rumors that our opponent took credit for work that other people did. Every time I discussed that in a call with someone who knew the real story, my candidate told me to give it up. My candidate thought that he would be able to claim the moral imperative to govern only if he never said anything negative about our opponent. In theory, that's wonderful. But it never really works in practice, and by not planning for or doing opposition research, we took an important weapon out of our campaign arsenal and decreased our chances of winning.

Near the end of the campaign, I spoke with a resident of the district who said that he really appreciated the positive tone of our campaign. Assuming he was one of our supporters, I thanked him and asked him to vote for my candidate. After all, you can't expect people to vote for you unless you ask for their vote. I was shocked when he said that he considered himself a member of the other party and he had no reason to switch parties in this election. At that moment, I realized we needed to make the case in our favor and against the other candidate. Our party was in the minority in the district, so we had to convince loyal members of the other party that our opponent didn't represent their views well enough.

We knew enough to be concerned about her fitness for office, but we were constrained by our candidate's refusal to go negative in the campaign. I knew we should have dug for more information; I knew we should have attacked. I let my candidate make the final decision, and I failed my candidate by not making the case for a comparative campaign well enough. And just like the Lee campaign, we lost. In fact, we lost big, by almost twenty points. We could have narrowed that gap and maybe even overcome it entirely to win, but to do that we had to put doubt in people's minds about our opponent. We let her control the agenda: the campaign was dominated by her strategy, and she won. My ultimate adage, the one certain truth I pass on to my students in campaign management classes today, is this: "To win, you must give people reason to vote for your candidate and against your opponent."

You have to do both. A campaign that just attacks its opponent never convinces people that their candidate is the better option. Just saying your opponent is bad without emphasizing the good things about your candidate may encourage people to leave the ballot blank or not vote at all. And campaigns that only tout the good things about their candidate will do nothing more than get their loyal base to support them. If you're managing the campaign of a popular multiterm incumbent with weak opposition, then that strategy may work. Most of the time, though, you're going to work for a challenger who starts twenty or more points down. If you don't give those supporters of your opponent reason to switch, you're going to lose no matter how high-minded and positive your campaign stays.

Planning and Managing Relationships in a Campaign

The Lee campaign schooled me in the 5P Rule quickly. Another lesson took longer. All my planning lessons dealt with strategy and doing the work of a campaign. But campaigns are also an intensely personal affair, and campaign managers must be able to work with people. More to the point, they have to manage people well and be able to navigate the delicate interpersonal relationships among campaign staffers and volunteers. I absorbed this lesson during another state representative campaign. I was lucky—at least at first—to have a couple of teenage volunteers. The two of them were dating, though, which became a problem. My two young lovers would do everything together, including volunteer for us. When they volunteered, they were remarkably effective. They would stuff envelopes, enthusiastically walk the district and go door-to-door, and make phone calls. If I had go-to volunteers, they were the ones. When they broke up, though, I didn't think much of it. They came to volunteer separately, until one day when I needed the two of them.

The young man arrived earlier than his ex. When she arrived, the tension in the room was thick. We managed to keep them apart until it was time to phone bank. I had established a call center with ten phones at our headquarters, and I needed every phone staffed. While we had everyone in one room making calls, they stared daggers at each other until one of them had enough, and words were exchanged. I don't remember who started it or what was said. I'll never forget the aftermath, though. Their voices got louder. Eventually, they let their animosity get the best of them, and they yelled at each other while in the phone bank room. The other volunteers were still making calls, and one of the shouters still had his line open. Their anger undermined our ability to call voters and get the message out. There were some callers who got complaints from our target voters that they couldn't hear us over the shouting. No matter how much we needed them, I should not have had those two people in the same room working on a common project at the same time. Another lesson in personnel management learned.

I was in a tough spot. I either had to eliminate both of them from the campaign or make damn sure they never entered campaign headquarters again at the same time. I was so burned out by their fight that I chose not to have either of them participate in any campaign events again. We didn't lose the election because we didn't have those two volunteering, but we certainly made things harder on ourselves, given what good volunteers they were before they broke up.

Managing brokenhearted teenage volunteers was relatively minor compared to dealing with a candidate's spouse. My first campaign debacle was a perfect storm, with a cavalcade of traps and problems that campaign managers might have to go their entire career to learn. I got them all in eight months. There has been, I'm sure, no greater lesson than my dealing with candidate spouses. Most candidates are married, meaning we all have to deal with candidate spouses when we're working on a campaign. Some candidate spouses are wonderful, helpful people. Some no-hoper candidates even have their spouses manage their campaigns. Almost every time a spouse manages a campaign, it's a recipe for disaster. Spouses are simply too close to the candidate to be objective. The spouse-manager doesn't help a lot and hurts a bit. But there are some spouses who hurt a lot. They are liabilities to a campaign, not assets.

The first time I managed a campaign from start to finish, the candidate's spouse was a real handful. She was a negative person at her core, argumentative and difficult. I was still a young man, inexperienced, and I think, looking back, that I believed everyone would just magically get along and do the work of the campaign. I never once thought that our biggest enemy would come from within. The campaign staff never knew if she would merely second-guess our decisions or outright yell at us. Once, in front of the entire staff, I got yelled at for getting lunch. You run out to get a sandwich, and the next thing you know you're the target of a tirade so nasty that Simon Cowell from *American Idol* wouldn't dare utter it. The other high-level campaign personnel and the candidate were all in the room. She called me an idiot, said that I wasn't committed to the campaign. She called me lazy. She called me other things that comedians refer to as "working blue." In other words, she cursed. Repeatedly. The effect of her rant was to undermine my authority and create a wedge between me and the candidate. When I would have a disagreement with the spouse, no matter what the topic, the candidate would side with his spouse rather than with me and the campaign staff. As a result, the staff learned either to defer to the spouse regardless of whether we thought she was right or to try to do things without notifying her. Being led around by the spouse, who had no political experience to speak of, meant we were constantly shifting our message and looked unprofessional. Some potential supporters told me in confidence (which is why

I will not reveal the name of this candidate) that she was the reason they did not contribute to or support the campaign. Many people liked my candidate but couldn't stand his spouse. When the spouse makes it a package deal, you have to develop a strategy to deal with that person. We worked in constant tension because of one very important member of the candidate's family. I will not say that we lost the campaign because of the candidate's spouse, but she certainly didn't help.

A spouse or a partner should be a valued component of the campaign. Spouses should be willing to help and defer to the staff. But sometimes it's up to the campaign manager to step in and establish boundaries between the candidate's spouse and the leadership of the day-to-day campaign. Campaign managers have to know that they are not just responsible to the candidate but the candidate's spouse. Establishing good relationships with the candidate's spouse is important. Again, like the teenagers run amok in my earlier example, one absolutely vital skill for a campaign manager is understanding how to work with the personnel, no matter what difficulties they might present.

As a result, I have a regular practice when I run a campaign—I meet first with the candidate and then separately with the candidate's spouse. The spouse is too close to the candidate, so there are two bits of information I need to learn from the candidate before I meet with his or her spouse: First, the candidate must let me know what kind of role his spouse will play in the campaign (if any); and, second, I want the candidate to let me know anything that he or she does not want the spouse to know. If there is a scandal in the candidate's past, the spouse should hear it from the candidate, not from the campaign manager or (even worse) in the newspaper. A spouse that will cooperate with the campaign and play an appropriate role is a wonderful asset to a campaign. A spouse that undermines the work of the campaign, though, can be destructive.

Planning, Fund-Raising, and Working the Phones

The 5P Rule has also helped me overcome one of my greatest fears going into the Lee campaign: asking for money or support over the phone. One truth of campaigning that I learned over time is never to be afraid to ask for money. In my fraternity training to recruit new members, I was asked by a national recruitment specialist, "Do you know why 90 percent of men don't join fraternities?" I answered no, and he told me, "Because they aren't asked." The same attitude holds true whether you're asking young men to join a fraternity, asking a potential donor to contribute to your campaign, or soliciting voters to cast a ballot for a candidate. You have to ask for money to get it, because nobody contributes or votes for someone unless they're asked. In fact, I've learned that some people even appreciate being asked to provide some form of support. But if you aren't ready to ask, you'll never get to find out.

My first attempt at campaign fund-raising occurred at the Lees' home, which was our campaign headquarters. Lee's wife met me in their downstairs apartment, so that I wouldn't be distracted by other campaign work going on. She handed me a list of people—the source of which I never quite knew—and told me that they were big potential donors. But I was given absolutely no preparation or training. With no preparation whatsoever, no script, and little knowledge of my candidate's position on many issues, I was supposed to extract money from the people I called. I was scared witless at the idea of calling people and asking them to donate money. Who was I to be making these calls? What if they said no? Could I live with the rejection and the shame? Those thoughts paralyzed me at first. Despite no experience, no training, and with much trepidation, somehow I had to turn that list into money.

I sat in the chair for half an hour, staring at the phone, trying to make sense of what I was about to do. I grappled with that unnamed fear all of us face whenever we ask for something important. I had asked people for money before, as a student on behalf of my university's alumni fund-raising efforts, but then I had a script. My university put every caller through a brief training session. That half hour was better than nothing, but afterward I was still nervous about calling our alumni. The people I was about to call for the Lee campaign were successful people in the community. The prospect of embarrassing myself to those leaders intimidated me, a young man of nineteen years. I still don't remember how I got through it, but I did. I called the names on that list. Not a single person gave money to the campaign. But the gradual beating of fear out of me had begun. I heard "no" a lot, but nobody yelled at me. Some were very firm, but they were polite. Maybe the politeness of the "nos" was enough to let me know that the world was not ending and nobody was offended that I was asking for money. Yet for years after, I still had the fear. Receiving a list and a phone still gave me a feeling of impending doom.

Later in the campaign, I joined other campaign staffers and volunteers on a phone bank. We were asking the voters in the district to go out and cast their ballots in favor of Lee. When I sat in front of that bank of phones, I felt the same fear I did when I was dialing for dollars. Maybe the fear of asking for support has to be beaten out of you, or drained out of you slowly. There's a natural human predisposition against asking people for anything over the phone. Telemarketers have made it even worse, giving those who call for any kind of support on the phone a bad reputation. Curiously enough, an event unrelated to politics helped cure my fear. I participated in Millikin University's alumni fund-raising phone drive during my years as an undergraduate there, and once while shopping I ran into someone I had called for a donation. The person was instead very pleasant. When I realized that my life would be unaffected by asking people for campaign donations and voting support, I eased up a bit. I knew I could ask for money and that I wouldn't be treated as evil.

I'm still not very good at asking for money, or at least I'm not very effective. I've done it many times now, and I don't normally get much. But now when I make calls, I'm unafraid. I credit that lack of fear to the regular rejection my pleas for money receive. One of the best ways to get over your fear of soliciting campaign contributions is to do it and get used to the rejection. Many, in fact most, recipients of fund-raising phone calls will tell you no. The more you hear "no" from people you call, the more you get used to it and the easier it gets to deal with it.

In addition, the 5P Rule can help more. Over time, I developed a packet of information any caller in a campaign could use. Two election cycles after my first failures, I had prepared a solid body of work to get the fear out of my callers. In 1996, when I was a running a state representative campaign for Tom O'Sullivan, I had script for fund-raising. A basic script does wonders for effective dialing. Getting people over their fear can be accomplished with some role-playing—and my university experience told me that it took only about a half hour to get people ready. Once again, preparation became my mantra. In the next election cycle, I had volunteers read the script with me in front of other volunteers. I played the role of receptive supporter, fence-sitter, and opponent. My goal was to ensure that volunteers never encountered a caller who was worse than the character I played in our skits. Volunteers might have felt trepidation at first, but a little bit of preparation did wonders for our efforts.

In preparing volunteers for calling, I tried to make the effort fun and to increase their confidence. If you are running a campaign, you will have to train volunteers to ask for money or a vote. The manager must be able to allay their fears by being comfortable with the idea of fund-raising. A campaign manager who displays the attitude, "Well, making phone calls isn't fun, but we have to do it," won't motivate his volunteers well. Being enthusiastic and positive about the calls, and participating in the training as a leader, are necessary to make volunteers effective at soliciting campaign support.

Sometimes it's the people you least expect will be nervous about fund-raising that you have to manage the most. During another campaign in 1996, with a bit of fund-raising experience under my belt, I told my candidate that it was time for him to pick up the phone and make calls to potential big-money donors. I'd never been on a campaign where the candidate had not done fund-raising himself before. One candidate, though, was more scared than I had ever been about fund-raising calls. The people we needed my candidate to call were people he knew well from his business connections in the district. Still, he did not want to make calls.

Of all the people you shouldn't have to motivate in a campaign, your candidate is at the top of the list. Sometimes, though, you have to get the candidate over his or her own fears. Role-playing and scripts, again, make the difference. Practice and preparation make things much easier. After my candidate practiced making phone calls with me, while I played a receptive donor, a persuadable donor, and then a combative nondonor, he got over his fears.

Fund-raising doesn't just happen on cold calls, though. Mail solicitation is also part of the process, and that takes planning too. When I started writing fund-raising letters for campaigns, I would never ask for specific amounts of money. I would include a letter, a response form, and a return envelope. I wasn't doing enough. By my second campaign in 1994, I was including a listing of suggested amounts, from $25 to $1,000. When I started graduate school at University of Missouri, I met former congressional candidate Rick Hardy, and he showed me how to make it easier to get donations in larger amounts. Rick's campaign for Congress set up a three-tiered fund-raising group of "clubs." You can name those levels however you wish: some of us use Red, White, and Blue; others use Bronze, Gold, and Silver. Either way, people respond to status, and giving a fund-raising effort a designation allows people to feel they have a higher status. Simple fixes like asking for specific amounts of money increased my success.

As my fund-raising efforts, phone calling, and mail solicitations became more effective, I noticed that some people enjoyed being approached about political contributions. Status can be extended to people in many ways, but one of the biggest ways to appeal to ego is to tell someone that they are a big shot. As I wrote more scripts for fund-raising, I became a bit more forward about complimenting the potential donor and casting the fund-raising request as a symbol of that person's status in the community, by hinting that only a real leader in the community would be interested in donating. That angle works with many people. Letting someone think that their donation is a special thing is a very effective method of boosting fund-raising.

Conclusion

Whether it's managing people, asking for money, or writing up a campaign plan, the real work of a campaign is done behind the scenes, often before anyone even knows who the candidate is or what office he or she is running for. Campaigning is like driving a car—you can just jump in and try it, but you're likely to cause a big crash. Practice, planning, and preparation are absolutely necessary if a campaign is going to be successful. There is no substitute for preparation. Most of the failures I have experienced in my campaigning have resulted from a lack of preparation. I have always benefitted from thinking ahead, whether about strategy, direct mailing campaign pieces, targeting voters, or managing people. In 1998, working for Patrick Henry's state representative campaign, I convened a "kitchen cabinet" of close friends and advisers with the candidate. That evening we brainstormed, planned the campaign, and set a process in place that would turn a first-time candidate with seemingly no hope into a contender. The Henry campaign was really the culmination of a lot of experience for me. For the Henry campaign, we had a playbook. Then we just went out and executed. I wish I could say we won, but when you take on incumbents, it's rare that you will win. We took solace in the fact that we were competitive, and having a plan helped our competitiveness. So I shall end as I began, by shouting my mantra one more time: Prior Planning Prevents Poor Performance. The 5P Rule is the triumph of reasoned planning over the rush of excitement that comes with a campaign. To campaign well, take the time to plan. It worked for me. So learn from my experience, the 5P Rule, or that old gospel song, because you don't want to build your ark after it's started raining. At best you're soaking wet, and at worst, you'll drown.

3

Long-Term Strategy in Local Elections

Stephen Daniels

Type of campaign: Mayoral, city council, ballot measure (general)

Role of author: Campaign planner, strategist

Lessons to look for:
- The rules and procedures under which campaigns operate matter.
- Planning, organization, and strategy matter.
- Campaigns are about taking advantage of opportunities.
- Incumbency, like inertia, is hard to overcome (but not impossible).
- Campaigns need both free and paid media to get their message out.
- Campaigning is a contact sport, sometimes played dirty.

Unlike the others writing in this collection, my life as a political scientist is not focused on campaigns and elections. Rather, I study law and politics. My reasons for political involvement are similar to those of the people with whom I have worked on various campaigns in my town—Downers Grove, Illinois, a Chicago suburb. We're interested in the quality of life in our community, good government, and so on. In the world of politics, people like us are referred to derogatorily as "goo-goos"—do-gooders who make a lot of noise but are seldom effective because of their political naïveté. As will become clear, although we may be "goo-goos," we see ourselves as "goo-goos" with an aggressive, pragmatic edge, and it has helped us to have some degree of success influencing elections in our town.

Most of what I've learned about campaigns and elections has been learned on the ground as a local officeholder, community activist, and head of a local citizens' group. This chapter chronicles that group's origins and key activities, and in so doing it reveals what we learned in the process and how we used that knowledge. Most immediately, it's a story of small town politics and how a community group can influence local elections. More generally, it's also a story of the importance of strategy for achieving success in the contingent world of politics—a world populated by a very interesting array of players.

There is one piece from my training in political science that I find increasingly useful and regularly reread—*The Prince,* by Niccolo Machiavelli. It's not a contemporary blueprint by any means, but it teaches about strategic action and how it must react to varying real world contexts over the long term. It is empirical, unsentimental, and pragmatic, and the work's insights into human nature and human failings always illuminate the context in which I play politics. At times, however, Jimmy Breslin's comic and now classic 1969 novel about New York City mobsters—*The Gang That Couldn't Shoot Straight*—may be more apt in trying to understand some of my group's political opponents and in charting a strategy to defeat them.

The Importance of Strategy

Decisions made on election day are powerful opportunities for achieving a wide variety of goals in the political system. Because self-interest drives elections, those goals may be virtuous or nefarious—it makes no difference. Elections are just a means to an end. In other words, they are a part of a strategy. Most simply, strategy is defined as a directed plan of action for achieving a goal or set of goals. As a result, strategies are usually judged by their degree of success rather than their normative virtue. And a good strategy is needed in an election. Otherwise, you lose.

Campaign organizations are the most visible manifestation of strategy when talking about elections. They are focused and easily observable as the formalized and structured version of a strategy. Strategy needs organization to coordinate and direct the parts, keep them on target, and make adjustments as the situation changes. Those three goals matter because strategies always play out in fluid environments—nothing is certain or predictable. Although a well-run campaign is necessary, it is not sufficient to reach a goal, and it is not the entirety of strategy. Strategy is broader than just the nuts and bolts of organizing and running a campaign. It is also about the goal animating that campaign, which may have a public face and a private reality—what is presented to the public and what the candidate really is after. Strategy is about articulating the substance of the public face and, if need be, shielding the private reality. A campaign is unlikely to be successful if it can't show why someone should vote for candidate X and not candidate Y.

In short, strategy is also about the politics of ideas and creating a narrative that defines the terms of debate for an election. Elections aren't just about competing candidates (or yes or no votes on a referendum). They are also about competing narratives—competing visions of the present (and the existence of problems or threats) and competing visions of the future (and possible solutions). The involvement of interested parties—like my citizens' group—can complicate the competition over narrative. An interested party may act in concert with one side or the other, or it may have different goals and try to turn the direction of the election's narrative. In our town my group is a repeat player wanting to drive the narrative over a series of elections and win the battle of ideas.

Even though my focus will be on strategy, I would be remiss if I did not again emphasize the importance and need for a well-run organization. Key members within my group make sure it is a well-run organization and that tasks are completed—and completed well. They take care of the finances; the scheduling; the design and placement of press releases, advertisements, and mailings; the website; and many other matters. Without them any strategy would be futile.

Context Is Everything

I ran for village council in 2001. The reason was a change for the worse in the town's administration and a concomitant change in the local political culture. In 1999, a well-respected mayor retired from office, and in the subsequent election a sitting village council member, who was her protégé, was defeated for the office. The victor was a younger candidate who grew up in town, was a star high school athlete, and became the chair of the township Republican Party organization. He was then and still is a politician with ambitions for higher office (especially one that pays a salary). In line with his ambitions, the new mayor's plans for our town were at times grandiose, expensive, and poorly thought out. Additionally, his way of doing business contrasted sharply to his predecessor's. Even today, many describe it as that of a schoolyard bully. In running for village council, my intent was to offer an alternative to some of the new mayor's plans and his way of doing business. I lost.

In retrospect, my goal was too narrow and my campaign strategy gave too little attention to the changing political culture. It's one thing to say your candidacy offers an alternative to the new crowd and their way of doing business and another to actually structure your strategy in ways that recognize the way things are actually working with the new crowd. A strategy based on the kind of political environment you want to see is not the same as one based on the environment as it presently exists. Again, strategies are not about virtue; they're about winning.

The new mayor operated on the basis of a strategy more politically sophisticated than seen in the recent past. It stretched beyond a single election and included a variety of ongoing, nonelectoral tactics. My strategy failed to adequately take this changed political context into account, but I learned some important lessons from that failure. And, it is important to note that these are not lessons I learned alone. They are lessons learned among a group who shared a concern for the future of our community.

Two key things changed when this mayor came to power. The first involves hard-nosed partisanship. Many local elections in Illinois—meaning town councils, school boards, and the like—are formally nonpartisan elections. Once in a while, things actually work that way. As a more general rule, one is better advised to assume that there is no such thing as a truly nonpartisan election. That became especially clear in the mayor's initial victory in 1999.

My town is located in a solidly Republican county. Like his predecessor, the mayor is a staunch Republican, but unlike his predecessor, his involvement in community affairs is driven by his long-term partisan interests and personal ambitions. The previous mayor, in contrast, left partisan concerns and personal ambitions aside when it came to community affairs (since retiring from office, she has become a leader in the local chapter of the League of Women Voters). The new mayor was, at the time of his election, and still is, the head of the township Republican Party organization and controls its resources, especially most of the precinct captains. He has the support of a number of regional Republican officeholders, and he never leaves partisan concerns aside.

The policy of the local Republican Party organization under the new mayor's leadership was to work at placing only loyal Republicans on nonpartisan municipal bodies whenever possible and to work against anyone considered to be a Democrat or an insufficiently loyal Republican (loyalty defined as fealty to the mayor). The local Democratic organization, such as it is, specifically eschewed such involvement in nonpartisan elections. The mayor and his supporters tolerated no rivals and went after them—sometimes viciously (and even their family members or business partners). There are stories, but for some of us it is a matter of personal experience. Such rough treatment had the desired deterrent effect: Many people were unwilling to publicly criticize the mayor.

In short, the mayor brought to the community a rougher, no-holds-barred approach to everything political. At the extreme, some of the mayor's supporters even used the police to harass opponents or subject opponents to public ridicule by using the public comment time during the televised village council meetings (the comment time, of course, is controlled by the mayor). These tactics reminded many people of the thuggish town politics in Cicero, Illinois (a former mayor was recently released from federal prison). Originally, the comparison was made in jest as a piece of dark humor, but this changed when the mayor hired a political consulting firm run by a Republican operative with ties to the Cicero political establishment.

The hiring of a high-profile, partisan political consultant represents the second key indicator of change in the local political culture—for lack of a better term, the modernization of politics in our town. Local politics was now being tied to the larger arena of Illinois partisan politics and the ways in which those politics are played. A key part of this is money and what it can buy. In the eyes of many residents, "pay-to-play"—the scourge of Illinois politics—came to town. Before, campaigns and fund-raising typically went into hibernation between elections, but the mayor's campaign never slept. Now fund-raising, particularly for the Republican Party, was an ongoing affair, and the prime vehicle has become an annual golf tournament. During his tenure, it was superbly organized by the new mayor's operatives with meticulous record keeping on who "participated" each year and to what degree. Those interested in doing business with the town and those with businesses in town were asked to contribute to the tournament's success—perhaps by sponsoring a hole or paying for refreshments or providing some other kind of support. There were prizes of various kinds, but the event is planned so that at the end of the day there was a substantial amount left to benefit the mayor's campaign fund. Of course, if golf isn't your game, you could simply write a check to the mayor's campaign fund anytime it seemed appropriate or was suggested.

Clearly, the political big dogs had moved in. Before, local nonpartisan elections tended to be inexpensive affairs with candidates spending in the low thousands. Campaigns were organized and run by friends and neighbors around someone's kitchen table with a meager budget of funds collected in small amounts from people in town during the campaign. It was relatively easy for someone to enter a race, and undue influence or reward as a result of large campaign contributions was not an issue. With the new political reality, entering a race became much harder and much more expensive.

The escalation in campaign spending says it all. Public records show that the mayor's initial 1999 campaign spent over $40,000 and his opponent just under $20,000. In comparison, the mayor's predecessor spent approximately $4,600 in her initial election campaign for mayor in 1991, and spent less than $3,000 in her 1995 reelection campaign. In the 2007 election, when the mayor was finally voted out of office (as I said, the "goo-goos" have had some success), his campaign spent over $75,000. The successful candidate spent just over $50,000. The new importance of money and the mayor's ability to raise it clearly stood as a major deterrent to a would-be challenger. And the mayor and his supporters also made it difficult for rivals to raise money. There is no better illustration of the challenger's disadvantage than the fact that the mayor ran unopposed for reelection in 2003.

If money was not a sufficient deterrent, then you also had to take into consideration the mayor's other resources. While you're trying to put a campaign together, the mayor had an ongoing political organization at his service. And even if the mayor's organizational resources were not enough to deter you, there were the likely personal costs. There was always the question of how much one was willing to tolerate in terms of threats and harassment (to family members too) from the mayor's supporters. In all respects of the term, these two factors—

organized, hard-nosed partisanship and money—kept the price of challenging the mayor very high. It wasn't just that the big dogs had come to town—they were junkyard dogs too.

Opportunities and Strategy

By the time of the mayor's unopposed 2003 reelection, his goal was evident and more comprehensive than many originally realized—consolidating his power and control over village government and public affairs. Some thought that goal had been reached with little prospect of altering the new reality. Why was the new crowd so successful so quickly? In retrospect, the answer is simple— the mayor saw an opportunity and devised a long-term strategy to exploit it systematically. Most of his opponents didn't fully appreciate what was happening at the time because much of the mayor's strategy was invisible to them. Even the few who did grasp the change weren't sure what to do in response.

The mayor approached his goal with a political strategist's eye. He waited for the right kind of opportunity and found it in his initial election. He ran for an important office with the potential for the exercise of power, rather than just any office. He ran for an open seat rather than challenge an incumbent, which leveled the field considerably. He had a slick, professionally designed campaign that created a compelling narrative of him as a local boy who made good (a lawyer and a CPA) and was active in the community, a family man (although he has no children, campaign brochures showed him in posed pictures with children), a youth athletic coach, and a church member. He presented himself as someone seeing a bright future for the community—of course, one with low taxes. In looking at the political context, he clearly saw that there was no ongoing political organization to fight. Everyone but him treated that election as nonpartisan, and he won as a result.

The mayor's success in consolidating power came quickly because there was no effective opposition after his initial election. A part of his strategy was to keep it that way by co-opting those he could and deterring significant opposition from others in ways consistent with the new political environment he created. Once firmly in power, however, the mayor started to show some surprising and troubling weaknesses when it came to governing. During his first term the village manager—a well-respected professional with a national reputation— was let go. The replacement didn't last long, and although the next manager lasted longer, he too was let go amid problems with the mayor.

In addition to the changes in the manager's office, a number of other professionals left the village's employ—some voluntarily, others not. Their replacements were not always as qualified, and a number of them also left in short order. Turnover became a serious problem; a number of community leaders began worrying that the town's reputation among municipal government professionals was suffering and driving top job prospects away. Much of the turnover came with the mayor's penchant for involving himself in the day-to-day operation of village government to the lowest levels. Given his goals, the mayor saw every position as one with the potential for the exercise of power. The problem was that the village's form of government didn't allow this kind of active mayoral control over village operations.

Ultimately, these problems revealed that the mayor and his supporters really were not as smart as they seemed. No doubt his victory came from a relatively superior strategy and superior resources, but it was also because he faced little real opposition. In other words, the mayor had not really been tested, and despite the image presented by his campaign narrative, he did not possess a strong body of applicable experience. Perhaps we overestimated him. It was not at all certain that these big dogs were really that big after all, even if they were mean. Those of us concerned about the mayor's new political order started organizing to challenge him.

Organizing for political purposes is always challenging because it means mobilizing people around a common cause that they care about. Most people have busy lives and multiple obligations that take up much of their time and energy. On top of that, the aggressive and harassing tactics of the mayor's supporters acted to deter activity by those not in the mayor's camp. We needed something to galvanize people—some event or action that affected enough of the right people personally so outraged them that they felt they couldn't take it anymore. We needed an opportunity.

Opportunities, however, do not occur on a regular schedule like elections. In fact, they may not occur at all, so you hope for the best and try to be ready to take advantage of what fate—or your opponent—offers. During the mayor's unopposed reelection in 2003, the prospects looked especially dim. In the aftermath, he appeared to be well on his way to fully consolidating his power. By mid-2004, however, an opportunity began to unfold. Ironically, it was supplied by the mayor himself, and it may well have been a by-product of his unopposed reelection—an overabundance of hubris that began to resemble a tragic play, although at times it looked as much farce as tragedy.

In the summer of 2004, the mayor began a series of what he called town meetings to hear from residents regarding their concerns. I was among the invitees to these meetings, and like most, I initially thought they were an outreach effort by the village government. But there were some questions because the meetings were sponsored by the mayor's ongoing campaign committee rather than the village. In reality, these meetings were a part of the mayor's political strategy, which became evident when a number of village council members angrily and publicly protested the meetings. They revealed that not only were they left off the invitation list but also they weren't even told in advance of the plan to hold the meetings. The town meetings were just a charade.

Unknown at the time, the mayor was quietly planning to circulate petitions to gain enough signatures to place a major referendum on the ballot in the April 2005 local election. The town meetings were apparently a part of that plan. By holding a number of well-attended, high-profile town meetings—with many of the invitees being community leaders—the mayor could use the emerging list of problems as proof of the need for the referendum he wanted on the ballot. The meetings would provide a compelling narrative pointing to numerous community problems and the need for some kind of solution. The mayor, through his referendum, would then propose a solution—a change in the village government to a "strong mayor" form of government—and he would be the model for it. Here was a vigorous, community-oriented mayor uncovering problems and acting forcefully to solve them. For some of us, it looked more like a coup d'état.

If successful, the mayor's referendum would have replaced the "weak council, strong manager" form of government with a strong mayor form of government. Under the former, the mayor and council are essentially volunteer public servants who set policy, leaving the day-to-day operations of the town to a professional village manager and the staff he or she hires. In the strong mayor alternative, the elected mayor is the chief operating officer—the person responsible for the day-to-day operation of the village government, including the hiring and firing of all employees. It would formally give the mayor the scope of power he always wanted but could not fully achieve without the change. It would also provide him with a substantial salary since the mayor would be a full-time official. An added benefit for the mayor's entourage was that they could seek election or appointment to other paid positions that would come with the new form of government.

The referendum effort, however, did not run as smoothly as the mayor had hoped. With this push for a strong mayor form of government and the town meeting charade, the mayor's strategy was now obvious to all who cared to look. He was intent on fully consolidating power in his hands in ways that would give him almost complete working control over municipal government and make effective political opposition impossible—and have a position with a six-figure salary. His initiative to change the village's form of government was the tipping point. It was the step too far in the eyes of many concerned people, and it provided the opportunity to mobilize people. Overlapping ad hoc groups began to form to discuss ways of stopping the mayor's plan. I helped to organize one of those groups. The challenge was daunting because we were starting from behind and had no strategy beyond trying to stop the mayor and his supporters—but it was still an opportunity. Indeed, a likely reason for the town meeting charade and the planned quiet nature of the referendum effort was to control the narrative and leave opponents with little time to organize and mount any meaningful opposition.

Getting Organized and Fighting Back

The ad hoc group of citizens I helped to organize and other existing groups scrambled to put together some kind of plan to defeat the measure. We assumed that the mayor's supporters would indeed get more than enough signatures to place the strong mayor referendum on the ballot—and they did. Fighting the measure once it was on the ballot would be especially tough because the April 2005 election would likely be a low-turnout election. There would be no state-wide or congressional races, and it would not be a mayoral race (the local elections with the highest turnout). In low-turnout elections, the advantage goes to the side better able to mobilize its supporters and get them to the polls. The mayor's organizational and financial resources, along with the head start, gave all of us pause.

A number of community leaders strongly expressed their opposition, wrote letters to the editors, and used their networks in an effort to mobilize broad political opposition with the hope of convincing the mayor not to formally file the petitions. Our group supported these various efforts, but it wasn't clear how well they would work. Because there was every reason to believe that the mayor would simply plow ahead, we began to do the research necessary to build an understandable and persuasive case against the measure at the polls. The more we learned, the more concerned we became, not only because of how fundamentally this would change local government, but also because of the poor track records of Illinois cities and towns with the strong mayor form of government. The question, of course, was whether a quickly constructed argument on the merits would work in a low-turnout election against a well-resourced opponent with a significant head start.

Fearing the answer, we also began exploring ways of keeping the measure off the ballot. Why go through the expense and risk of trying to defeat a ballot measure at the polls if you can keep it off the ballot in the first place? For this reason opponents will check signatures on nominating petitions or look for violations of other statutory requirements, such as the deadline for filing or the precise wording of a ballot measure. Problems with one of these matters—or others—may be sufficient to keep a candidate or a measure off the ballot. Such problems can be the bane of any campaign if the organizers are not careful to thoroughly research the relevant requirements because petition challenges provide wonderful opportunities for opponents willing to invest the time and effort. Some may consider such a tactic to be "winning ugly," but the idea, after all, is to win any way you can within the rules.

I was among those pushing hard for this tactic. Although the mayor (himself a practicing attorney) and his supporters (key ones also practicing attorneys) were known for their bare-knuckles approach to politics, they were not known for their careful attention to detail or depth of knowledge. Usually they didn't have to worry about such things because their aggressive tactics were sufficient to deter opponents (who didn't always do their homework either). Additionally, I had used this tactic successfully over a decade before in keeping a referendum issue off the ballot because it was not filed within the statutory deadline.

There was another reason for trying this tactic, which had to do with a second, very different, referendum issue that could also appear on the April ballot.

This one was, in some ways, the opposite of the strong mayor question. If both matters were on the ballot, we would have been in the position of fighting a bizarre, two-front war. A group of residents opposed to some of the mayor's recent economic redevelopment efforts and their costs for the taxpayers—especially a multimillion-dollar parking structure—had begun a petition drive to strip the village of its "home rule" powers. If both questions made it to the ballot, we would easily be stretched beyond our capacity to act effectively, and so we hoped to keep at least one referendum, if not both, off the April ballot.

Without going into the legal details, home rule authority in Illinois gives municipalities significant independent power to pass ordinances on a variety of matters unless the Illinois Constitution or a statute prohibits it. It allows greater leeway for local governments to respond to their needs in ways most appropriate to that locale. Much of what the village had done with regard to redevelopment and what it planned to do involved its home rule powers. There was, and still is, substantial controversy surrounding the village's various redevelopment efforts. The group fighting home rule hoped to tap into the discontent surrounding redevelopment.

In early January 2005, this group filed petitions with the village clerk's office to place a binding measure on the April ballot asking the voters to rescind the village's home rule powers. After examining the signatures on the petition sheets filed with the clerk's office, members of my group quickly filed a formal objection to this referendum with the village election board. Our challenge was simple—a count showed that the petitions were over 1,000 signatures short of the statutory requirement. In response to our challenge, the village election board ruled that the home rule question would not appear on the April ballot. One battle won.

We hoped to be equally successful in keeping the strong mayor question off the April ballot too, but something other than the number of signatures would be needed. When the mayor and his supporters formally filed the petitions to place the strong mayor question on the ballot, they had more than enough. After substantial research, one member of our group (not an attorney) found a fatal flaw in the wording of the question on the strong mayor referendum that voters would face. Voters would actually be asked to decide two questions: (1) to abolish the current form of government and (2) to adopt the strong mayor alternative. That meant it was possible to vote yes on the first and no on the second, which would be nonsensical.

We pooled our funds and hired a lawyer, a municipal law specialist with experience in challenging ballot measures. He refined our challenge and laid the necessary groundwork to file it once the mayor formally filed his petitions. The mayor and his supporters knew of the potential legal challenge we were planning, but it is not clear that they actually believed that we would file it—or that we would be successful. Because challenges to this kind of ballot measure had to be filed in the circuit court and have a hearing that was essentially a full-blown trial, perhaps they felt we didn't have the resources or nerve to do it and that we were just bluffing. If so, they were dead wrong. We filed our challenge with the circuit court, and we were confident that we would win.

By this time, the atmosphere in town was very tense—it was like a game of chicken and the question was who would swerve first. On the day of the hearing, the courtroom was packed, and the tension was palpable. Interestingly, even some key village employees sat on our side of the courtroom. To everyone's surprise, just as the court clerk called the case, the mayor's lawyer stepped forward and told the judge that the strong mayor petition was being withdrawn. The mayor swerved first. The judge suggested that she was likely to have ruled against the mayor had the petition not been withdrawn. We and the other opponents of the mayor's attempted coup d'état prevailed and did so publicly. A second battle won.

Even though we won this battle, the mayor and his supporters weren't going away (and neither were the anti–home rule people). The mayor said he wasn't giving up on the strong mayor idea and would pursue other avenues to the same end—primarily through changes in village ordinances, which of course needed village council approval. As a result, the April 2005 elections for village council took on a special importance. The mayor could increase his strength on the council and further his strategy, but the election also gave us opportunity to elect good people and thwart the mayor. In other words, the game was on if we wanted to play. The publicity surrounding our successful challenges to the two very different referenda positioned us well and helped to announce the existence of our group—now formalized as the Community Advocates.

Staying Organized: The Community Advocates Are Born

We learned some very important lessons about the political environment created by the mayor since his initial election. Two stood out: (1) Combating the mayor and his agenda required a strategy of our own, and (2) a successful strategy needed a sustained organization because it would involve working over a number of elections. While we were challenging the two referendum matters, we decided to formalize our working group and create our own organization—the Community Advocates—and I became the president. Those challenges were actually our first formal actions as an organization and stood as our announcement that we intended to be a major player in the public life of the community. With the success of the strong mayor challenge we also learned—and hopefully others saw—that the mayor was not invincible and his success not inevitable. He could be beaten. For all his strengths, there were serious weaknesses that could be exploited. He and his supporters were a living example of hubris.

We had to find a way to take advantage of the opportunity provided by the mayor, starting with the kind of organization we wanted to create. It was our first strategic challenge. Since we would be a good government group, we quickly ruled out involvement in partisan political matters. Since we assumed that our resources would be limited, we could not involve ourselves in every matter. We agreed that our group would be active in nonpartisan, local elections and in local elections involving referenda of special importance. We agreed to focus our energies where we could be most effective rather than weigh in on every issue. We'd have more credibility if we chose our battles carefully.

We wanted to send an important symbolic message by the makeup of our group. The Advocates needed to form a stark contrast to the mayor and his supporters in order to drive the narrative and win the battle over ideas. We also wanted to be a stark contrast to those in town—like the anti–home rule group—who reflexively oppose everything and offer few, if any, constructive ideas. To establish our credibility, the Advocates was designed to be a diverse group of residents with substantial experience in community service and wide connections throughout the community. In short, we wanted to show that we knew what we were talking about. Among those involved were current or past members of the village council (including a former mayor), the park board, the library board, the school boards, and other community groups (including the League of Women Voters). In addition, to have the widest appeal and to provide an alternative to the highly partisan political environment the mayor was creating, we consciously included Republicans, Democrats, and independents along with members of some of the larger churches in town.

Having decided on the kind of organization, the next challenge was the name. This challenge carried great symbolic importance because we needed to position our group in the community's eyes. The wrong choice could be disastrous. Above all, we wanted to emphasize the organization's reason for being—the best interests of the community. Accordingly, having the word "community" in the group's name seemed obvious. It would be a clear signal of what we're about and what we're not about. It is community that drives us, not personal, political, or other ambitions, not the interests of some larger group like a political party, a commercial interest, or those contributing money to political campaigns.

Tougher still was the choice of the word to describe what we wanted to do. We did not want to be mere boosters or watchdogs. We saw a need for leadership, and we wanted to be actively engaged in the important issues ourselves rather than leave the engagement to others. Since we saw ourselves as representing or advocating the community's interests, the word "advocates"—like the word "community"—seemed a good choice. It would best describe our reasons for organizing because an advocate speaks not for him- or herself but for some cause or issue. That cause or issue was the community, amply demonstrated by the diverse group of people organizing the Advocates. We believed that "Community Advocates" sent the right symbolic message as a key part of our strategy.

By the beginning of 2005, we had begun putting together a website and mapping out our basic plan, which would take us through a number of election cycles. Our ultimate target was defeating the mayor, but the immediate target was the upcoming village council election. Three council seats would be contested, and our goal was to deny the mayor a working majority on the council in light of his interest in changing the village government. Our most important initial decision was to formally endorse candidates for the village council election: The Advocates began scouting likely candidates. We hoped that if we put our name and support behind the right kind of candidates they would have a better chance of success.

In preparation for the endorsement of candidates, we conducted our own background research on them. We decided to send a short questionnaire to announced candidates asking about general background information (education, job history, etc.) along with experience in the community and public service activities. Our research went further than just those areas, and in the case of one candidate—one of the mayor's strong supporters—we became aware of what we believed to be a serious problem (more on that later).

Before making our endorsements, we planned a public forum at which we asked candidates a series of questions about their reasons for running and about the issues we believed to be the most important. Our per-endorsement plan also included an informational mailing to people we identified as "super voters," those who had voted in the past three local elections. We saw those people as most likely to vote in the upcoming election, and targeting them was the most efficient and sensible use of our meager resources. Using a list obtained from the county board of elections of all registered voters in town and some of our own time and effort, we were able to cull the super voters from that list. The informational piece we mailed to them was a simple, single sheet that reminded the recipients of the upcoming election, included the names of all those running for office, and provided some basic information on the Advocates (mailings with our endorsements would come later). It was another way to announce our existence, who we are, and what we are about—and that we would be active in the election.

Once we made our endorsements, we did a variety of things to publicize the endorsements and help those candidates, including a press release that was ready to go the day of the endorsements. Shortly after the endorsements were announced, we scheduled a well-publicized "meet and greet" so that interested voters could spend time talking with our endorsed candidates. Regardless of attendance, the publicity surrounding the event—both before and after—was the key. The Advocates also put together a mailing sent to our list of voters announcing our endorsements, placed a series of advertisements in the local newspapers, and sent a postcard to voters the weekend before the election with our endorsements. The postcard also told voters to take it with them when they went to the polls.

Although our techniques are not unique, two things were important: our consistent message and our way of spreading it. In fact, the latter was itself a part of the narrative and the contrast we wanted to make to the mayor. Our initial informational mailing was scrupulously neutral. We conducted an open and public forum that was nonconfrontational and to which all candidates were invited and attended. All were treated in a respectful, professional manner. When the endorsements were made, we simply announced them without saying anything negative about those we did not endorse. The meet and greet for endorsed candidates was well-publicized and open to the public—and free. Our mailings, press releases, and advertisements were well designed yet simple, informational, and inexpensive. There were no slick, multicolor brochures. The fact that we were able to do these things stands as evidence of the need that any similar organization you design must be well run.

As I noted above, one of the candidates the Advocates did not endorse was a strong supporter of the mayor. He was a leader in a local men's club that involved itself in a variety of community issues, including political matters. Additionally, if someone was facing harassment for their political opposition to the mayor or his agenda, some club members were among those who supplied the harassment. In doing research on the candidates, the Advocates learned that this candidate had sent to and shared with club members a number of e-mails that an outside observer could consider to be sexually charged, misogynist, and even bigoted. A number of these e-mails became public and were made available to the press. They raised serious questions about this candidate's character and his ability to appropriately represent residents who were not just like him. The candidate made no apologies for the substance of the e-mails and instead defended them as private correspondence within a club. Some of the candidate's (and the mayor's) supporters came to his defense and lashed out at his critics, questioning their motives. I was among those critics singled out for censure.

There was, however, more to the story, and it came out after the candidate's supporters (including a former village council member who was also one of the mayor's key operatives) began their aggressive and public defense of the candidate's character and fitness for office. It was a long-past arrest record and conviction. In itself, an arrest and even a conviction from years past isn't necessarily a problem. It depends on the specifics—the nature of the offense and its seriousness. And of course, it depends on whether the candidate is the one who brings it up. We learned that this candidate pleaded guilty to a very embarrassing misdemeanor charge centering on a public sex act that placed some of the sexually charged e-mails he shared with his club members in a new light. After reviewing the official record, the local newspaper reported on the specifics. The mayor, needless to say, tried to distance himself from his candidate. However, despite his claim not to really know this candidate, the local newspaper also reported on the close ties between this candidate and the mayor.

We never understood why the mayor backed this candidate and why he, the candidate, and their supporters thought that none of this would become public. If nothing else, it would cause great embarrassment for the candidate and his family. Needless to say, they all looked ridiculous when the guilty plea material became public in light of the earlier defenses. When asked, the Advocates indicated that in our view the best course for the candidate would be to withdraw from the race. He eventually ended his campaign after the information about his guilty plea became public. Because he waited too long to formally withdraw, his name remained on the ballot, and he finished dead last.

Once that candidate's full criminal record became public, the mayor and his supporters reacted quite strongly, even attempting to have some members of the Advocates arrested for extortion and harassment because we suggested that the candidate end his campaign. They blamed everything on the Advocates—making the e-mails public and turning the guilty plea material over to the press. To this day I do not know who made the material public or who supplied the material to the press. Not surprisingly, the local police and the county prosecutor's office declined to do anything since there was no evidence of a crime. If nothing else, having the mayor and his supporters place all blame on the Advocates and come after us so aggressively did suggest that we were now seen as a major adversary. It was an interesting sign of our success and potential influence—even if we were "goo-goos."

All of the candidates endorsed by the Advocates for the village council, as well as for the park board and the school boards, won in the spring 2005 election. Some of us paid a price for this success at the hands of the mayor's supporters, including being personally attacked at length by the brother-in-law of the candidate with the criminal record during the public comment section of two televised village council meetings. Of course, such personal attacks during the public comment section of a council meeting can only go on if the mayor allows them since he is the presiding officer. As personally painful as these activities were to us, they served our strategy and our narrative well. We didn't have to publicize the tactics used by the mayor and his supporters—their activities spoke for themselves. To the very end of the mayor's second term and his resounding defeat, the mayor and his supporters never seemed to realize that they were the best spokesmen for the Advocates, our message, and our goals. They were the political gift that just kept giving—they were the gang that couldn't shoot straight.

It Is a Continuing Strategy—Not Just One Election

Because the Advocates does not see ourselves as an organization weighing in on every local issue, but only the most important ones, the Advocates largely withdrew from visible activity after the 2005 elections. This did not mean that we ceased operations. We invested money and time in our website, which we now maintained on an ongoing basis. Among ourselves, we continued to monitor local events and to talk to people in our respective networks to keep some momentum alive. In early 2006, we decided to become visibly active again. Another anti–home rule referendum petition emerged from the same group that pushed the earlier one. This group was quite persistent, and they wanted to place the same question on the March 21, 2006, primary ballot.

This time they succeeded in getting more than enough signatures, but the Advocates again filed an objection. If nothing else, we wanted to send the message that this was an issue the Advocates thought was so important that we were always prepared to fight. This time we alleged that there were so many irregularities in the sheets of signatures, some bordering on fraud, that all the signatures should be rejected and the question not placed on the ballot. Despite painstaking examination of every signature and every sheet of signatures, our objection was not successful this time. There is some room for judgment by the election board in weighing the evidence in such a challenge, and it probably didn't help that the mayor chairs the village election board. In the view of some of the Advocates, the mayor's position would be better served if the measure made it onto the ballot but was defeated and he could be the key actor responsible.

While the Advocates were preparing their formal challenge to the ballot measure, we were also doing the necessary research and strategizing to defeat the question if it was placed on the ballot—and we were working with other activists and groups who shared our concerns. Collectively, the pro–home rule coalition made a strong, easily understandable, and well-communicated factual case on the merits for our town to keep home rule. We used multiple mailings and paid ads in the local newspapers to present factual information on the costs and benefits of removing home rule—especially the change in what residents would pay in property taxes, which would increase despite the claims of the anti–home rule forces.

Looking forward to the 2007 mayoral election, the Advocates had to make sure something else was a part of the campaign narrative. The anti–home rule forces focused on the idea that withdrawing power from the village government was the only way to stop the kinds of public projects to which they objected—especially the parking garage mentioned earlier. It was the only way in their view because—to no one's surprise but theirs—they had utterly failed in the electoral arena. Knowing by this time that there was growing dissatisfaction with the mayor and his actions, the home rule opponents were hoping to capitalize on that dissatisfaction by arguing that you can never "vote the bums out." In contrast, the Advocates strongly emphasized in communications and campaign materials the idea that the voters can and should vote the bums out, not cripple for years to come the village government's ability to deal with local matters adequately and appropriately. Given the Advocates' growing visibility and success by this time, we hoped that enough voters would take our argument to heart. Because of the efforts of the Advocates and other community-minded activists, the home rule question was overwhelmingly defeated—over 70 percent of those voting voted to keep home rule.

The Advocates hoped that our role in defeating the anti–home rule referendum would help lay some groundwork for a campaign to defeat the mayor in the 2007 election by strengthening our position in local politics. We were becoming more optimistic about the chances, and some information we garnered regarding the mayor buoyed our hopes and affected our planning. We heard informally from a reliable source that some county Republican leaders saw our mayor as a problem and that his prospects for political advancement outside our town were slim. In other words, he was seen as a problem, but he was our problem—meaning our town's problem. He might not find greater opportunity outside of our town, but whether he had a future in our town was up to the town. The message appeared to be that a move to defeat him at the next election would be fine—presuming, of course, the challenge was not a move by the Democrats to invade traditionally Republican territory. Some of us saw an opportunity—the mayor really was politically vulnerable.

Because our plan in trying to defeat the mayor in the 2007 election was to focus on his ethics and style of governing, the Advocates continued monitoring the mayor's fund-raising activities and spending. We were particularly interested in who contributed large amounts to the mayor and whether they received benefits from the village (such as a sales tax rebate for a business) or did business with the village (such as a no-bid contract for professional services of some kind). Although Illinois had no limits on campaign contributions or spending for local elections at that time, there were regular and detailed reporting requirements for both. In addition, municipal contracts of any kind are public information, and the village is required to have a public notice published annually that indicates the identity of all contractors and the value of each contract. Any special benefits granted to a local business—such as a sales tax rebate to a car dealer as an inducement to locate or stay in the village—must be passed by the village council in an open meeting. With a little work and perseverance we were able to match contributions to contracts and benefits, and it yielded important ammunition for the upcoming mayoral election. Indeed, it appeared that "pay-to-play" had come to town.

The broader political context at the time had the potential to help our plan. The federal prosecutor in Chicago had recently won a string of high-profile political corruption convictions. Many involved Chicago Democratic officeholders and political operatives, but not all. An equal opportunity prosecutor, he went after Republicans as vigorously as Democrats. In the spring of 2006, the corruption investigations reached the highest level of political office in Illinois with the conviction of former Illinois governor George Ryan, a Republican. A key to the prosecution was the testimony of Ryan's former chief aide—a member of a prominent Republican family in our county. This local boy had earlier pleaded guilty to corruption charges and was serving time in a federal prison. Other members of Ryan's administration had also been convicted or pleaded guilty to corruption charges. News reports of federal investigations, trials, and convictions in the Chicago area continued throughout the fall of 2006 and into the beginning of the campaign season for local elections in the spring of 2007.

While the mayor was building his campaign war chest—it would hit $100,000 and then some—the Advocates began scouting potential candidates who shared our goals to run for mayor and for the three village council seats that would be contested (again, even if the mayor won reelection, we wanted to deny him a council majority). It was important for us to find serious, compelling candidates because this election was crucial and potentially brutal. We believed that the mayor could be beat, but we had to convince potential candidates to agree and that we could help them. We had already laid the groundwork for the election's narrative—ethics, money, and pay-to-play.

We were successful in recruiting candidates, including two potentially strong mayoral candidates—one a sitting village council member and the other a former longtime member of the school board. Eventually the sitting council member filed to run for mayor, and the former school board member filed for village council. The Advocates and others believed this was the best arrangement politically because the sitting council member was a Republican and the former school board member a Democrat. Running a known Democrat against the mayor would be to the mayor's advantage and play to his political strengths. Running a known Republican could substantially neutralize these advantages. Running a Republican smart enough to visit local and regional Republican officeholders, explain his candidacy, and ask not for their support but their neutrality in the election would be especially effective in neutralizing the mayor's advantages. Paint the election as a purely local matter involving a problematic mayor that was best left to the town's residents to sort out (the candidate we supported did all those things).

In encouraging candidates to run, we assured them of our help if we endorsed them, including access to the results of a survey we were planning. We took a random sample of 1,000 names from our list of super voters (making sure that no more than one voter in each household was in the sample) and then mailed each a one-page questionnaire about specific issues of concern in town as well as more general questions. The latter were designed to elicit people's views about local campaign financing and spending, the traits and experiences they valued in local officials, and partisanship in local politics. Each mailing included the questionnaire, a cover letter from the Advocates explaining who we were and what the survey was about, and a stamped, self-addressed return envelope. With minimal follow-up we had a 51 percent response rate.

This survey was at the heart of our plan for the election, and it had a number of purposes in addition to providing information to the candidates we supported. First and foremost, its purpose was to lay out the narrative we wanted to guide the election and set the terms of debate. If we could control the battle over ideas, the candidates we supported had a better chance of winning. The survey was sent out early in the fall, well before the December filing deadline for candidates and well before much active campaigning. In short, we wanted to be out there first.

The survey asked nothing about specific candidates or officeholders—only about the issues noted above, as well as some demographic information on respondents. In addition to getting information on people's attitudes, we wanted to get them thinking and talking about these issues in the context of the upcoming local election. It was not a question of changing people's attitudes—we didn't believe we could accomplish that or, more importantly, that we needed to. Given the broader political context at the time and the general disgust in the Chicago area over corruption, along with the growing impatience with highly partisan political warfare, we believed all we needed was to turn that general disgust and growing impatience to local concerns. In other words, we needed to channel what we believed to already be there.

Receiving over 500 usable responses with no real follow-up sent a clear message to us. The Advocates was an excellent brand despite attempts by the mayor and his supporters to discredit us collectively and individually. People—or at least those who pay the most attention to local affairs and vote most often—cared about the issues we believed to be important. They believed that a candidate's integrity, character, and independence are very important, whereas a candidate's party affiliation, age, and gender are not. Money in campaigns bothered them, with most saying that contributions should only come from people in town rather than interests from outside the town. When it came to how much a candidate spends, less was clearly preferred: 44 percent thought $10,000 was too much, 76 percent thought $25,000 was too much, and 88 percent thought $50,000 was too much. By the end of 2006, the mayor's campaign fund was approaching $100,000. Forty-two percent said they did not have confidence in public officials, only 24 percent said they did, and the remainder weren't sure. A full 80 percent of the respondents agreed that the town needed an ethics ordinance.

Once we had those 500 surveys, we began running the numbers and publicizing some of the findings. We posted them on the Advocates website, placed some in a press release, shared a few with other groups, included still others in a mailing to the super voters, and began to share the findings with potential candidates. Again, we wanted to drive the narrative for the upcoming election, and we succeeded. The combination of the information we uncovered on the connections between contributions to the mayor's campaign fund and certain benefits, and the findings of our survey, made a compelling narrative.

The narrative quickly took on a life of its own. Others started looking at the available public records and making additional connections that pointed to pay-to-play politics. When those findings were publicized, village council members not up for reelection began talking about the issue during village council meetings, even raising questions about specific contributions and specific contracts or benefits. One council member referred to a specific contribution as "tithing" because it amounted to 10 percent of the value of the contract with the village. In addition, one of the people running for a council seat (and backed by the mayor and his supporters) provided more grist for the mill. He had made a number of sizable contributions to the mayor's campaign fund, and his firm had consulting contracts with the village—contracts in the past and at least one that was current at the time. At first this candidate failed to understand the issue because he didn't see the need for his firm to stop doing business with the village. Initially, the mayor tried to ignore the money/ethics issue, believing it was a nonissue despite the visibility it had been getting. His professionally designed campaign centered on a picture of him as a civic-minded public servant who had successfully accomplished much while keeping taxes low. His campaign also wanted to control the narrative, but it couldn't. Too much of the discussion centered on factual matters in the public record that could not easily be explained by the mayor or his supporters. Whenever they tried, someone would go to the publicly available records and contradict them, which only gave more credence to our narrative and eroded the mayor's credibility. Some of the mayor's own attempts to explain things away at candidate forums would be videotaped and put on YouTube and then contrasted to information from the public record.

Perhaps the most damaging item was an analysis of the mayor's fund-raising and spending reports that appeared as an ad in the local newspaper, paid for by a local group. It showed that the mayor raised over $500,000 since his initial election and spent over $400,000. Less than 5 percent of those funds came from individuals living in town. Most came from businesses. As to a claim made by some of the mayor's supporters that a substantial amount of the money raised actually went to local charities, the ad showed that less than 7 percent went to charities or nonprofits. Six percent went to purchase tickets for the mayor to attend sporting events. More was paid to a business co-owned by the mayor for services performed for his campaign. Each time the mayor or his supporters tried to respond to the money/ethics issue, his credibility eroded more.

The election was perhaps the most intense in recent years, featuring more than its share of crude tactics by the mayor, his supporters, and the outside political consultant used by the mayor's campaign. The Advocates followed the same basic plan we had used in the 2005 election, putting out various flyers and advertisements, running e-mails and content on our website, holding a candidate forum, and making endorsements. All the candidates we endorsed for village council won, as did our endorsed mayoral candidate. In fact, he won an overwhelming victory, beating the mayor by a 2 to 1 margin. His campaign was built around the idea of change—that it was time to change the way things were done in town. A key platform issue for him was the need for an ethics ordinance.

Another key to his campaign was the people he attracted to work on it. Some members of the Advocates moved over to help run his campaign, as did some of those people involved in fighting the strong mayor referendum. The new mayor was able to effectively mobilize discontent. He helped to bring a new set of younger people into local politics, which was important because it would help sustain the victory and the long-term prospects for our goals. The now former mayor and his supporters had been defeated, but they weren't leaving town.

After the 2007 election victories, the Advocates again withdrew from public visibility, but we did not ignore what was happening. We had helped to vote the bums out and bring about a major change in town government—or at least the potential for major change. It was time to wait and see if the potential proved real. One of the first real tests was the promised ethics ordinance, and one was indeed passed that was stricter than any in surrounding communities and stricter than the state's requirements. There was also a noticeable, positive change in the style of leadership during the council meetings and in village affairs more generally. We regrouped in the fall of 2008 in preparation for the spring 2009 local elections. There would be park board and school board elections, but most importantly three village council seats would be on the ballot, giving us an opportunity to consolidate the gains of 2007 and keep the former mayor from gaining ground back.

The Advocates had developed a successful model for influencing local elections, but now there was one big difference. We were not on the offensive, mounting an attack on something that needed substantial change. Instead, we wanted to protect and consolidate the gains made with a new mayor who had a solid majority on the village council. The biggest threat was likely to come from the former mayor, who continued to have a hard time accepting and understanding his staggering loss. A number of names circulated as possible candidates, including some well-known, close supporters of the former mayor. When the filing deadline came in December, none of those visible players filed their candidacy for the village council election (one most likely because he would be asked about his business dealings in town). The former mayor put up only one candidate, even though three council seats would be contested. Although a long-time resident, this candidate was a virtual unknown, with no record in community affairs aside from a recent appointment as a Republican precinct committeeman. He was one of the weakest candidates to run in a council election in recent years, and he came in dead last despite the active support of the former mayor, his supporters, and the township Republican Party. Needless to say, the three candidates endorsed by the Advocates won. This meant that after the 2009 election, the mayor and the other six members of the village council were candidates who sought and received the Advocates' endorsement and support.

The Challenge of Success

The Advocates now face an interesting challenge in terms of strategy. We helped to completely change municipal government. We won almost every time we entered an election as an active player. Since our first foray into local electoral politics in 2005, only two candidates we endorsed—one for a school board and one for the park board—lost. We had achieved our original goal. Did this mean we could retire from the field? No, because one all-important lesson we learned was that although the opposition may not be very smart and may have lost in a series of elections, they weren't going away. If we retire from the field, they will happily step in and retake the ground they lost.

The Advocates need to rethink our strategy to maintain the gains we made. It will be especially challenging because we need to do it in a completely different fiscal environment than the one in existence just a few years ago. The change has to do with the nation's severe economic downturn. Local governments have been hit hard in Illinois because much of their revenue is tied to taxes that are very sensitive to economic conditions, especially sales taxes. Like many, the village council is struggling with the budget cuts that must be made in the face of sudden drops in revenue. We have not yet come up with a strategy and a narrative for maintaining good government and the quality of life in our community in the worst economic conditions in recent memory. That is our current challenge.

In reality, one overarching lesson is that you never fully reach your goal. It's just an ongoing series of battles. It's a lesson best summarized in the phrase that serves as the refrain in a well-known song by Texas singer-songwriter Robert Earl Keen: "The road goes on forever and the party never ends."

PART 2
Money, Media, and Staff

4

Funding Hillary's 2008 Presidential Campaign

Vladimir Gutman

Type of campaign: Presidential (primary)

Role of author: Fund-raising staff member

Lessons to look for:

- Money matters.
- All campaigns are basically local affairs.
- Particularly for fund-raising, the rules and procedures under which campaigns operate matter.
- Planning, organization, and strategy matter.
- Campaigns need both earned and paid media to get their message out.
- Even for volunteers, campaigns are about taking advantage of opportunities.
- Planning fund-raising events is not easy; a poorly planned event can embarrass the candidate.

A Chance Encounter

In January 2007, the presidential election was almost two years away, but the campaign had already begun. Tom Vilsack, the former governor of Iowa, was the first serious politician to announce his candidacy for president, and he did so less than a month after the 2006 midterms that swept the Democrats back into control of Congress. I was then a junior political science student at Northwestern University, just north of Chicago. Like many of my friends, I paid close attention to the speculation surrounding the high-profile candidates, especially the two hometown favorites—Senators Hillary Clinton and Barack Obama. I argued endlessly with my friends, and occasionally with my professors, about what various events meant and how to interpret them. I didn't have a strong sense of who I wanted to be our next president, but I was concerned that the country wasn't ready to elect either a woman or an African American. Knowing only that I was a Democrat, and despite living through six years of a Republican administration, I was worried that simple prejudice could prevent a change in the party that controlled the White House.

A chance encounter changed things. Several weeks before Senator Clinton formed an exploratory committee for her presidential campaign at the end of January 2007, I was with a few friends in a downtown Evanston eatery located across from a Barnes and Noble bookstore. After we'd been sitting for a few minutes talking about nothing in particular, someone tapped on my shoulder to get our attention and asked us who we thought would be the country's next president. Convinced at the time that Hillary Clinton would eventually win the nomination, I expressed my concern that she was unelectable both for her gender and her background. The man strongly disagreed with me, and began citing a slew of recent polls demonstrating Hillary's strength. He introduced himself as Terry McAuliffe, the former chairman of the Democratic National Committee (DNC) and a close associate of the Clintons. He had chosen to talk to us at random—merely seeking a sample of the average Northwestern student. He was friendly, engaging, and willing to debate politics with an overeager college student he had met at a fast food restaurant. We talked numbers for a while, and when my friends and I walked out with him, he told us that he was speaking at the Barnes and Noble bookstore across the street as part of his book tour. We followed him to the bookstore and listened to him talk, discuss his experience in politics, and explain to the people gathered why he was supporting Senator Clinton for president.

I went home inspired and spent hours reading about Senator Clinton's past and her positions, and I recognized myself in her views: a social liberal with an appreciation for the free market and an internationalist who still believes that US power can and should be projected around the world to promote human rights and thus secure our own security. The more I read about her, the more I agreed with her. The more I read, the more I was inspired and the more I came to believe in Hillary. I wanted to work in politics, and I wanted to work for her.

Acting on Inspiration

Junior year was far off from graduation and the real world, but I knew that a career in politics was possible only if I demonstrated an early commitment. I also knew that at least for the first several years out of college, I wanted to work in politics, actively pursuing the policies and governing style that I thought our country needed. Several months after my chance encounter with Terry McAuliffe, I started applying for internships in Washington, looking for a position in a congressional office or on a campaign. After much effort and plenty of disappointment, I was asked to volunteer at a Hillary fund-raiser in Chicago. That was just the beginning.

It was a small beginning. On June 25 I arrived in the lobby of the Palmer House Hilton in the heart of downtown Chicago. The hotel is in a beautiful old building with painted ceilings, columns, and heavy velvet drapes. It is a regal setting, and the 500 guests attending the event were dressed in magnificent suits and dresses. The room was full of some of the most successful, famous, and rich people in the city. J. B. Pritzker was among the billionaire heirs to the Hyatt Hotels fortune, and Jerry Springer, the television personality, sat at the head table right in front of the stage. I was assigned to be an usher, helping people navigate the large ballroom to their assigned table in preparation for the dinner and speeches that were to come.

As I would later find out, this was only the second event Senator Clinton's Illinois finance team had put together since being formed a few months prior. It was significantly larger than the small event they had organized at a law firm a month earlier. It was a chaotic evening. Hundreds of people arrived in a short, half-hour time span. Lists of attendees were not available, and the seating assignments were confused. After forty-five minutes and many frustrated donors, dinner was served. I was surprised to find out that these people who had donated $2,300 to Hillary's campaign were served a surprisingly bland chicken dish with rice and a salad. This, I learned, is the hallmark trait of a Democratic fund-raiser: The less you spend on food, the more of the money you can keep and spend on actual campaign expenses. Though my experience with Republican fund-raising is limited, it seems that they operate differently. At one point several months later, the campaign successfully flipped a longtime Republican bundler. He organized an event for us, and because his acquisition had political value in addition to financial value, he got free rein over the planning. It was done the way he was used to doing things before his switch from the Republican side: 100 guests at the upscale Morton's Steakhouse.

The Illinois campaign's finance director was swamped for much of that night, but I eventually got some time to speak to him. I told him I was a committed supporter of Hillary's and that I wanted to get involved with his work in the state in any way I could. He was courteous and polite, but I was already one of several people who had approached him with the same pitch. The next day I sent him an e-mail and didn't expect to hear back again. Luckily I was wrong. A few weeks later, on a Wednesday, I received a call from the deputy finance director asking me to volunteer again. This time they were preparing for a major conference of trial lawyers to be held in Chicago, and they needed me for four days.

I spent the first day in the office making calls and stuffing envelopes. The next two were spent on my feet, walking around the conference and inviting people to a low-dollar fund-raiser planned for Sunday, the last day of the conference. I spent eleven hours on both Friday and Saturday distributing fliers, while other hopeful volunteers only did several one-hour shifts and went home. The result was that most of the lawyers at the conference recognized my face and said hello whenever they saw me, and our fund-raiser was oversold while the Obama and Edwards campaigns had nearly empty rooms. On the last day, the finance director approached me and asked me to start coming in every day as an intern. It was my first and most important lesson in politics: Persistence pays off. Some people get jobs and internships because they know someone who can give them a leg up onto a campaign or another political position. In fact, all the other interns I worked with benefited from this type of assistance. But for those like me who don't have such connections, doors are opened because when your shift is over, you don't leave.

On the Inside—Opportunity

The team I joined was small. When I started in July 2007, there were two paid staffers, the finance director and his deputy, and two full-time interns. I was the third intern. The office space we occupied was minuscule. The Illinois finance office was a spare room we rented for an exorbitant rate at a law firm in down-town Chicago. The room was thirteen feet by thirteen feet, with a round table in the middle that the law firm forbade us to remove. This tiny space was home to five people, three phones, a fax machine, a printer, and all the materials we received. Among them were countless T-shirts, bumper stickers, rally signs, yard signs, posters, literature, blank name tags, posters, and so on. At one point, the national office inexplicably sent us six enormous signs that measured ten feet by five feet, months after the Illinois primary when they could have been useful. As I was also to learn, that sort of gross inefficiency was unfortunately quite common in this campaign.

At first the setting concerned me. I wanted to be part of the central action of the campaign, and this operation seemed like a small part of it. Over the next year I spent the bulk of my time working in this office with the same staffers and a fluid cast of interns, and I quickly grew to appreciate the experiences and relationships that grew out of my time there. I also had the opportunity to work in larger parts of the organization, including several days at the national head-quarters, and it quickly became apparent that working in a smaller setting had its benefits. In the larger offices junior staff and interns, like me, were taken for granted. With tens and sometimes hundreds of people working in a building, it becomes more difficult to get noticed.

The campaign in Illinois was different. It gave me opportunities that the national office couldn't. The finance operation eventually yielded 12,000 donors to Hillary Clinton's campaign and successfully staged many large, complicated events. The two paid staffers could not possibly handle the workload involved in running such an operation. This meant that the interns could, with persistence, become more central to the process. By being one of five rather than one of hundreds, I had more opportunities to demonstrate my talents, knowledge, and skills. Working so closely with the fund-raising staff and the finance committee also gave me more chances to learn and practice the communication and recruitment skills that are so critical to politics.

As time went on, I gradually proved myself to the finance director and his deputy, as well as to various members of the volunteer finance committee we assembled. I made myself available at a moment's notice and stayed informed. I learned how to communicate the campaign's message to hesitant donors, and discovered what it takes to keep members of the finance committee involved and engaged. By demonstrating my commitment, I gained the trust of the paid staff and began to take a greater role in the day-to-day decisions of the operation. I was still asked to make phone calls and work on everyday tasks normally given to interns, but I was also given the opportunity to grow and develop in my position. The finance director began inviting me to attend meetings with donors and participate in calls with the national office, and he trusted me to run portions of fund-raisers, such as managing small battalions of volunteers and working rooms full of high-profile contributors.

A Thousand Here, a Thousand There—
Pretty Soon It's Real Money

Over the next several weeks, I spent much of my time phone banking, cold calling long lists of potential donors to recruit people for various upcoming events and to reach out to politically active individuals in the Chicago area. It is tedious work, hours spent on the phone frequently leaving the same voice mail many times in a row, occasionally having a short conversation with someone if they picked up the phone. I also helped the staff organize meetings with our most generous contributors and in doing so gained an understanding of how a federal fund-raising operation is structured. Perhaps the most critical difference between federal and nonfederal races comes in the area of fund-raising. State election laws place giving caps at substantially higher levels than the federal government allows for congressional and presidential races. Some states, Illinois included, do not provide for any cap whatsoever and even allow corporate giving.

This distinction fundamentally transforms a campaign. The federal limit is adjusted for every cycle to compensate for inflation. In 2008 it was set at $2,300. By restricting contributions, the federal limits prevent any single individual from bankrolling a campaign. Ideally, they should decrease the role of specific individuals in influencing the policy choices later made by elected officials. Of course, as many commentators have observed, these caps do not decrease the influence of a small group of donors. Before, candidates would look for contributors with the deepest pockets; now they seek those with the largest Rolodexes. Prominent officials, professionals, labor and business leaders, and especially those with traditional ties to the Democratic Party, like lawyers, still provide the backbone of any good fund-raising effort.

Because of the prominent positions occupied in private life by such people, they are able to function as "bundlers." Bundlers recruit large numbers of donors to give separately to a candidate, thus assisting a campaign with more money than they can legally contribute on their own. They can do so because there is no shortage of people who wish to get in their good graces. An afternoon of phone calls, an e-mail blast, or a large mailing from these contributors can free up tens of thousands of dollars, depending on the particular bundler in question. After the low-hanging fruit of individual contributions has been picked, dedicated donors still have large networks of people with the means and the interest in either politics or in currying favor with these leaders to contribute to a candidate. For some bundlers, especially ones from major families like the Pritzkers, these networks are national in scope, but for most, networks form around friends, colleagues, and clients. The networks may be wide, but they are still overwhelmingly local.

The payoff for the most dedicated bundlers is greater access to campaign staff, senior advisers, and, if you're a large enough contributor, to the candidate herself. The most generous and effective bundlers, along with those people in whom the finance staff saw fund-raising potential, were organized into an external finance committee. Although we earnestly tried to return phone calls from everyone who called our office, including callers who did not have any giving potential, members of the committee would get a return call as quickly as possible, usually from the Illinois finance director. Membership on the finance committee was coveted for the honor of the title, which implies a certain degree of connectedness, but mostly because it provided the supporter with an institutionalized way to influence the campaign. Several times a month we gathered the finance committee to brief them on the status of the finance operation and the broader political effort, as well as to solicit their advice on both fronts. Because of the broad networks members commanded, they usually understood the zeitgeist of the campaign—the buzz going around political and business communities and the general mood of the public. On national staff calls, we were frequently asked to report what our finance committees thought of some news item, campaign effort, or policy initiative.

Senior advisers to the campaign would sometimes be sent on tour to various major cities where they would lead intimate briefings and question-and-answer sessions with members of the finance committee. Former DNC chairman Terry McAuliffe, former supreme allied commander Wesley Clark, Clinton-era cabinet officers, and numerous other famous and influential people would be flown in to thank and motivate donors. Members of the committee would also be given influence, or at least we would create the illusion of influence, over the way the local finance staff ran the fund-raising operation, including everything from language to the minutest details of event planning. The most effective fund-raisers would get even more attention: regular meetings, phone calls, and meals with the finance director, as well as face time with traveling advisers. Sometimes that involved taking them to meetings or picking them up from the airport. For some, occasional phone calls with Hillary or even meals before or drinks after fund-raisers were arranged as well.

For the first several months on the job, raising money was fairly easy and successful. Our finance committee had wide networks of willing donors, and we were able to put together several successful fund-raisers. My first big event, in June, was a multitiered fund-raiser that included a standing reception, a seated dinner, and a klatch (a private get-together with the candidate). The event raised approximately $1 million. A one-hour reception at the lawyers' conference, mentioned above, brought in $50,000 in smaller donations. We arranged a house party in Chicago's northern suburbs, which raised $100,000, that Hillary attended after a successful but bland union-organized debate at Soldier Field. In fact, we proudly noticed that in the third quarter of 2007 we had raised over $500,000 in Illinois, tantalizingly close to Obama's $800,000. Our national office in Arlington, Virginia, was very pleased. All the regional staffs were reporting successful fund-raisers, and everyone was hitting expectations.

The Anatomy of a Major Fund-Raising Event

Most Fund-Raising, Like Politics, Is Local

Our fund-raising activities reflected the curious organization of a supposedly national campaign. Hillary for President ended up spending just under $230 million in about seventeen months. At its peak it employed approximately 1,000 people, a small army of consultants and senior advisers, hundreds of interns and unpaid staff, plus countless thousands of volunteers. Although we were ostensibly part of a national campaign, the fact that convention delegates were awarded principally through individual state primaries meant that the real campaign winds up a balkanized effort. The national headquarters was responsible for compliance, communications, scheduling, vetting, and advance operations, but the bulk of the campaign existed in semi-autonomous operations spread across the country. Major parts of the ground operation, from organization to get-out-the-vote efforts, were left to the discretion of local staff with only sporadic input and oversight from the national headquarters in Arlington, Virginia. The fund-raising operation was no different. The political side was balkanized because of the splintered nature of the electoral process, but the finance operation was balkanized because fund-raising networks are naturally local. The result was a slew of semi-independent regional fund-raising offices like ours in Illinois.

Finance directors and the teams they put together had great responsibility and freedom of movement within their states. National finance staff set goals, pursued certain targets of critical significance, and occasionally put together a national initiative like the volunteer fund-raising phone banks we organized after the stunning loss in Iowa. But generally speaking, we were left to our own devices in Illinois. At various points in the course of planning an event, we checked in with various national departments to approve our decisions, but the great majority of the planning and all the donor recruitment were left up to us. A national campaign like ours, then, is essentially a collection of many smaller efforts. Even though it gives the campaign incredible flexibility to respond to diverse and fluid circumstances, it creates problems of its own, as when meticulously crafted plans had to be scrapped and quickly, sometimes hastily, redesigned after one of the national departments disapproved of some aspect of our proposal.

Planning a Fund-Raiser

Over the course of several fund-raising events, I grew to understand the logistics of putting on a large political event, the way to communicate both optimism and urgency to the bundlers we needed to stay active and committed to the cause, and how to interact with and convince potential contributors to give money. I also came to understand how these events reflected the essentially local nature of a national campaign. One of our largest events took place on December 18, several weeks after a November debate between the Democratic candidates for president in which Hillary Clinton gave a less-than-satisfactory answer to a difficult question on driver's licenses for illegal aliens. This question was a political landmine, and her answer, although not actually that bad, hurt her because it gave the impression of waffling. We started preparing for the fund-raiser about a month before it was scheduled. It took some wrangling with the national scheduling staff, but we finally were able to arrange for Hillary to arrive in the early evening and spend the night in Chicago. With this much time, we had the flexibility to put together several tiers of events for the night. The finance director and his deputy, along with me and one other intern, spent several hours each day discussing possibilities and capacity. How much money could we expect to raise? How deep was the interest in Chicago for a large, multitiered event?

It took about a week to plan out the entire trip in coordination with national scheduling. There were a number of hour-long conference calls that included members of our finance committee. Depending on the call, as many as fifteen committee members would join in, and we would brief the callers on the current state of our plans and ask them for their suggestions. Generally, such calls were not really useful to staff. They took large amounts of time out of our day for very little benefit. It was difficult to have a productive conversation with fifteen disparate voices, especially when large egos were involved who were at times more interested in pursuing their own private interests. Nonetheless, we included the finance committee members in these discussions as part of our on-going effort to give our top donors a sense of ownership of the campaign.

In addition to the morale boost such calls provided to our fund-raising leadership, there was at least one critical reason they were necessary. We raised money by virtue of the connections we developed with people who commanded large networks of their own. In determining the feasibility of various plans we put together, it was necessary to get a sense from these donors of how realistic our ideas actually were. Did our finance committee think they would be able to attract 500 people at $50 each on a Tuesday night? How about an additional 500 people at a high-dollar event to follow? No matter what we thought of the reasonableness of various plans, our finance committee members knew their networks much better than we did. We ignored their advice at our own peril.

After several days of back and forth among all the various actors, and after reaching out to a number of venues for price quotes, we wrote a final plan to submit to headquarters. We were about three weeks out from the date of the fund-raiser, and we proposed two events. One was a double-tiered, high-dollar fund-raiser at the Drake Hotel in the swanky, North Michigan Avenue area of downtown Chicago. It would include a $1,000 general reception for 500 people and a $2,300 VIP reception that included a photo with the senator. The second was a low-dollar event for 1,000 people with $100 admission, which was to take place at the Alhambra Palace Restaurant in the trendy West Loop area of Chicago.

Because months of easy fund-raising had made us somewhat overconfident, we decided to make this our first and only open press event. It raised the stakes for us significantly. Campaigns have an almost pathological fear of having their candidates appear in an empty room, and for good reason. If someone of Hillary Clinton's stature can't attract a few hundred people, it shows tremendous weakness and a lack of popular support. This concern is greatly magnified if the press attends an event. In the past, if we failed to put together a successful event, the only people who knew were the donors we had managed to gather. With this event, if we could not attract enough supporters, our failure would be broadcast on the evening news that night, along with more positive reports of Senator Barack Obama's polling gains and fund-raising prowess. This event would be our attempt to prove that even in her opponent's backyard, Hillary Clinton was strong, that in the depths of Obama country, we could gather over 1,000 people to loudly express their support in a rally-style fund-raiser.

Before we could release news of this event to the public and begin recruiting in earnest, our invitation and choice of venues had to be approved. To recap, we had committed ourselves to recruiting 1,500 donors in less than three weeks and organizing the detailed logistics of an evening that would include events occurring practically one after another across town. If this seems somewhat last-minute, it's because it was. A wedding with this many guests would be carefully planned months in advance, but because a campaign needs to be able to respond to any significant change in the political environment fairly quickly, scheduling extends for no more than about one month out. Time, then, was of the essence, so when the vetting department informed us that we would have to start over on the low-dollar fund-raiser, we were shocked and concerned.

Every important aspect of an event is sent through vetting to ensure that no hidden embarrassments result. The bundlers listed on the invitation as the host committee, the locations, and the speakers are checked by vetting professionals whose sole job is to keep the campaign out of media trouble. The location we chose, the Alhambra Palace, was a large, beautiful restaurant and one of the few locations able to accommodate so many people on such short notice. Unfortunately, it is located right next to an adult video store. The concern was that the press corps, which would inevitably take pictures and video of the venue as Hillary was walking in, would have a number of shots with the words "Adult" in the background. That was not acceptable. One of us called Alhambra to tell them of our decision to cancel. Though it was not a requirement and not even something we asked about, the owners were huge supporters of ours and were devastated at the news. We got a call back an hour after canceling asking us to reconsider—Alhambra had contacted the owners of the video store and asked if they could pay to have the sign covered up for one evening. The adult video store, also owned by a Hillary supporter, excitedly offered to do it for free, but vetting would not budge. Someone from the media might find out, or simply know, that it was an adult store anyway and report on it that night or the next morning. With very little time left, we had to find a new place with the capacity to handle 1,000 people on December 18.

The second place we found was approved. The Hyatt Regency, along the Chicago River in the center of Chicago, was able to accommodate us. Though we found this new venue fairly quickly, it still took three or four valuable days before our plans received final approval. With just under three weeks left, we had only just announced the event to the public and were only now able to begin inviting people to attend. In the meantime, national news about Hillary's candidacy had steadily grown worse. Polling showed the race narrowing slowly but consistently for several weeks. Worse than that, we began getting reports from other regional finance operations about events that couldn't be filled without substantial admission discounts and goals that were not being met. I remember hearing about a large low-dollar event similar to the one we were planning that took place in early December in St. Louis. The price of admission was comparable to or a bit lower than ours, but in order to reach the number of attendees that would make the hall look full, people had to be admitted for free or with substantial discounts. That event missed its goal by over $100,000. By this time, the webpage for our event had been posted for a few days and we had begun recruiting, but few people had actually accepted.

I was spending several hours a day on the phone calling through long lists of potential donors. One of my responsibilities on the campaign was to constantly find new targets for fund-raising outreach. I would do this in any number of ways, such as acquiring membership lists for prominent and exclusive clubs around the city. Frequently, some of the best cold-calling targets were individuals who gave to multiple candidates or who supported a single presidential candidate whose political chances were declining and whom everyone had all but written off because of anemic fund-raising and poll numbers. Using federal campaign contribution disclosure reports, I would gather the names and contact information for supporters of opposing candidates. In addition to the lists I assembled, we received similar information from finance committee members and the national office. We also had an extensive list of people who had attended various events of ours as guests of donors, and we mobilized a Young Leader group we had been developing for a few months to help increase attendance. Every day we arranged for a few volunteers to come in to call through these lists, using scripts we wrote up for them. If there was a free phone or if a volunteer failed to show up as promised, we would make the calls ourselves.

Slowly the response became better, but even with the improved results, people were not signing up fast enough. Just over a week before the event was scheduled, we decided that we needed to take steps to ensure that we had the right number of attendees. The first thing we decided was that we would be willing to make deals to encourage people to come in spite of the cost. One man called us saying that he had five people who wanted to attend, but that he couldn't afford the $500 it would cost to admit all of them. After talking to him for a few minutes, I agreed to let his whole party in for $250. We received a donation from him later that day. This kind of deal making was kept strictly under wraps. The event was still a fund-raiser, and the effect of announcing that we were open to deals like that one would be to prevent new people from signing up at the full price, in addition to the inevitable anger from the people who had already put down the $100.

Cutting deals had additional benefits. For instance, the potential contributor mentioned above had never given to us before, even though we had reached out to him previously. The people he brought along were also new to the campaign, and the goodwill that I fostered with them by allowing his group in at a deep discount paid off. A few months later I checked our donor database and saw that between the five of them, they had contributed an additional $500 to the campaign right at the times when we needed contributions most. As effective as this method was at increasing participation at fund-raisers, it took some getting used to. There was a time when I could double the contribution if an interested donor called after we had closed admission, a technique that would sometimes raise a few thousand extra dollars for an event.

Even with such efforts, on December 11, a week before the event, we had a problem. It was clear that though we had not yet filled up the high-dollar receptions at the Drake, that event would likely succeed. Senator Evan Bayh of Indiana had agreed to raise money among his fifty largest supporters in exchange for a klatch with his wife and Senator Clinton. Our finance committee had also managed to recruit a few hundred people to attend, and RSVPs to our invitations were still coming in at a steady pace. The low-dollar event was a different story. By this time, only about 400 people had responded. We comforted ourselves by saying that a significant portion of responses to fund-raisers came in a couple of days before the actual event. That was true, but given that there were always no-shows, especially during the cold snap the city was going through, and given the fact that we had recruited barely half the desired numbers, we knew something else had to be done. This was an open press event, and the last thing we needed was for press cameras to show an empty room.

The ballroom we had reserved could be split into smaller rooms, so I suggested shrinking the actual size of the space by blocking off one of its subsections. That would decrease the capacity of the hall to about 800. We would still need more people, but not quite as many as before. We had already reported to the press that the event was slated for 1,000 people, and there was no need to inform them of the change of plans. Reporters would arrive, film a full ballroom, and air the story of a successful Hillary fund-raiser in Chicago, likely using the figures we had already provided them. This may have worked, but we were reluctant to try it. There was no guarantee that the press would be fooled, and the deception itself was a cause for concern.

The solution emerged one day when the campaign managed to win the committed support of Chicago alderman Danny Solis, a relative of Patti Solis Doyle, a close associate of Hillary since the Clinton administration and the current campaign manager. Solis agreed to raise $40,000 and bring 400 people to the event. I was tremendously relieved, as was the rest of the team. The hotel informed us that even though the room we were using had a 1,000-person capacity, it would look full at about 800. With the alderman's contribution, we would have 800 attendees and would be able to present a room that was loosely full but visually acceptable. Solis intended to find 400 of his constituents and let them come for free while relying on seventeen of his top donors to give maximum contributions of $2,300 to Hillary for President. Just as Senator Bayh requested a klatch for his people at the Drake fund-raiser, Alderman Solis requested a similar gathering for his group at the Hyatt Regency. A few days after he agreed to help us with his supporters, we arranged for him to come to our offices. He arrived with his senior campaign and aldermanic staff, and we sat down with him to work out the details and thank him for his generous support. Campaign chairman Terry McAuliffe called in to speak to the assembled group to thank them for their support and to hear their advice and thoughts on the campaign.

Three Days Left

Over the next few days, more people signed up, and it became clear that the event was going to be important, even if not as successful as initially anticipated.

Our estimates showed that we would miss our goal of $800,000 by about $200,000, but we predicted about 1,200 people at the low-dollar event and 500 people for the high-dollar event. We asked approximately eighty volunteers to join us on Tuesday to help keep the event running smoothly. That was entirely too many people, but an overabundance of caution led us to recruit as many as possible. Even if we were overstaffed, volunteers provided bodies to fill the room, creating a picture for the cameras that was that much more impressive.

Three days before the event, national staff began arriving. The first person to arrive was the finance event coordinator, who spent most of his time on the road. He arrived a few days ahead of nearly every fund-raiser we organized and took over much of the direction and organization of the event. The local finance staff does the bulk of the planning in the weeks preceding the event, but at the end of the day, our focus was fund-raising and not event planning. The event coordinator's focus was on the flow and function of the evening. As soon as he landed, we took him to what would be the first of many walk-throughs. Because of the size and complexity of the night we had planned, a single walk-through could take over an hour. Both hotels had to be toured with an excruciating attention to detail. Ballrooms, spaces for klatches, hold rooms, the walking path the candidate would take, driving directions for the move from the Hyatt to the Drake, timing, the location of rope and stanchion, how the press would be organized, the shape of the press risers, positioning of volunteers, and many other details had to be covered. The event coordinator would correct and improve the plan we had put together based on his much greater expertise. Similar walk-throughs, though with much less detail, were arranged for others as well. We took the finance and host committees on a tour, ostensibly to get their input and adjust the event according to their wishes, but generally speaking by the time these groups got their walk-throughs, all the decisions had been made. As I mentioned previously, a lot of effort goes into developing and keeping bundlers and supporters involved. These tours are a prime example of this effort. They yielded no immediate benefit to us and took up large amounts of time, but our supporters felt appreciated and respected. I don't remember ever changing the flow of an event based on input received during these tours. Similar walk-throughs, with even less detail, were arranged for volunteers and the rapidly arriving national and advance staff.

The most important tour came the day before the event, on December 17. In the morning we greeted agents of the Secret Service. When other members of the campaign make a logistical request, there is room for debate and negotiation. Compromises are reached to create optimal efficiency. There is, however, no arguing with the Secret Service. After several events, we became fairly good at predicting the security demands of the agents. Precautions that would never have even occurred to me before became second nature. Windows, for instance, had to be covered at all times to ensure that a shooter could not aim through the glass. Hillary and Bill Clinton always had to be on the same level as the rest of the crowd (stages were permitted) to make it more difficult to get a vantage point from which to aim a weapon. The flow of an event mattered as well. A certain space bubble had to be maintained around the guarded individual to allow the agents to be able to intervene physically at a moment's notice. Most of the time, the flow we put together was approved, but when it wasn't, the result was intense discussion and sometimes wholesale redesign of certain portions of an event, again with an emphasis on the littlest detail. For this particular event, only minor changes had to be made.

By the day of the event, many more staffers had arrived from around the country. Finance professionals from neighboring regions were often the best kind of help. They dealt with similar work in other cities and so were used to the kinds of challenges presented by our event. In addition to the visiting finance staff, members of the campaign's national advance team arrived right before an event. Advance staff travel the country a few days ahead of a candidate and take over day-of management of events in coordination with the planning staff, in this case the Illinois finance office. They are presented with the plans as they stand at that point, make final adjustments, and run the detailed logistics throughout the day. Their attention to detail is impressive but also frustrating to fund-raisers, whose chief focus is raising money. Putting together events such as these was merely the means to that end, and so people in finance have a naturally big-picture view of the actual day of the event. Advance professionals focus only on the particular event at hand. Their job is to pay attention to the things nobody else is concerned with. Should tables have trimming to hide their legs? Should there be additional rope and stanchion in a particular section? Which path should a photo line follow? The work they do takes place at the most high-stress times in a campaign. Problems constantly come up and must be resolved. A myriad of tasks require attention, and the person who sees and judges your performance isn't just a normal campaign staffer, but Hillary Clinton or one of her prominent surrogates. That could be Bill, Chelsea, or celebrities from the political or entertainment establishments. Advance staffs, inevitably, are not fun to deal with. They are constantly stressed, on the go, and frequently worked up over what, at the end of the day, are minor issues at best.

The Event

On the day of the event, we spent several hours making name tags for the high-dollar donors. Name tags are used to manage traffic flow. In a low-dollar event where there is essentially a single destination for the bulk of the attendees, there is no need to create methods of quickly sorting the group, but our high-dollar event at the Drake, like most of the ones we put together throughout the year, had multiple stages and sections. We had to be able to quickly direct people to prevent large pile-ups and long lines. Name tags have different stickers depending on which areas the wearer is allowed to enter, and volunteers are distributed throughout the event and told to admit only certain people. Mistakes must be minimized: There is no better way to upset high-dollar donors than to make them wait in line for an hour for an event they paid over $2,000 to attend.

I saw the inside of the low-dollar fund-raiser only briefly, and that was before most of the donors had arrived. Reporters milled about, interviewing people about Hillary and what it was like to support her in the middle of Obama country. Guests and volunteers struck defiant notes, something that I found to be common among Hillary supporters in Chicago, where it sometimes seemed like absolutely everyone else supported Obama and thought our preference was ridiculous.

Between the entrance to the hotel and the area that we had rented out for the day, there were people posted at frequent intervals, ready to direct groups of excited supporters. We had far too many volunteers, but they were a great asset. They spent much of the time talking to each other about how great it was to be there and what they thought of some recent piece of news, and generally projected an aura of excitement and happiness to arriving guests. This being a rally-style fund-raiser, the more energized the crowd, the better. The news reports that night showed Hillary emerging into a sea of enthusiastic, exuberant, loud faces—precisely the impression we wanted to communicate to the rest of the city.

I was assigned to the VIP reception at the Drake. I organized a group of volunteers and told them what to expect, and spent much of the first several hours walking around the room, talking and interacting with groups of people as they arrived. By this time I had been on the campaign for about six months and was acquainted with every member of the finance committee and with many of the donors who had attended multiple fund-raisers. While working the room, I always made a special effort to have a conversation with the bundlers we depended on most.

Talking to high-profile donors is a tightrope act. As a representative of the campaign, I had to stay on message. National communications would intermittently send out talking points to all staff and interns in order to keep the campaign consistent. As I have since learned, talking points that political organizations put together are always painfully rudimentary. They provide only general outlines of fairly elementary concepts focusing on issues that the campaign is currently pushing, basic responses to the most recent controversy, and occasionally arguments against opposing candidates. On a national campaign, these talking points are heavily tested through polling and focus groups to provide the optimal phrasing and topic selection.

They should have been helpful in situations like this one, where I was required to work a room and communicate the message of the campaign, but that was not the case. In interacting with voters or donors, it is critical to respond to the target at their level of sophistication. For the political operation, in which most communication takes place with people on the street or during canvassing, basic talking points usually suffice. But I was a member of the finance team, so I was interacting with individuals who invested significant resources and time into the political process. In a VIP reception, the average level of political understanding far exceeds that of most common voters because this group is self-selecting: If an individual is willing to commit the funds and time to attend, it is because politics interests him. In these conversations it was necessary to balance honest political analysis with the message coming from headquarters. As I mentioned above, this was a time of growing pessimism on the campaign, and our trouble raising the funds necessary to hit our goal drove this home to me and everyone else on the team, but a donor who has assumed defeat is not one who will continue raising money. Keeping our contributors energized and happy was, therefore, vital to the continuing success of our finance effort. In the face of falling fund-raising and narrowing polls, we had to maintain a constant façade of optimism without appearing blind to events unfolding every day, even after we ourselves had stopped believing in our candidate's chances. That took practice.

According to the plan, Hillary was supposed to arrive at the low-dollar event at about 7 P.M., but because of a snowstorm, her plane didn't depart Iowa until after 7:15. The supporters gathered in the room grew frustrated but stayed patient. I'm not sure the featured speaker was ever on time for any of the events I worked on, but the presence of an open bar coupled with the anticipation of the speaker's arrival usually kept people in reasonable humor. Fortunately, this particular event attracted a number of prominent Hillary supporters from across the Midwest, so political heavyweights like Ohio governor Ted Strickland and other elected officials spent time interacting with people at the reception and, in a buildup to Hillary's arrival, delivered speeches emphasizing the health of the campaign and the wonderful future that awaited an America with Clinton as president.

After what must have been a two-hour delay, Senator Clinton arrived at the Drake. She was given a few minutes to prepare herself in a holding room and then rushed to the Evan Bayh klatch. The thirty people gathered in the room we had reserved for the gathering burst into applause when Hillary arrived with her Secret Service entourage. She addressed the group along with Susan Bayh, Senator Bayh's wife. Hillary first thanked everyone for their support and spoke warmly about Senator Bayh and all he was doing for her campaign. She then spent a few minutes discussing her prospects and the political landscape. After a few questions, she spent some time greeting and shaking hands with everyone in the room. A lot of people asked for pictures, and some addressed her with policy concerns. She spent time with every family and couple there, always listening attentively and responding to substantive questions thoughtfully, with the campaign message always in mind. She would round out an argument with a request for support for the campaign, or would pepper a comment with references to the need for continued involvement. It was impressive how naturally she was able to meld a policy response with political messaging, and everyone came away with a sense that she was sincere, committed, and needed their continued support, even if the necessarily short answer did not address all the concerns raised.

Seeing her interact with supporters in a variety of contexts, both at high- and low-dollar events, confirmed for me my original decision to support her. She connected with people from all sorts of backgrounds and was able to respond in a way they understood and could appreciate. When a number of supporters criticized her for accepting contributions from lobbyists while Obama was claiming not to, she did not dissemble or avoid the issue but responded to it directly. In situations in which I observed her engaged in a conversation on policy, it was clear that she was committed and deeply informed. In conversations she acknowledged the narrowing poll numbers but would then present other evidence and anecdotes that suggested strength. The senator accepted challenges to her positions but would also push back and explain another interpretation or a mitigating consideration. She achieved credibility with her audience not by denying individual facts, but by arguing that they didn't represent the entire truth.

From the klatch, it was on to the main VIP reception. The 200 people gathered here had to be herded into a long line that snaked around the room. One after another, or sometimes in family groups, the person at the front of the line would approach Clinton, speak to her briefly, maybe have a photo taken with her, and then move on to the larger general reception. Hillary kept smiling and engaging everyone who approached her. The photo line is a particularly political phenomenon. I can imagine few other situations where people are willing to pay so much for so little. Photo lines were reserved for VIP receptions where the cost of admission was $2,300. In exchange for this exorbitant contribution, donors were given the privilege of mingling in a room for over two hours before being ushered into a line that could last an additional hour. At the end of the wait, you get less than a minute with the candidate and a hasty snapshot taken by a photographer who has already taken hundreds of similar photos already and whose priority is to keep the line moving. As you exit the room, a staffer, usually from the advance team, hands you a card directing you to a website. The website hosts thousands of similar photos taken at events across the country. Once you locate your image, you can order a print for no less than $40, but as much as several hundred if you prefer yours to be mounted in a commemorative frame. Because I ran several of these events, I had the opportunity to tag along at the end of a line and get myself a picture as well. I did this a few times with both Bill and Hillary, and not once did the photograph come out even halfway decent. I didn't spend any serious amount of time studying the site, but I'm convinced that not one of the other images turned out well either.

Running a photo line is among the most tiring experiences imaginable. Even with the help of the advance team, this process is chronically understaffed.

Keeping a mob of people in an organized line while an accessible celebrity is standing in the room is next to impossible. Everyone is eager to rush in, take a picture, ask for an autograph, or start a conversation. The line must keep moving, and because Hillary would never be rude to a donor or supporter, it was left up to the staff to gently but firmly maintain the flow of the event. Push-pull, as the process is called, is met with resistance by nearly everyone in attendance because everyone wants to have a longer conversation. By the time the general reception speeches were about to begin, I was entirely too exhausted to listen, especially since Hillary and her surrogates delivered basically the same stump speech every time. Any changes were reflected in the talking points anyway. After the event had wrapped, Hillary made a special point of asking the Illinois finance staff to be gathered so that she could personally thank us for a successful event. Even after an incredibly long day, she walked up to us beaming and radiant. She thanked each of us individually and chatted with our four-person group for a few minutes about the event and its planning, as well as the campaign in general. It was not the end of her night, however. She was still scheduled to have drinks with J. B. Pritzker in her rooms upstairs. So after a brief conversation, she was ushered away to prepare for her final task of the evening.

Postscript to the Event

It was a particularly rewarding evening not only because of the success of the event, but because of what followed. Terry McAuliffe was staying in a large suite at the Hyatt Regency where the first event was held. After final business had been taken care of, he invited all the finance staff and a couple of donors to join him to unwind—scotch, wine, plenty of food, and some pool. We discussed politics and the campaign, but mostly it was a relaxing evening of stories and jokes, alcohol, and food. I stayed until four in the morning, even though I was more tired than I had been in ages. Not only was I having a great time, but when you're in politics, the business of relationships, an invitation to interact with a political superstar like Terry, senior finance staff, and high-profile donors, is not optional. Terry was boisterous and energetic, much like Hillary had been, quick to start a conversation and even quicker with a dirty joke. The sound was muted on the television, but it was turned off entirely when the anchors discussed the campaign.

Terry gave a few press interviews before the evening wrapped up. We had raised about $650,000 that day, but he told the media that we had just pulled off "a million-dollar day here in Chicago." Financially speaking, the event was not the success we had originally hoped for. We had come up about $200,000 short of the goal. Alderman Solis avoided us for weeks after that night. It was clear to us that he was unable to come up with the $40,000 he had promised. For the next month he had aides answer calls, and on several occasions they told us that the checks had been messengered that day. It wasn't until mid-January that we finally received four checks totaling $9,600. We never heard from the alderman again. We started referring to this kind of behavior as the Solis Special, and though this example was more egregious than most, this wasn't entirely uncommon no matter what part of the campaign we were in or what the political news was. Nonetheless, we had made a strong political statement by rallying such a large crowd in Chicago, and we had successfully executed an extremely complex event while keeping donors happy, which itself led to additional contributions down the line that mitigated some of our original shortfall.

By the end of the night, I was excited and satisfied. The entire evening felt surreal. My journey had started barely eleven months before this when, in torn jeans that were wet from the melting snow and a drab hoodie, I had run into one of the most powerful Democratic politicians in the country while getting a sandwich. Now I was shooting pool and trading barbs with the same man in his hotel room. It was immensely gratifying—I knew that I had achieved this because of my commitment and my skills, and I knew that my experience, at least in this sense, was not unique.

The Dark at the End of the Tunnel

As I noted, the trouble began after an early November debate when Hillary Clinton answered a question about driver's licenses for illegal immigrants. The question was a difficult one. The answer she gave didn't provide any good sound bites and reflected a degree of nuance that many interpreted as waffling, specifically Senator Chris Dodd, who pounced on her response immediately. That both Obama and John Edwards provided nearly identical responses to the question over the next several weeks didn't matter. The damage had been done. In postmortems on Clinton's candidacy, different analysts and politicos gave varying start dates for the campaign's decline. Some pointed to Oprah Winfrey joining the Obama campaign in December, which had a profound effect on polling of African Americans in South Carolina. Others cited an admittedly dismal— at least compared to Obama's—turnout operation in Iowa. Although it was all true, from my perspective, the beginning of the end was that debate. Although the effect was not instant, I began to notice new difficulties attracting donors, and the finance committee was no longer able to as effectively recruit new people either. Previous to that debate, Hillary Clinton's performance had been consistently strong. She had won all or most of the preceding debates, appearing confident and in control of the issues. Polling placed us far ahead of all of our competitors. When she tripped up on that question, it was as if everyone saw the first sign of fallibility, saw for the first time that our candidate was not invincible, and it quickly became harder to convince people to invest in her campaign. Once that happens, a candidate's chances begin to fade, and the light at the end of the long campaign tunnel starts to darken.

The experience of working on a campaign, especially a prominent one that receives significant attention from the media and the public, is an unparalleled roller-coaster ride and at least as thrilling. I still remember the tremendous dejection and sense of hopelessness that set in the week after the Iowa caucuses and our string of losses in February, and I can remember few feelings of elation like the one after our victories in New Hampshire, Texas, and Ohio. If you work for a candidate or cause you truly believe in, as was emphatically the case for me, this thrill is complemented by the understanding that your work is truly purposeful. Though the campaign did not conclude as any of us had hoped, it was nonetheless a watershed experience for me. Working for Hillary taught me how to deliver a political message and communicate effectively in a way that no amount of education could have, and it provided me the opportunity to meet and work closely with a range of successful people, which encouraged me to pursue my own ambitions. My political instincts and the career I have since proceeded to build were profoundly shaped by a chance encounter with Terry McAuliffe one day in a sandwich shop, and the work that happened to follow it.

5

Media, Money, and Mud in Illinois's Eleventh Congressional District

Tari Renner

Type of campaign: US House (general)

Role of author: Candidate

Lessons to look for:
- All campaigns are basically local affairs.
- Planning, organization, and strategy matter.
- Campaigns are about taking advantage of opportunities.
- Incumbency, like inertia, is hard to overcome.
- Money matters, and it matters most to challengers.
- Campaigns need both earned and paid media to get their message out.
- Campaigning is a contact sport, sometimes played dirty.

In May 2003, I decided to seek the 2004 Democratic nomination for US Congress in Illinois's Eleventh Congressional District against Republican incumbent Jerry Weller. I had ideological concerns that our country was taking the wrong track on important policies facing us—the economy, energy, health care, and foreign affairs. My views on these issues were not reflected in the votes cast by my congressional representative. Weller consistently voted for the policies I thought were wrongheaded. In fact, the incumbent supported the Bush administration's position on virtually everything. I was convinced that I would do a better job of making policies to effectively address the nation's problems. In addition, as an academic, I had the intellectual curiosity of a political scientist who had studied elections all his life. At many levels, I wondered what it would be like to challenge a congressional incumbent in a potentially competitive district. However, the race for Congress in 2004 was not my first run for elective office. In 1998, I ran for the McLean County (Bloomington/Normal area) Legislature and defeated a Republican incumbent who had come in on his party's tidal wave four years earlier. I was reelected without opposition in 2002.

There were contextual factors indicating an upset victory was plausible. Few incumbents lose, but when they *do* lose, they do so in congressional districts like Illinois's Eleventh. It is a marginal or competitive district in presidential elections. The Eleventh was Illinois's most evenly divided congressional district in the 2000 presidential race. Republican George Bush received 50 percent of the vote to Democrat Al Gore's 48 percent, leaving 2 percent for the Green Party's Ralph Nader.

The Republican incumbent rarely provided himself with political cover by trimming toward the ideological center. He had a 100 percent voting record in support of the Bush administration. A clear case could be made that Weller's votes on key issues such as prescription drug coverage, a patient bill of rights, and special tax breaks for oil companies reflected the positions of powerful special interests that contributed large sums to his campaigns. In addition, there were political scandals involving his fund-raising that could potentially be exploited by a challenger. The Federal Election Commission (FEC) had ruled in 2003 that his campaign received over $100,000 in illegal contributions. Further, there were rumors among the activists and media throughout the district of a shady land deal Weller negotiated in Nicaragua. Given these potential vulnerabilities and the fact that I would be an "experienced challenger" (the term analysts use for those who have held an elected office, as opposed to "novice challenger"), I reasoned that the contextual factors could make for a competitive race.

I also realized that the chances of pulling an upset of the incumbent would be magnified if some national political winds developed favoring the out-party (in this case, the Democrats). My strategy was to attempt to replicate the 2000 Gore/Nader vote totals in my district. Gore's and Nader's combined vote slightly exceeded Bush's total. Our logic was that, if the choice was clarified, these voters would support a Democratic challenger over a Republican incumbent who voted with George Bush 100 percent of the time.

There were also some sobering realities that I knew would limit my chances under the best of circumstances. First of all, it would be very difficult to raise the money necessary to get our message out against an incumbent in a sprawling district. The natural difficulties of challengers would be magnified in this situation for several reasons. The Eleventh reaches into eight counties and three media markets (Chicago, Peoria-Bloomington, and the Quad Cities). This meant that the costs of communicating via television would be very high and inefficient. Further, Weller's three previous challengers (in 2002, 2000, and 1998) raised very little money beyond their own contributions to their campaigns. In fact, the most recent challenger in 2002 was virtually invisible and spent only $30,000. So, our campaign would have to start from scratch since there was literally no donor base of people who had consistently given money to defeat the incumbent. Finally, although I was an elected official and had served as a political commentator for eight years on the NBC affiliate in Peoria/Bloomington, my home base represented less than 15 percent of the district's population.

Nevertheless, the Eleventh District was clearly one of the few across the country that was winnable for either party. That was an important strategic consideration in my decision to run, as well as a critical starting point in recruiting and motivating volunteers; receiving endorsements from prominent politicians, bloggers, and interest groups; and soliciting money from potential contributors. Our campaign kept making the case that this district could be won. It offered one of the few opportunities to pick up a seat and help shift the control of the US House to the Democrats. However, much of our campaign and initial strategy would be eclipsed by an issue no one expected. The political firestorm resulting from it created much free media for our campaign, but it all came with a mixed blessing.

The Dictator's Daughter

Over a year after I decided to run, a strange and twisted series of events unfolded that would forever change the dynamics of our campaign. As we arrived at the first of many Fourth of July parades across the district, in 2004, a local activist who was working the event for another Democratic candidate came up to me and asked, "Did you hear that Weller's got a big announcement of some form coming? One friend of mine on the GOP side of the aisle says that he's getting married. Can you believe that?" I thanked him for the heads-up on a brewing rumor, but neither my campaign manager Matt Glavin nor I paid much attention to it since we thought that it, even if true, would be largely irrelevant to us.

Three days after the parades, I was contacted by Kurt Erickson, a reporter from the *Bloomington Pantagraph*. Kurt asked me if I knew that Weller's fiancée was Zury Rios Montt, the daughter of former Guatemalan dictator and army general Jose Efrain Rios Montt. I had known Kurt for many years, and he had interviewed me dozens of times as a political commentator long before I ran for Congress. So, at first, I thought he might just be joking with me. I snapped back, "Yeah, right, and I'm marrying Hitler's granddaughter next week." He responded, "No, Tari, I'm serious! We were scratching our heads over this last night in the newsroom." After realizing Kurt wasn't kidding, I asked if I could call him back with an "official reaction." I immediately called our campaign team together: Matt Glavin, Gretchen Grabowski (finance director), Jake Posey (pollster), Pete Giagreco (direct mail and message specialist). Matt and Gretchen were on-site with the rest of the staff at the Bloomington campaign headquarters, and Jake and Pete joined us in a conference call from their firms' offices.

The engagement seemed extremely bizarre to all of us, since his fiancée was clearly part of a genocidal regime and no one in the district had ever seen the two of them together. It was also unique: No member of Congress had ever married a member of another country's parliament. Beyond that, however, Jerry Weller had a conflict of interest because he was a member of the House Foreign Affairs Committee and its subcommittee on the Western Hemisphere. The latter had jurisdiction over US foreign policy and aid to countries in the region. It was, in fact, because of his committee membership that he met his fiancée, Zury. The two were introduced when Weller was on a fact-finding trip to Guatemala.

Our campaign debated how to handle this news. Ultimately, we issued a press statement on Thursday, July 8. The headline was "Renner Calls on Weller to Denounce Ties to a Brutally Repressive Guatemalan Political Party." The statement was short and to the point: "Weller's fiancée, Zury Rios Sosa, is a Guatemalan member of Congress and the daughter of Guatemalan Army General Jose Efrain Rios Montt, who was charged with genocide from [*sic*] the killing of thousands of innocent citizens. Congresswoman Sosa represents her father's political party, the Guatemalan Republican Front (FRG)." The statement continued with a quote from Frank Boyd, a political scientist who specialized in Latin America: "Rios Montt was the most brutal dictator of the 1980s. He was the Slobodan Milosevic of Guatemala." Another quote was from a Nobel Peace Prize nominee, who said Rios Montt was "to Guatemala what Pinochet is to Chile." It included the specifics of Rios Montt's military regime and his reign of terror, noting that by the end of direct military rule in Guatemala in 1985, 400 villages had been razed, more than 100,000 people had been killed or simply disappeared, and hundreds of thousands more had been driven into exile or a political netherworld at home. There were no direct quotes from me in the statement. Matt, as the campaign manager, played the bad cop. He was quoted as saying, "Jerry Weller's renegade diplomacy puts US foreign policy at risk. While the State Department was distancing itself from Rios Montt, Weller was courting the dictator's daughter, who is herself a leader of a political party which ruled by torture, intimidation, and murder."

The long media controversy began that morning shortly after the statement went out. The proverbial "gloves came off" from both campaigns as Weller and I had live radio interviews sequentially on WJBC (the number one commercial news radio station in the Bloomington area). Weller was on first and was asked about the engagement and any conflicts of interest. The campaign staff, several volunteers, and I were listening to this live interview in the campaign headquarters (I was to call in immediately after Weller went off the air). Representative Weller began with a very powerful response: "This is a personal matter! Zury is the best thing that's ever happened to me. She's an incredible woman. Only the lowest form of politician would try to take advantage of something like this. It's sad that the professor has stooped so low that he is attacking the woman I love. The woman I am going to marry. The woman I hope to raise a family with." The show hosts, Beth and Jim, gently prodded Weller to more directly answer some of the concerns about the Rios Montt regime and any possible conflicts of interest as a result of his service on the Western Hemisphere subcommittee. Weller's response to every attempt to address the controversy was exactly the same. He repeated, almost verbatim, the same sentences: "This is a personal matter! Zury is the best thing that's ever happened to me. She's an incredible woman. Only the lowest form of politician would try to take advantage of something like this and attack the woman I love . . . the woman I'm going to marry and raise a family with."

After several rounds of this, Beth and Jim tried another tactic. They quoted Frank Boyd's statement from the press release, saying, "Well, Congressman, the Renner campaign quotes a specialist in Latin American politics as saying that Rios Montt is the 'Slobodan Milosevic of Guatemala.' What's your reaction to this?" Weller kept to his script by saying, "Well, you're quoting one of the professor's left-wing buddies. As I said, this is a personal matter! Zury is the best thing that has ever happened to me. She's the love of my life. Only the lowest form of politician would try to take advantage of something like this." Ultimately, Beth tried to press him by asking, "But, if your fiancée continues to support a brutal regime, isn't that a political controversy and not a personal one?" Weller stuck to his script by saying, "No, this *is* a personal attack on my fiancée, the woman I'm going to marry, the woman I'm going to spend the rest of my life with. Only the lowest form of politician would stoop this low." Beth and Jim finally gave up, congratulated him on his engagement, and wished him a happy birthday. In the interview, Weller had repeated his standard response ("This is a personal matter!") a total of nine times! After the third time Weller repeated his lines, Matt started his typical pacing around the campaign headquarters, wearing a grin rivaling that of the Cheshire cat in *Alice in Wonderland* and saying, "This is great! This is great! He's more of an idiot than I had ever imagined. We've got him now!" The only time Weller deviated slightly from the script was when he acknowledged at one point during the interview that he didn't even know who Zury was when they met.

I called in after Beth and Jim concluded their interview with Weller. They started by repeating Weller's claim that this was a "personal matter." I responded this way:

> Genocide is not a personal matter. National Security is not a personal matter. Congressman Weller sits on the House Foreign Relations Committee and the subcommittee on the Western Hemisphere. . . . It is supposed to protect democracy and promote human rights abroad. Mr. Weller's fiancée is a member of the Guatemalan Republican Guard. She is her father's key political operative in parliament who is trying to get him back into power. There are obvious possible conflicts of interest here. God forbid, what if she is successful in getting this butcher back into power? You don't have to be a rocket scientist to realize the possible national security problems, perhaps even unintentional, if that were to happen. These are important political, not personal, questions and Mr. Weller pretended to be a martyr and dodged them all.

They then asked me about Weller's response to Boyd's quote in the press release (Rios Montt was the "Slobodan Milosevic of Guatemala"). I responded,

"If Congressman Weller doesn't believe Frank, then I suggest he consult what's called the *Encyclopedia Britannica* and the website of the State Department of the United States of America. Both make it clear that nearly 20,000 people died during his regime and nearly 200,000 during the civil war."

After our interviews, the radio station's phones rang off the hook for several hours with callers reacting to what they had heard. Virtually all were anti-Weller. Some were appalled at the connection with a genocidal dictator, but most were mad that he not only refused to answer Beth and Jim's questions but also gave exactly the same response over and over. The first caller said, "He sounded like a 'Stepford Husband,' merely repeating the same old lines over and over as if he were 'brainwashed' or something." As caller after caller came on the air to bash Weller, Matt's grin turned into a beaming glow. After an hour or so, he said, "If this keeps up, it'll become the 'Renner News Network.'"

There were several empirical realities that tempered my interpretation of the callers' reactions. First of all, they were Bloomington/Normal (McLean County) area residents who didn't know Jerry Weller very well (that portion of the district was added after the 2001 redistricting, so he had represented the area for only three years). I wondered if he would have greater political "body armor" in the areas of the district he represented for over a decade. But, most importantly, these callers actually heard both interviews. Weller appeared more disingenuous as the questioning continued. This is not how the controversy would be reported as it spread throughout the district.

This interview was only the beginning of an explosion of national and international news over the congressman and the dictator's daughter. There was saturation coverage in virtually every major news outlet in the district and in the Chicago area on Thursday and Friday. We were contacted almost immediately by journalists throughout the United States and in Guatemala for interviews (including *Good Morning, Guatemala*). The *New York Times* sent its Latin American reporter to interview me at our Bloomington headquarters on Friday, July 9.

As the controversy unfolded, all of us learned much more about the scope of the situation. The Guatemalan journalists, for example, talked to me off the record after the interviews and all indicated how horrified they were about the legitimacy that the marriage would give the rejected Rios Montt regime throughout their region. After I gave dozens of telephone interviews all day Friday, *Times* reporter Steve Kinser arrived a little before lunch and spent much of the afternoon with the campaign. He interviewed me, Matt, Gretchen, and several volunteers and took dozens of pictures. At some point in the middle of the afternoon, Kinser walked the streets of downtown Bloomington and asked passersby their opinion of the story. He and I had half a dozen conversations throughout the day. I was mixing our discussions with press interviews from around the country and the globe. After spending several hours with me and the staff, Kinser said, "I don't know much of anything about this Weller character, but I can tell you, I know Zury. She is Machiavellian to the core! She doesn't blink without a cold cruel calculation. There were political motivations behind each of her other three marriages." It turned out that the Weller campaign even got the number of her previous marriages wrong. At thirty-six, she had already been married four times.

And on it went. At 3:30 P.M., Matt, Gretchen, and I had to leave to get to Springfield by 4:30 so that I could be interviewed at the capitol news bureaus of the major Chicago networks for their 6:00 news programs. The off-the-record reactions of most journalists were exemplified by the comments of one Chicago news anchor that evening. With about sixty seconds before our taped interview began, he said, "I honestly didn't think you had much of a chance against Weller until this broke. Wow! Talk about a 'gift from the gods.'"

My years of experience as a television political commentator came in handy during this particularly intense barrage of press coverage. Within hours, I had shifted from dozens of interviews by print journalists and reporters from radio stations (some live and some taped) to a totally different medium, conducted in a highly controlled studio environment, with an exceptional premium on visuals and very concise remarks (one that is, in many respects, the most difficult and least forgiving). In Springfield that late Friday afternoon, I had three waves of television interviews (for each of the three major Chicago networks). I wasn't the slightest bit uncomfortable talking to someone in Chicago while staring into a camera lens in a studio 200 miles away. It was in this environment, while wearing an earpiece and a microphone on my tie, that I had become conditioned to being the most succinct in my remarks.

We were getting media attention because of Weller's engagement, but also we were picking up allies. As we returned from the major network interviews that evening, Matt received word that the Democratic Congressional Campaign Committee (DCCC) jumped on the bandwagon that Friday, July 9. The DCCC issued a press release criticizing Representative Weller for having a "clear" conflict of interest, "serving on the committee that sets American policy for Central America while he's marrying into the family of a Guatemalan dictator." The press release noted that

> GOP Rep. Jerry Weller (IL) has responded to questions about his engagement to the daughter of a murderous Guatemalan dictator by saying, "love knows no boundaries."
> Fair enough. But should Rep. Weller continue to serve on the House Foreign Relations Committee and the Western Hemisphere Subcommittee when he is marrying into the family of Efrain Rios Montt, whose tenure the State Department declared "the most violent period" of Guatemala's 36 year Civil War? . . . Congressman Weller has a clear conflict of interest serving on the committee that sets American policy for Central America while he's marrying into the family of a Guatemalan dictator . . . Rep. Weller can do as he pleases in his personal life, but he doesn't have the right to influence America's foreign policy.

"Feeding Frenzy": The Second Wave

In a campaign conference call between the staff and the consultants on Monday morning, July 12, we decided what to do next. The unanimous consensus was that, given Weller's terrible response to the firestorm around his engagement, we needed to hammer home the conflict of interest and dramatize the human rights problems in Guatemala. We would specifically call for Weller to resign from his committee position, something several newspapers had already done. The actual stories of massive physical violence, torture, and countless murders were incredibly gruesome, but I refused to push the envelope too far by taking advantage of tragedy. We compromised by holding a series of events with a representative from a Guatemalan human rights organization located in Chicago. He highlighted the core reasons that his organization was concerned about the legitimacy this marriage would bring to the rejected Rios Montt regime. He was understandably nervous about speaking in front of reporters throughout the state, so we had our message consultant Pete's associate, Stacy, come along as an interpreter.

The second wave of publicity was almost as massive as the first (at least within the state of Illinois), primarily because Weller's campaign answered none of the questions we raised and patently refused to acknowledge any conflict of interest or entertain the possibility of resigning from the committee. On Thursday, July 15, I did a live call-in interview with Bloomington-based WJBC at 7:30 A.M. (I called in on my cell phone as Matt drove up to Chicago), in which I formally called on Weller to resign his seat on the Foreign Relations Committee and the Western Hemisphere subcommittee. The interview was conducted by Colleen and Scott on their morning show. Colleen started by asking, "Why are you pressing this issue? Congressman Weller says this is just a personal matter!" I responded, "The Congressman and I are both 'public officials' who are obviously entitled to personal lives. But, when your personal life involvements have clear public consequences, you've got to set things right—at least to ensure there are no clear conflicts of interest." My comment led Colleen to follow up with the next logical question, "Well, what's the problem here?" I responded:

> Jerry Weller is certainly entitled to marry whoever he wants but, as a member of the House Western Hemisphere subcommittee which oversees US foreign policy and aid to the region, his very presence on that committee gives legitimacy to the rejected murderous regime which his fiancée is trying to bring back into power. In addition, specific votes on matters of importance to the region could very easily pose serious conflicts of interest. I join the *Chicago Sun-Times* and other newspapers in the state which have called upon him to resign his committee post.

Scott interjected,

Hey, let me tell you I Googled this guy, Rios Montt and his daughter, Zury, and let me tell you this is just crazy! She is not just the daughter! She's his party leader in their legislature and led much of his campaign to regain power last year. You're just calling for him to resign from the Committee. I can't imagine how we could even have someone in Congress who's tied to this kind of regime. This is just crazy!

Scott's remarks permitted me to play the good cop during the remainder of the interview.

Next, we stopped in Joliet, 95 miles north of Bloomington, for a live 9 A.M. radio interview. We left there after a quick taped interview and began our Chicago news conference, where we met Stacy and the gentleman from the Guatemalan human rights organization at a downtown hotel at 11 A.M. Representatives from the major radio and television stations were in attendance, along with reporters from the *Sun-Times* and the *Tribune* and some local Spanish-language newspapers and radio stations, and the room was full. We promptly got back in the car to drive back down to a Bloomington press conference at 3 P.M., which was covered by the local television and radio stations and the *Pantagraph.*

As the press onslaught continued, the Weller campaign's only concession after several weeks was a promise to abstain from any vote having to do directly with Guatemala. This response was fairly meaningless from a substantive perspective, but it might have blunted some of the media feeding frenzy if it had come immediately. At the very least, it would have been better than outright denial or Weller's often-quoted line that he "wouldn't comment on Guatemalan domestic politics." That was certainly the consensus of our campaign's consultants and any journalists who were willing to comment to us off the record.

In addition, Representative Weller's reputation for arrogance showed in the few press interviews he gave during this time. This behavior began to alienate many journalists, particularly since our style was very different. Several reporters told us how irritated the incumbent was at the very mention of the subject, and it became painfully apparent in a rare live radio interview after the second wave began. Weller agreed to appear on WJBC, as long as he was interviewed by the station manager (he refused to be interviewed by most of the reporters at the station, presumably because he viewed them as being too hostile). Weller was gently but consistently pressed to give answers directly addressing the "conflict of interest" concerns by the station manager. After repeated attempts to get Weller to get off the "Tari Renner is the lowest form of politician to attack the love of my life" line of attack, the interviewer said, "But, Congressman, it's not just the Renner campaign that's bringing this up. Our phones were ringing off the hook, with many of your constituents calling in who had very similar concerns about this situation. How do you respond to them?" While never wavering from his script, Weller was apparently so incensed at the line of questioning that, after the interview, he threw his headphones down on the counter and stormed out of the studio.

An indication of how this situation soured his relationship with the press came from an opinion column written by Tom Collins in the September 1, 2004, edition of the *LaSalle News Tribune:*

> He [Weller] has ignored our repeated calls for an interview. He has never is-
> sued a single press release about it. Clearly, he wants the whole subject to sim-
> ply go away. There is just one small problem. Jerry Weller is a member of the
> United States House of Representatives and his association with the daughter
> of a Third World dictator has raised grave questions about Weller's standing
> on issues of foreign policy. The one person who doesn't seem to grasp this
> simple fact is Weller himself. Oh, the Morris Republican had no problem
> showing off Zury Rios Sosa for the flash cameras. Weller's Guatemalan bride-
> to-be is a stunningly beautiful woman. . . . But when Zury's lineage surfaced
> in the news—courtesy of Weller's opponent, Bloomington Democrat Tari
> Renner—Weller was no longer in the mood to talk about Zury and her pop.
> Here's why: Gen. Jose Efrain Rios Montt is a butcher. . . . [H]e wiped out
> enough Guatemalans to roughly match the population of LaSalle County . . .
> Weller only broke his stony silence to accuse Renner of playing dirty pool.
> "Professor Renner owes my fiancée an apology," Weller said after I finally
> cornered him. "His vicious attacks to smear my fiancée are character assassi-
> nations.". . . Remember this, Mr. Weller: Renner didn't introduce Zury Rios
> Sosa to the world, you did. Now start talking.

Where's Weller? Not Here!

In our third wave of press coverage, we tried to take advantage of the media momentum surrounding this situation by stressing a related but different line of attack. We wanted to suggest a pattern of behavior on Weller's part. Matt and
volunteers working on the opposition research uncovered several pieces of information that we could weave together into an attack. The three dots we would
connect were as follows: Weller had sold his primary residence in Morris and
now claimed to be living in part of a rental property next door (which he owned).
He had also bought a condominium in downtown Chicago. The congressman's
financial records indicated he owned investment property in Nicaragua. We
would suggest that these actions indicated how out of touch and physically removed from his constituents the incumbent had become. He sold his home inside the district and bought a condo on Chicago's lakefront to go along with his
vacation property in Nicaragua. The press release headline was, "Where's
Weller? Not Here!" The release did not just focus upon the residence and property issue, however. It ended with the following reminder:

> Weller has recently come under criticism from human rights groups for re-
> fusing to repudiate the regime and political party of Gen. Efrain Rios Montt,
> a former Guatemalan dictator who presided over one of the most brutal mili-
> tary campaigns in modern Latin American history. Weller has also refused to
> step down from the US House Committee on Foreign Relations . . . despite the

fact that he is engaged to Zury Rios Sosa, the daughter of Rios Montt, who is also a member of Congress in Guatemala and a leader of the party that had tried to restore the murderous Rios Montt regime to power in 2003.

To go along with the press release, we called a press conference in front of Weller's former residence in Morris, hitting him for being out of touch with the district. I was to make the following points: "We have full-time problems in this district, and we need a full-time congressman, not a part-time jet-setting congressman. We need a congressman who will live in and be grounded in the Eleventh Congressional District. Last time I checked, neither Chicago nor Nicaragua was in the district. We need a congressman who will spend more time in Coal City than Guatemala City" (Coal City is a small community in Weller's home county).

The coverage surrounding this third wave was strong but not as wide as the first two. The press conference itself in front of Weller's former and current legal residence was somewhat eventful. A local Morris, Illinois, radio station had reported that we were going to be there a couple of hours before the event. The early report gave Weller's campaign time to organize an opposition protest at the site. Matt had arrived on the scene about thirty minutes beforehand and called John, who was driving me up from Bloomington. He warned us of the situation and advised us how to change direction and arrive from the south so as to avoid direct confrontation with the several dozen Weller supporters (who were carrying "Weller for Congress" signs). As we discussed the logistics, it seemed clear that we weren't going to be able to avoid such a confrontation. Several reporters were already there interviewing the Weller supporters. Matt called some of our local supporters to see if they could show up at a moment's notice. He was concerned about the visuals because Weller's supporters clearly outnumbered ours at our press conference.

Under the circumstances, we positioned our sidewalk location so that the cameras wouldn't be facing the Weller supporters but rather the former residence. I decided to alter my remarks slightly to "blend in" with the situation. I stressed how healthy it was to have contrasting views and free and open discussions and public debate. Unfortunately, many countries don't enjoy these fundamental freedoms (implied wink at Guatemala). And, even in our great country, many incumbent members of Congress don't come out into the open for such public discussions, which help educate voters. "Yes, unfortunately, many incumbents in Washington are simply out of touch with their constituents. I pledge to be a congressman who stays grounded in our district." I then went on to maintain that Weller's latest actions demonstrated that he was becoming more of a jet-setting member of Congress than one who stays in touch with his constituents.

A Morris city council member who was a strong Weller ally came to stand right next to me during the press conference and offered contrary views to my points during the question-and-answer period with reporters. It turned into the equivalent of an impromptu debate, which many of the reporters found to be highly amusing. She made points such as, "I see Jerry out here jogging all of the time," and said, "He and Zury are looking for another home in Morris so they can raise a family." Our tone remained civil throughout. I ended by noting how great it was to have contrasting ideas and hoped that Weller would come out of his shell to debate in the future—rather than operate through surrogates.

By the middle of August, just as we thought the story had finally begun to die, Representative Weller asked the Federal Election Commission (FEC) if his fiancée could participate in fund-raising and other campaign activities. Under federal law, foreign nationals are not permitted to make monetary contributions or anything of value to campaigns. The FEC, however, ruled that she could volunteer for the campaign as long as she didn't help set strategy. Weller's attorney said, "The important thing here is that they recognize that the congressman and his fiancée may attend political meetings together and give speeches, and that's important" (Associated Press, August 14, 2004). Weller's request and subsequent FEC ruling produced yet another wave of publicity on the controversy. However, it was clear from the coverage (page 3 or later) that the media's interest in the story was waning.

An Uneven Payoff

In many respects, the benefits from this "media momentum" were unmistakable. The firestorm over Weller's engagement, the resulting perception of a conflict of interest, and our ability to capitalize on these events increased my visibility and name recognition in the district and made me a more viable challenger. It also aided in fund-raising efforts. In my fund-raising calls to prospective donors, people were much less likely to hang up on me and were more likely to contribute to our cause. After introducing myself as the Democratic nominee for US Congress in Illinois's most marginal congressional district, I would now add, "You may have read or heard about the latest twist in our race, which has received national and international attention." Invariably, the prospective donors had heard of the story (even if they didn't know anything else about Weller or me). Beginning a conversation is more than half the battle in cold call fund-raising. In many cases, the people who took my calls wouldn't have taken them before the story broke. Sometimes, prospective donors kept *me* on the phone, asking about my take on this situation and what impact it might have on the race. John Schmidt, for example, was a former assistant attorney general of the United States in the Clinton administration who had run for statewide office twice himself (for governor in 1998 and attorney general in 2002). He took my call for the first time and was very honest in saying, "Quite frankly, I didn't think that you had much of a chance before this dictator's daughter situation.

But, this is just so bizarre that it's anyone's guess how it will play out over the course of the campaign." Schmidt not only took my call but made two very generous contributions and hosted a fund-raiser for us in his downtown Chicago law firm.

The percentage of cold calls that translated into actual donations rose significantly after the dictator's daughter stories. The size of the average donations rose as well. Prior to July, for example, it wasn't unusual for me to spend eight to ten hours in call time (mostly to strangers), raising as little as a few hundred dollars a day. It was rare for me to hit the $1,000 mark. By mid-July, the eight- to ten-hour calling days almost always yielded over $1,000 and usually several thousand. In addition, in the aftermath of the story, it wasn't unusual for prominent people to call *us* with offers of support. The most prominent caller was Representative Jesse Jackson, Jr. His office called our campaign headquarters with the message that he really liked how our campaign was taking Weller to task and wanted to meet with me.

The volunteers also poured into the campaign headquarters, and the crowds were larger and more enthusiastic throughout the district. Democratic activists were really pumped up. In our first fund-raiser following the first and second waves of press coverage, we had an overflow crowd of nearly 300 at a small bar in the very small town of Diamond (in Jerry Weller's home county). As Gretchen drove me and my son Max up to this event, we thought something was wrong because we arrived a few minutes early and couldn't find a parking space. The turnout was nearly three times what we expected. The increased enthusiasm was consistently apparent at all our campaign's fund-raisers, events, and appearances in the month after the story broke. In McLean County, for example, Gretchen had worked with Jeanine, a full-time volunteer, on an Artists for Renner fund-raiser. Jeanine, herself a Bloomington-area artist, had considerable success in persuading her colleagues to donate their work to be auctioned off at our event, with the proceeds going to the campaign. We had the venue and other logistics worked out months in advance. Several weeks before the artists' fund-raiser, it was announced that Barack Obama would be delivering the keynote address at the Democratic National Convention—within minutes after our event was to begin! Gretchen made arrangements to have a large high-definition television delivered and hooked up so that attendees could watch the Obama speech but became very pessimistic about our likely success. However, despite the "time conflict," we had a large crowd and received several thousand dollars more than our initial goal.

There was also a substantial increase in our visibility within political circles outside the state. The DCCC had not only sent out a press release during the first wave of this story but also listed our campaign as the featured race in its biweekly online newsletter. We used this as leverage with prospective donors and the political directors of various Democratic-leaning political action committees (PACs) to urge them to "jump on board" by contributing to our cause.

Many left-leaning blogs (Daily Kos, MyDD.com, Archpundit) listed us as one of the increasingly competitive races to watch on their websites. We were already on the radar screen of some groups before the story broke because of our work behind the scenes, the district's competitiveness, and Weller's ideological voting record. It's just that the blip on their radar screen had become much larger. We mentioned these lists to political directors of labor and ideological PACs as further evidence of our campaign's progress. At that point, however, there were no real tangible results from the PAC community. They were still taking a wait-and-see attitude. Their political directors wanted to see what additional progress our campaign would make before deciding whether to get into the race. In contrast, the financial impact from individual donors was clear: The third quarter of 2004 (July 1–September 30) was the only one in which we raised six figures ($100,000 or more), and virtually all this money came from individuals. One reason for this success was my increasing effectiveness on the phone in fund-raising and the increased visibility of our race.

Another positive result of the dictator's daughter story is that the media throughout the district, and even the Chicago-area media, got used to covering our campaign. In the process, Matt and I began to develop relationships with journalists outside my McLean County base. In most conversations with reporters, I always tried to show them some part of who I really was as a person. In our conversations, I wouldn't hesitate to concede an obvious counterpoint (rather than rigidly sticking to the script). Ultimately, our campaign never had a bad story (one that was primarily negative or critical in focus). To be sure, there were many, if not most, that we would have liked to rewrite in order to stress different things, but none of the mainstream press stories were really bad.

The clearly negative side of the dictator's daughter situation was that it became very hard to change the subject in the eyes of the press. For example, even when we held press conferences on other subjects (health care, overtime, or economic stimulus programs), the dictator's daughter controversy often came up in one of two ways. Either reporters would ask a question about Weller's nuptials, or they would include background information about the situation in a story about the unrelated policy proposals. The only relevant link was that it was a previously popular story generated by our challenge to the incumbent.

Weller's extreme reluctance or outright refusal to answer the core questions on his engagement kept the story alive in the minds of many reporters. In the short run, our consultants Pete and Jake thought it was great for our campaign, but it may not have been so good in the long run. For example, almost two months after the engagement, Matt received a call from the CBS Peoria television station, wanting to interview me after the local Mitsubishi automotive plant in Normal, Illinois, announced more layoffs. Matt and I were both thrilled because it would permit me to use one of our campaign's "silver bullets" (highlighting the incumbent's votes for special tax breaks that had the perverse effect of encouraging outsourcing of US jobs overseas). However, when the reporter and camera crew arrived at our campaign headquarters to begin the interview, they made it clear they didn't really care about the "smart corporations" plan I was supporting to change tax incentives to reduce job outsourcing. They said, "No, we're here to talk about the dictator's daughter. Congressman Weller angrily avoided our questions about it at the Mitsubishi plant this afternoon." In my response to her questions, I tried to shift the conversation to highlight our differences on tax policy, but those comments were totally cut out of the story as it appeared.

As we approached the traditional Labor Day kickoff of the fall campaign, it was clear we had a great deal of momentum resulting from earned media coverage of Weller's engagement to the dictator's daughter. It had, however, been primarily focused upon the Rios Montt situation. The cylinders in our systems were really beginning to fire. Volunteers were pouring in to help us. Our phone operation was working full-time, and the field operation was taking shape (although it was nowhere near what I had envisioned a year earlier). The fundraising had finally picked up but still was going to be far short of what was necessary to get our message out effectively to swing voters throughout the district. The Washington PAC money was either nonexistent or trickling in very, very slowly. And the late summer poll showed weaknesses and softness in the incumbent's support but the results weren't good enough to shop around for national PAC money. Consequently, while all of us were pumped by the progress of the summer, we were mindful of the problems ahead. The stories on Weller and Zury Rios Sosa may have given voters a reason to vote *against* the incumbent, but we had to get back to why they should vote *for* us! The engagement was both an opportunity and a challenge to our campaign.

National Trends and the Obama Factor

Besides our own initiatives such as my smart corporations proposal, we also hoped to give people a reason to vote for me by relating my campaign to national trends. Specifically, our campaign was hoping for a very favorable national partisan trend toward change to help us defeat the Republican incumbent. As the fall election season progressed, however, the national political environment didn't seem to be moving toward either political party. The polls showed the presidential race to be just as tight as they had throughout the year. The so-called generic ballot question (asked without candidate names in order to assess the likely aggregate vote for the US House among the 435 districts) was still virtually unchanged. The average of the polls indicated that Democrats had a slight lead but, historically, the generic ballot question has a slight Democratic bias. So, the broad macrolevel indicators seemed to suggest that 2004 would be similar to the nearly deadlocked election of 2000. If that were the case, our campaign would have to prevail against the Republican incumbent without any national partisan winds to our back. There was, however, always the hope that a last-minute movement toward the Democrats might materialize, just as one had for the Republicans in the 1980 elections.

In addition, there was a possible impact in all races in Illinois from what might be called the Obama factor. That is, we had an extremely unusual race for US Senate. Then state senator Barack Obama, the Democratic primary winner, was a strong, charismatic figure who achieved rock star status after his now-famous speech at the Democratic National Convention in the summer of 2004. The Republican nominee was Alan Keyes. Keyes lived in Maryland until July of that election year and was recruited at the last minute by the Illinois state Republicans after the primary election winner, Jack Ryan, had to step down following a sex scandal. Keyes's candidacy proved to be one incredible embarrassment after another for the state's GOP. Not only was the recruitment of someone from out of state a severe image problem, but Keyes spent much of the campaign receiving negative press coverage for a serious of controversial actions and statements. In one prominent interview on a major Chicago television station, for example, Keyes became extremely nasty toward the reporter conducting the interview (including interrupting him and yelling at him on live television). Keyes started a five-minute tirade because he didn't like the way the questions were phrased. To say the least, Alan Keyes had an incredible image problem. And, of course, the Republicans could ill afford such difficulties when facing one of the strongest nonincumbent Democratic candidates in recent memory. The fall polls showed Barack Obama leading Alan Keyes by over 40 points. Ultimately, Keyes lost by more percentage points than any major-party candidate for the US Senate in the history of Illinois.

It was clear to those of us on the ground during the fall campaign that the so-called Obama factor was having a positive effect on the size and enthusiasm of crowds at Democratic campaign events throughout the state. I was with Obama or his wife, Michelle, at dozens of events at community centers, union halls, black churches, or on bus tours, both before and after his famous speech at the Democratic National Convention in August. The crowds gradually became larger after his primary victory in March, but their size paled in comparison to the explosive increase after the convention. Obama's presence at an event, or that of his wife, always ensured that hundreds of party loyalists would show up in order to meet or catch a glimpse of Land of Lincoln's new political rock star. That was the case throughout the Eleventh District, whether we were holding rallies in urban centers such as Joliet, Kankakee, and Bloomington or smaller communities such as Morris, Ottawa, or De Pue. And, of course, there was always substantial press coverage of any Obama-attended event. The flip side of this coverage was that other candidates such as myself barely got an honorable mention in the articles and stories. Still, I found Obama's presence invigorating.

Three weeks before the election, Barack Obama came to Bloomington to host a fund-raiser for our campaign at Fat Jack's, a downtown establishment where we had held several previous fund-raisers. His presence drew a large crowd and saturation-level media coverage in the Peoria/Bloomington side of the district. The front-page headline read, "Obama Boosts Renner Bid as He Campaigns for 'Team.'" At the event, as reported in the October 15, 2004, edition of the *Pantagraph,* Obama said, "Politics is a team sport. And, if I'm going to be successful in Washington, then I've got to have a team of Democrats going with me to Washington that can help me carry that progressive banner . . . Here we are 19 days from Election Day with an enormous opportunity to take back a seat that has been controlled by Republicans . . . The only thing that is preventing Tari from winning this thing at this stage is whether he's got enough money and enough troops to get his message out" (*Pantagraph,* October 15, 2004, pp. A1, A10).

This fund-raiser also illustrated the dilemma for us (and other candidates as well) of Obama's candidacy. The crowds were larger and there was much better coverage with him, but our campaign's message was more difficult to get out in the earned media since Obama was obviously the focus of the news stories. It was our event, but we got lost in Obama's star power.

Weller Strikes Back

On October 27, 2004, just six days before the election, Representative Weller and I were scheduled to debate that evening in my hometown of Bloomington when Weller's campaign began airing radio commercials featuring a new line of attack against me. They claimed that I was for the legalization of drugs and received support from a drug legalization website that included instructions for how to shoot up heroin. The radio ads were reinforced with a direct mail piece sent to all the district's voters. I even received one. The direct mail piece made the same claim: "What is Professor Renner's answer to the War on Drugs?—Legalize them!" The text continued: "Sounds like the easy way out of an important problem. How will Professor Renner stand up to crime in our cities and the war on terrorism when he backs down so easily on other issues? Don't let Professor Renner's college campus values jeopardize Illinois families!" The visuals on this piece were very dramatic. On the front there was a picture of me smiling next to some young girl engaged in illegal drug use. The back of the piece had a "Drug Free School Zone" sign on a schoolyard fence with the word "NOT" written in red capital letters near another picture of me smiling. Weller's name did not appear on the headlines or message of the piece. If you looked carefully, you could find his name on the return address ("Weller for Congress"), the obligatory box ("Paid for by Weller for Congress"), and his campaign's website address, all in very small print.

The presumed basis for these attacks was that someone who established the DrugWarRant website endorsed me over Weller and sent our campaign a check for $200. A few days earlier, Matt had brought it to my attention, and we decided to send the check back. However, federal law requires that we report all individual contributions of $200 and above, and at this point in the campaign, we had to report contributions to the FEC within forty-eight hours of their receipt. The Weller campaign was likely monitoring everything we were doing during this period, searching for new lines of attack.

The so-called drug ads seemed to have an immediate impact. Our phone banking operation, which made thousands of calls each day, instantly picked up systematic concerns about my position on legalization of drugs. There were consistent responses to the drug ads, such as, "Isn't he the guy who wants to legalize drugs?" or "I don't support him; he wants to give kids heroin!" Our callers, of course, assured the people that I was, in fact, opposed to the legalization of drugs. However, it was clear that these ads were having a distinctly negative effect.

In response to the attack, Matt began working the phone lines, pointing out to the electronic and print media throughout the state how outrageous and desperate the Weller ads were. Beyond that, however, there was very little our campaign could do to respond except through the earned media. We had spent the entire communication budget on seven waves of direct mail and radio ads so there was very little money left for further paid communication. I could hardly hold more fund-raisers or call enough people to raise sufficient contributions to pay for an effective response. It was now Wednesday, and we only had a few days left before Election Day! A conservative estimate was that it would take an additional $100,000 to effectively respond through direct mail and radio ads.

Given our inability to respond in kind, we decided we would need to do something dramatic at a candidate debate scheduled for that evening. I worked with Jake and Pete to construct a response for the upcoming debate that evening. There was some concern about whether a "debate stunt" would merely draw attention to the charges. At one point during our conference call, our field coordinator, Josh Worell, walked into the campaign headquarters and weighed in: "I received the mail piece this morning and heard this commercial at least five times before lunch. People are going to be bombarded with this attack. You've got to respond!"

I had already memorized my introductory and closing statements for the debate. In order to stay on message during these opening and closing remarks, we didn't want to address Weller's attack in either of them. Instead, we agreed that I would have a "planned blowup" at Weller over the drug ads at some point during the debate itself. I was to express carefully controlled outrage at his campaign tactics. Our hope was that the dramatic conflict would be the theme of all media stories covering the event. If that did occur, I would get my response out as effectively as possible in the earned media.

That evening, I arrived at the debate with my sons about fifteen minutes early to scope out the situation and work the crowd before the debate. Matt,

Gretchen, Josh, and dozens of volunteers were already on-site. The large auditorium in the Bloomington Interstate Center was packed with people and reporters. One press estimate was that there were approximately 300 people in attendance. About five minutes after we arrived, Weller marched in with his entourage, including his fiancée, Zury, who sat only a couple of rows away from my sons. They were sitting with my ex-wife, Judy, who joked to me and Matt, "We'll keep an eye on the boys and protect them from the murderous dictator's daughter."

As I walked onstage, the lights were so bright that I couldn't see many people in the crowd. Although the intensity of the lights was disconcerting at times, it was good because it forced me to speak to the cameras and concentrate on what I was saying, not how people in the audience were reacting. The debate began with our opening statements. Weller had written out his remarks and he read from them, whereas I had memorized mine so that I could speak directly to the camera. Weller began by recognizing his family in the audience and his fiancée Zury and said, "Zury, you're the best thing that's ever happened to me!" He then proceeded to list a range of projects and legislation for which he was taking credit, saying, "I've taken care of central Illinois!" He continued: "My opponent . . . is a left-wing college professor with views out of the mainstream. His views have earned him the endorsement of a radical group that wants to legalize drugs. Interestingly, its website (drugwarrant.com) gives instructions on how to shoot up heroin and how to make a contribution to my opponent's campaign. It's clear my opponent is a left-wing college professor and I've worked hard."

The moderator then recognized me, and I stuck to my planned script even though I was dying to confront Weller immediately on his drug assault against me. I began by noting that my sons were in the audience and that being a father of two was the most important thing to me. I then spoke about my diverse experiences in order to clarify that I was more than a college professor. I noted that I had served two terms on the McLean County Legislature and that I had worked for the FBI, EPA, and the International City/County Management Association in Washington. I spoke of my background growing up in a single-parent household in which my mother and I were on and off welfare for many years, saying, "I worked my way out of poverty." I maintained that my diverse background and bipartisanship had motivated the newspapers on this side of the district, the ones that know me the best (the *Bloomington Pantagraph* and the *Peoria Journal Star*), to endorse my campaign for Congress. Those same papers endorsed Republican George Bush for president. I continued:

> This election is about choices but not the ones Mr. Weller has referred to. I believe, for example, that we must change our tax policies to stimulate the economy and create jobs in America and not send jobs and corporate headquarters abroad. In contrast, Mr. Weller voted for billions of dollars in budget-busting tax breaks to do precisely that—give companies incentives to outsource—companies that contributed to his campaign. I believe we need to lower

prescription drug costs for our seniors on Medicare by negotiating with the drug companies. Mr. Weller has consistently opposed negotiating prices. Not coincidentally, the congressman gets massive campaign cash from the pharmaceutical industry. I believe we need a responsible energy policy in which we invest in alternative energy resources and move toward energy independence. Mr. Weller claims he's in favor of these policies, but he votes to give crumbs to alternative energy while voting for heaping loaves to the oil and gas industry, which, of course, are major contributors to his campaign. I believe they earn enough at the pump! The choice will be clear: Politics as usual in Washington, on the one hand, with influence peddling catering to wealthy special interests, and, on the other hand, I pledge to be a strong independent voice who will work tirelessly for real reform and change.

We then proceeded to answer several rounds of questions. Each question was directed at one of us, but the other candidate received one minute to respond. The person who answered first would get an extra opportunity to respond after the opponent's answer. The questions were posed to each of us in turn to ensure fairness and equal time. During each of the questions, I took every opportunity to hit the incumbent on giving tax credits to companies to outsource American jobs or charged him with selling out to narrow special interests that distort the public interest. At one point, for example, there was a question from the audience directed at Weller on penalties for Internet hacking. He explained why he supported increasing penalties and cited his work to protect children from Internet predators. In my response, I merely noted that I didn't disagree with the incumbent on this point and spent my time calling for the use of Internet to help hold public officials in Washington accountable. I supported requiring the websites of members of Congress, which are paid for by taxpayers, to include posting the members' nonunanimous votes and the sources of their campaign contributions. "So, with two clicks on a mouse pad people could see whether or not their congressman, like Jerry Weller, has sold out."

During the question-and-answer period, I kept searching for an opportunity for my planned blowup over the drug ads. In answering an unrelated question on the sneak-and-peek provisions of the Patriot Act, Weller mentioned the word "drugs" in passing. In my response, I quickly seized upon it as my opportunity. I turned my face slightly toward Weller (so the cameras could still clearly focus upon my face), gestured at him with a closed hand (pointing is supposed to be way too rude), and raised my voice dramatically.

Well, since you've mentioned "drugs," Mr. Weller, I want to make one thing very clear. Your ads and your charges are absolutely incorrect! I don't support the legalization of drugs and you know it! Ronald Reagan was endorsed by the Klu Klux Klan in 1980, and no one blamed him for cross burnings. That would have been going over the line. You went way over the line! And not only that, but you're not a parent! I'm a father of two, and let me tell you that you have no idea what it's like on a daily basis to protect your kids from evils of all forms—including drugs. So, don't lecture me . . . Mr. Weller!

There was immediate clapping and cheering after my blowup. This reaction actually violated the rules since the audience was asked to withhold applause until the very end.

Weller's response to this was, "I presume I get my full forty-five seconds. [Weller was delayed in his response by the applause from the audience.] Where was the professor when they tried to link President Bush to a victim, an individual who was chained to the back of a pickup truck? They ran ads against him, and the professor was not there to defend President Bush." He then shifted to an attack on what he viewed as my inconsistencies in responding to the sneak-and-peek provisions of the Patriot Act (the original subject of the question).

Even without the planned blowup, throughout the debate there were constant sparks, if not a blaze, between Weller and me. In fact, there were no questions during which one of us didn't take a shot at the other at some point in the exchange. Weller stressed how left-wing I was, and I stressed the need for change and reform because the incumbent represented politics as usual in Washington.

Immediately after the debate, the press swarmed around me as I left the podium, asking a range of questions, mostly surrounding my reaction to Weller's drug attacks. In answering each question, I gave some version of this response: "It's despicable behavior like this—with outrageous and false charges—that turns many people away from politics today. This is why we need a change in politics as usual in Washington. Jerry Weller is the poster child for this type of politics."

A few questioned me about my response to the Project Vote Smart questionnaire in which I indicated that I supported decriminalization of marijuana. I said, "I merely support a policy that would not throw both George Bush and Al Gore in jail. They both admitted they tried marijuana in their youth. That's not legalization! I have always opposed legalization of drugs!" After the flurry of interviews, my conversations with neutral and not-so-neutral observers in attendance were consistent with Matt's observation: "If we could get the voters across the district to see this debate—Weller would lose in a landslide. He was horrible!" We all realized, however, that few voters would actually view the debate. However, there was substantial coverage of the debate across the district in the print media and through radio. The only television coverage was in the Peoria/Bloomington area. Most of the coverage was favorable to our campaign, but it could not possibly convey the dynamics of our interchange. It would have been very different to be there or to watch it on television. Several radio stations played our closing statements and a quote from my blowup. The print coverage that most closely illustrated the dynamics of the debate was in the *Bloomington Pantagraph*. The massive top front-page headline read, "Weller, Renner Debate Gets Heated" and was accompanied by large pictures of my facial expression and hand gesture toward him during the blowup and Weller's glare at me. In fact, the article filled the vast majority of the front page.

In the final articles and stories over the weekend before the election, though, it was still the drug ads and not the debate that dominated the news coverage. For example, the October 29, 2004, edition of the *Chicago Tribune* reported:

> After months of being battered over his decision to marry the daughter of a brutal former Guatemalan dictator, US Rep. Jerry Weller of Morris struck back Tuesday with news that Democratic challenger Tari Renner has been endorsed by the pro–drug legalization Internet site DrugWarRant.com. The endorsement, which Renner's campaign characterized as an unwelcome surprise, links to Web pages that detail how to safely shoot, snort, and smoke all sorts of illicit substances. . . . Weller cited the endorsement as a sign that Renner has "an agenda that will put Illinois children, families and values at risk." But Renner's campaign has returned $200 in donations from Guither, spokesman Matt Glavin said.

Stories like the *Tribune*'s were problematic for at least three reasons. First of all, voters were being bombarded with Weller's negative ads claiming I supported legalized drugs. Second, we had no ability to respond. Third, the ads produced wrap-up news stories that focused upon them. It was clearly not the sort of media coverage our campaign had hoped for as we attempted to seal the deal with swing voters in the last few days of the campaign. And, regardless of the coverage, which made it clear that I was not in favor of drug legalization, our phone banking continued to pick up the political hemorrhaging over these ads (at least in the calls outside the Peoria/Bloomington area).

During the last few days, many friends and supporters called me and/or asked Matt, Gretchen, or Josh some version of "How is Tari holding up? Those drug ads are awful. I can't imagine how tough this is on him." The reality was that I was psychologically at ease. Weller's attack ads were certainly aggravating, but I knew that one way or another, the long campaign was going to be over within a few days. At that point, I realized there wasn't too much I could do about the onslaught. It would either backfire on the incumbent or take me down.

The Results and Conclusion

When the votes were finally counted, Weller, the Republican incumbent, won 58.7 percent to 41.3 percent. The only area I won was my home county of McLean. Contrary to my initial hopes as I entered the race in early 2003, the national partisan tide in the district had swung toward the Republicans. This is apparent from the 4 percent increase in the vote for George Bush from 2000 to 2004. In 2000, the Gore and Nader totals in the Eleventh District exceeded those of Bush. In 2004, however, Bush prevailed over John Kerry by a 54 to 46 percent margin in the Eleventh District (Nader was not on the ballot in Illinois that year). Consequently, the way in which the national trends played out in the district would have made it extremely difficult for a challenger to have prevailed over the incumbent under the best of contextual circumstances. As I mentioned early in the chapter, I was hoping for some national partisan winds behind my back but, instead, experienced a backdraft.

Also, we could only get so much mileage from the dictator's daughter. In the end it turned out to be a mixed blessing. The dictator's daughter incident helped our campaign obtain substantial earned media coverage that most challengers would savor. This attention helped raise our campaign's profile and made it easier to raise money in the last few months. However, the downside was that we found it difficult to control the earned media coverage to move beyond that story. We tried to clarify that it was only one part of why the incumbent was out of touch and had lost his way. In order to do that effectively, our campaign needed a much larger paid communication budget. The financial data from the FEC on the race indicates that the incumbent spent nearly $1.8 million to our $320,000. The difference in our respective campaign war chests also meant that we lacked the necessary financial resources to both drive home our message and effectively respond to the last-minute attack ads on drugs. It seems that no matter what advantages incumbents might throw in their challengers' laps, challengers still can't win without enough cash. Unfortunately, this case study confirms what has become the fundamental empirical reality of modern congressional elections in the United States: Money doesn't just matter; it matters more than anything else.

6

Working on Bill Clinton's 1992 Research Staff

Kevin Anderson

Type of campaign: Presidential (general)

Role of author: Research staff member

Lessons to look for:
- A campaign must know and research its candidate as well as its opponent.
- A good research office and a rapid-response team are part of good planning, organization, and strategy.
- Campaigning is a contact sport, sometimes played dirty—that's one reason a campaign needs a good research office.
- Life as a campaign staff person is hard work and can be an emotional roller-coaster, but ultimately is fun.

I have always loved politics. The combination of the high ideals of public service, along with the emotional edge of partisan competition, appeals to me in ways that I still cannot fully describe. I have always wanted to know why things happen, who is in charge, and why they make the rules the way that they do. I enjoyed majoring in political science as an undergraduate, but even though I had some political experience, I knew something was missing. I knew my political education was incomplete. Then, in the fall of 1991, the opportunity to enhance my knowledge of politics came to me and taught me lessons I will never forget.

In October 1991, Arkansas governor Bill Clinton declared his candidacy for the presidency in my hometown of Little Rock, Arkansas. It was a daring candidacy due to both the popularity of President George H. W. Bush in the wake of the first Gulf War (his approval ratings had reached 90 percent at one point after the war) and the fact that Clinton, although a gifted politician, was not widely known outside the South. I was a graduate student working on my master's degree at the University of Arkansas at the time and would occasionally attend meetings of the College Democrats on campus. The sense of excitement surrounding a local politician running for president led the campus chapter to organize a November trip to Des Moines, Iowa, for the Democratic Party's Jefferson-Jackson Day Dinner to support the governor in the first public event featuring all the declared presidential candidates. We loaded up on a bus in Fayetteville early on a cold November Saturday morning and drove nearly six hours through occasional heavy snow in order to arrive at the dinner on time. The trip proved successful: Governor Clinton had the largest base of support after Iowa senator Tom Harkin, and our passionate cheering for the governor when he was introduced earned us some brief camera time on the C-SPAN show *Race for the White House*. We met with Bill and Hillary Clinton briefly after the dinner and were thanked for our support and informed that we could not know how effective those images of us cheering would be for the momentum of the campaign. A few months later on the night of the New Hampshire primary, as Clinton walked out to celebrate his surprise second-place showing and claimed the moniker "Comeback Kid," I thought I understood the power of media images. In reality it was only later, after a six-month experience inside the Clinton-Gore presidential campaign, that I truly understood the power of images and ideas in politics; only then did I recognize what was incomplete about my personal political education.

From Volunteer to Staff

As I approached graduation in the spring of 1992, I had no concrete plan for the future. I was trying to decide between law school and Ph.D. programs in political science. One of my faculty advisers at Arkansas, Professor Diane Blair, had taken leave from the university in order to work on the Clinton campaign. After an intense primary season in which the governor survived a number of attacks that had sunk other candidates, Bill Clinton had emerged as the presumptive Democratic nominee. My adviser invited me to come in and volunteer "for a couple of days" after graduation to help out in the office and see what a presidential campaign was all about. A few weeks later, I visited my adviser inside the bustling and cramped building that served as the first Bill Clinton for President headquarters. It was a small, ordinary building in downtown Little Rock that had housed a small printing company that had closed a year earlier. It had large windows in front that were plastered with "Bill Clinton for President" signs. Inside, it had what seemed to me to be an impossible number of cubicles stuffed into too tiny a space. I noticed the division of duties and multiple tasks going on as Diane gave me an impromptu tour of the campaign office. She quickly introduced me to people in the press office, the advance team (the people who traveled ahead of the campaign to set up rallies, meetings with local officials, etc.), the scheduling office, the policy shop (domestic and foreign), and the research department. This office was divided into Opposition Research, which dug for information on Clinton's opponents, and the Arkansas Record, which was dedicated to defending Bill Clinton and his public policies. As an undergraduate, I had been an intern in the local office of Arkansas representative Tommy Robinson (Second District) and for the state Democratic Party, but to see the passionate, chaotic, and exciting atmosphere of a national campaign up close made me realize that I really wanted to be a part of this, no matter what role I would have. I quickly volunteered to do whatever was necessary. After my first visit, I volunteered for a couple of weeks working alongside Professor Blair in the Research Office until I was asked to be an official member of the campaign team. To become official, I had my picture taken for a staff identification card, and I was put on a list of staffers who were paid "monthly meal expenditures." It wasn't much money, but I didn't need or want much else at the time. Unlike several of my new colleagues, I could live at home, so my expenses were low. And I knew exactly where I wanted to work. Professor Blair, as a longtime friend of the Clintons and an expert on Arkansas politics, was working in the research department as a part of the team digging through, interpreting, and defending the Arkansas Record. This team was, in many ways, the heart of the campaign. I told Professor Blair that as an Arkansas native, I wanted to be a part of this team. I felt comfortable with my knowledge of Governor Clinton and my home state; plus, this department appeared to be at the competitive edge of the campaign, aggressively seeking to define the Clinton legacy in Arkansas while always on the lookout for the next charge leveled by the Bush campaign. It was at once the most mundane and exciting place to be in a presidential campaign.

The Arkansas Record

By the time I officially joined the campaign in May 1992, Governor Clinton had managed to survive a number of charges, allegations, and political attacks, from an accusation of marital infidelity by a Little Rock nightclub singer named Gennifer Flowers, to a charge of evading the Vietnam-era military draft (generated by a letter Clinton wrote to a University of Arkansas ROTC officer after receiving a draft notice at Oxford, where he was a Rhodes scholar), to a clumsy answer to a question about his past drug use (Clinton infamously answered that he had tried marijuana but didn't inhale). Nothing could sink the Clinton campaign. The candidate and campaign proved resilient enough to be competitive yet was still polling behind President Bush and H. Ross Perot, the Texas billionaire who was generating a lot of speculation that he would be a serious independent candidate for president.

After moving ahead in delegates and clinching the Democratic Party nomination, the Clinton campaign moved to bigger and better offices in the late
spring of 1992 in the locally famous Gazette building, the former headquarters
of the *Arkansas Gazette* newspaper, which at the time it ceased publication in
the fall of 1991 was the oldest newspaper west of the Mississippi River. The research department was located on the third floor of the building in a space consisting of four rooms, one of which was big enough to hold four large desks in
a semicircle. There were several "Bill Clinton for President" signs along with
our campaign motto, "It's the Economy, Stupid," on every wall, and there always seemed to be an exploding pile of paper on every desk in the room. Several televisions in the corners of the room were constantly tuned to either cable
news or what we came to call "BCTV," or Bill Clinton Television. It was the
satellite hookup from the campaign trail; we could watch any live Clinton event
whenever and wherever it was happening. In the days after the Democratic National Convention, as the campaign embarked on the famous "Bus Tour"
through the country, BCTV gave those of us at the Little Rock headquarters a
sense of how well the campaign was doing, how large the crowds were, and
how effective the message of the day appeared to be.

The research department was headed up by Betsey Wright, a smart, tough
political operative. She was former chief of staff to Governor Clinton and had
known him for twenty years. She understood the governor's strengths and weaknesses and was determined to defend the truth of his record against any and all
attacks, including personal broadsides against a man who had admitted to making "mistakes" in his marriage. Through her knowledge and loyalty, Wright defined what we needed to look for in order to best defend the governor, and that
included knowing his public record better than anyone and putting it into context for those who challenged the campaign's public statements.

The bulk of the staff in the research department consisted of well-educated
people in our mid-twenties with a passion for politics and a belief that the Reagan-
Bush years needed to end. Most had taken leave from graduate school or law
school, joined the campaign during the primaries, and worked their way up to
a staff position in the national headquarters. It was an interesting and exciting
group to be a part of, although I admit that at first, I felt a little bit out of place.
This feeling, however, was never due to my being the only African American
working in the department. What caused me to pause was that Harvard, Yale,
Princeton, Bowdoin, Tufts, and the University of Pennsylvania were some of the
alma maters my fellow staffers claimed. I had received a B.A. from the University of Arkansas at Little Rock, and I had a newly minted M.A. in political
science from the flagship campus of the University of Arkansas. Although that
might be a major achievement for some, this was an elite group of young, politically active talent. In fact, only one other staffer in the research department
had even attended college inside the state of Arkansas. As I later discovered, a

large number of local college students and activists were participating in the campaign, but they were spread across diverse departments such as scheduling, the advance team, policy, and other areas. My status anxiety quickly subsided after a few lunchtime discussions of politics, books, and ideas at local eateries such as Vinno's Pizza or Your Mama's Good Food. Not only did we share a passion for politics, but we discovered that we all had debated some of the same intellectual ideas despite having varying collegiate backgrounds. I think that to some degree, we all saw joining a presidential campaign as a way for each of us to translate words into deeds and intellectual theory into action. I came to realize that Plato and Thomas Jefferson read the same, whether they were read in Cambridge, New Haven, or Little Rock. Our common love of American politics brought us to the campaign, and we all saw this office as our opportunity to be a part of a seminal political moment.

Arkansas Record: Day-to-Day Activities

A typical day started with a review of the clip files. In the pre-Internet days, all relevant campaign stories were cut from newspapers and compiled into a large morning briefing book of major newspaper headlines from all over the country. Every story that mentioned Governor Clinton, plus editorials and op-ed pieces on key issues that shaped the agenda for that day, were included. This bulky file was compiled by the Media Office and then photocopied and distributed to each department. That news review set up the morning briefing, which discussed what was on the daily schedule, what the message was for the day, and how the governor's record would be useful in conveying that message. In the evening, around 6:30, a second staff meeting was held to discuss the events of the day and the plans for the next day. I found this structure fascinating in terms of its interconnectedness. The news defined the issues, the issues defined the message, and the message defined the campaign. These meetings were later immortalized in the D. A. Pennebaker and Chris Hegedus campaign documentary *The War Room.*

The Arkansas Record was essential to structuring the message, which meant that our job of defending Governor Clinton was central to what the campaign was attempting to accomplish. After the morning briefing, we went to work digging for information to supplement the policy agenda and protect the Arkansas Record. How do you best know the record? You go through it, year by year, or in our case, box by box. From the time that Bill Clinton was first elected Arkansas attorney general in 1976 and then governor in 1978, nearly all his public acts had been recorded and boxed up for future analysis by historians and archivists of Arkansas politics. This time capsule of Arkansas politics and government in the late 1970s and early 1980s, fascinating to scholars, was both a treasure trove and mine field for a political candidate seeking the highest office in the land. The policy implications of being the governor and having his influence on state politics for the last ten years was enormous. Every bill the governor had signed, every speech he had given, every debate he had engaged in, along with correspondence with state legislators and other state officials, were all ripe to be exploited by his political opponents. Given the charges and attacks from the primary season, the necessity of doing this job and doing it well was paramount for the fall campaign.

A rather nondescript room on the second floor of the new campaign headquarters was the sealed home of the Clinton records. It was an old storage room with boxes stacked on metal shelves from floor to ceiling. The shelving was roughly eight feet high and there were typically three to four boxes per shelf, all labeled by policy and year, except correspondence, which was just labeled by year. This room was kept secure; you had to know the four-digit code to get into the room. I sometimes fantasized that it was a high-tech vault and that those of us with access to it were Central Intelligence Agency (CIA) employees sorting classified material. The archaeology of the Clinton record was ultimately trusted to a small group of research staff collectively nicknamed the "Box Boys." Adam Samaha, Steve Simon, Joe Trahern, Mike Sweeny, John Monroe, and I were the bulk of the team, although we often had help from other research staff as we dove into boxes, trying to establish context for everything from education policy to death penalty cases. As the campaign began to pick up speed after the convention in July, our task often transformed in hours from the mundane to the critical as public policy and campaign politics clashed on the way to Election Day 1992.

Research as Department of Defense

In the days after the primaries and before the Democratic National Convention, the sharp edge between politics and policy began to blur. The tendency to think that what your department is doing is the most important part of the campaign was true for those of us in Arkansas Record, but the bigger picture of the campaign began to come into focus when the subject of choosing a vice president came up. After Governor Clinton cinched the nomination, the speculation intensified as to whom he might pick as a running mate. As the media consensus was building around an older Democrat with Washington experience, I kept hearing the name Al Gore. The Tennessee senator had run for president in 1988 and seemed like a formidable candidate in 1992, but had chosen not to run. I personally could not see two southerners running together, regional balance on presidential tickets being one of the things I remember reading about in a class on the US presidency. Nevertheless, staff discussions of Gore seemed to indicate that he offered all the essential elements that Clinton was looking for: Washington experience; foreign policy credentials; a strong policy record on environmental issues; and as a fellow Baby Boomer southerner, a compatibility that might make a partnership work. The campaign research department was involved in some vetting of potential vice presidential nominees, but overall those of us in Arkansas Record were left to speculate much like the public. And speculate people did! Press reports heated up that Indiana representative Lee Hamilton was going to be the pick. However, the advantages of adding Al Gore seemed to multiply rapidly. Within days, Gore arrived in Little Rock to accept the vice presidential slot on the ticket.

The momentum of the campaign was also building faster than I expected. Governor Clinton took his first lead in public opinion polls after the selection of Gore. Just as the Democratic National Convention was in full swing and the campaign was building momentum, we caught a break. H. Ross Perot suddenly announced that he was getting out of the presidential race. The Texas billionaire had energized a segment of the population with his direct talk and perceived political independence. The Perot candidacy was serious enough that both the Clinton and Bush campaigns were conducting opposition research on him, research that he later cited as part of the reason why he initially got out of the race. Perot also claimed that he had reports that Republicans were planning to disrupt his daughter's upcoming wedding. This claim caused Clinton campaign strategist James Carville to quip: "How do you mess up a Texas wedding? Everybody goes home sober with the woman they came with?"

The campaign, and especially the research office, knew that life was about to get hectic after the convention. It was whispered that Betsey's department had something of a siege mentality, always on the lookout for the next attack, leak, or quote that had been misrepresented and appeared as the harbinger of liberal doom. This mentality could have made us seem paranoid, but I believed it served us well, although an old corporate espionage tactic may have made us a bit more paranoid than most. For several days in a row, our department received deliveries of flowers addressed to female staffers from "secret admirers." The flowers were addressed to different female staffers and had different floral arrangements, but they had one thing in common. They were all bugged! In retrospect, it seems a little funny to think that we all immediately assumed that the flowers had been bugged by members of the local Republican Party as a way of finding out what we were doing. We made a joke out of the flower deliveries by standing around the flowers and whispering about the "October Surprise" that would win us the election, but as President Bush began attacking the governor over his lack of experience, his perceived tendency to raise taxes, and questions about his "character," we knew that we could not take anything for granted. All of these attacks were meant to induce fear of his purported liberalism and to raise doubt about his fitness to serve as president. The Box Boys' attempts to refute these attacks and correct the record were part of a larger campaign strategy to make the race about issues and not personalities, turn the focus around and make the campaign about the voters and not the candidates, try to advance the understanding of policy as opposed to the popularity of the party, and use a charismatic leader to generate excitement and change built around a rejection of the Reagan-Bush era.

To do these things required all the campaign staff, including us Box Boys, to avoid the mistakes made by the Dukakis campaign in 1988. The incumbent president, although embattled due to a lasting economic downturn, was still a formidable opponent, and his political team had succeeded four years earlier in turning Democratic nominee Michael Dukakis, who had emerged from his convention in 1988 with a seventeen-point lead, into a losing candidate and the butt of endless late-night talk show jokes. We knew that we needed to have rapid response for every charge made by the Bush campaign, no matter how trivial and no matter how false. Our rapid-response mentality was in pointed contrast to the Dukakis campaign, which allowed itself to be sunk over charges it either answered late or not at all. The infamous Willie Horton ad charging that Dukakis was soft on crime was the most obvious example of the Dukakis campaign failing to control the framing of the issues and the images of the Democratic nominee. In contrast, we used a rapid-response model of challenging accusations with research-based responses, and we did it in ways that helped frame the debate to our advantage.

The speed, coherence, and subtlety of our responses to political attacks taught me an effective lesson in the art of campaign politics. I learned that there was no need to shout at the top of your voice that your opponents are lying. All you have to do is refute the allegations with facts and use your emotions to decry the tactic rather than the opposition. In one notable incident, however, the passion of the campaign team spilled out into a public debate. James Carville, chief strategist of the Clinton campaign, was debating Bush campaign strategist Charles Black on *Face the Nation* one Sunday morning from headquarters while a number of us stood nearby, watching the in-house studio feed. After several instances of Charles Black distorting the Clinton record and talking over him, Carville, in his thick Cajun accent, snapped at Black: "Excuse me for speaking while you are interrupting!" There was an audible gasp over the feed, and for once, the aggression of the campaign served notice that we were ready to counterattack at every provocation.

As the Republican Convention began in August, our task in research became one of anticipation and response. What were the themes of the day, and how could we respond? If there were attacks on Clinton's education initiatives, we produced copies of education legislation, test scores, and policy analysis comparing where Arkansas was before Clinton was governor and where the state was in 1992. We used the recommendations of policy experts inside and outside of the state to frame the issue and then presented the governor's policy solutions. If the issue was crime, we again and again attempted to juxtapose the problem, the debate, and the policy response against previous attempts to solve the problem. The point was not to portray Governor Clinton in the best light possible in every instance but to demonstrate an engaged leader attempting to solve the myriad problems facing a small southern state. Our actions contrasted sharply to the implied and often explicit charges of moral laxity, insufficient patriotism, and general political radicalism that had worked to demonize Democrats in previous campaigns. Our spirited desire to change the nature of political debate ran into the tried-and-true formula of fear-and-smear politics.

Often as we Box Boys were spending days sifting through musty boxes of speeches on education policy, we would listen to conservative talk show host Rush Limbaugh during the day. His radio program, although strangely entertaining, also proved useful in that a number of rumors and increasingly strident attacks on Governor Clinton either got their start or were given media airplay on the commentator's show. The show seemed to be something of a clearinghouse for negative attacks against the governor. Over time, we were treated to the host or his callers breathlessly declaring that

- Governor Clinton had burned an American flag in Red Square while on a trip to Russia during his time as a Rhodes scholar. (There were pictures of this too!)
- Governor Clinton had facilitated a drug-running operation in the small town of Mena, Arkansas, for the CIA in order to help fund the contras in Nicaragua, and now the CIA was paying him back by making him president.
- Governor Clinton was widely known to have fathered a child by a black prostitute.
- Bill and Hillary Clinton had used the Rose Law Firm in Little Rock as a base of operations for their political careers and had used the firm in order to intimidate and sometimes kill political enemies.

Each of these stories was fairly easy to rebut by showing public records that directly conflicted with the stated conspiracy. For example, we found and produced the picture of Clinton on his trip to Russia while he was a Rhodes scholar: He had grown a beard that made him look like a late 1960s radical, but there was no flag to be found. When Clinton was accused of helping to facilitate drug deals in small town Arkansas, his public schedule showed him to be at Disneyland with his family. We even found pictures of Clinton at Disneyland with his daughter, Chelsea, who was wearing Mickey Mouse ears. The press office handled the bulk of the questions about these charges, yet we were always on alert about the next wild accusation.

At each stage of the campaign, what I had learned in textbooks and classrooms converged with what I had observed as an unabashed political junkie, yet the gaps in my knowledge filled in by this new experience taught me things I had never considered. How do you respond to charges like the one peddled on the Limbaugh show? How do you refute rumors and innuendo when negative information is often more easily remembered and harder to dislodge than the simple truth of the matter? We answered these questions by first presenting the facts as best we could. Second, we tried to establish the context of the one leveling the attack. In other words, we hit back. We questioned the political motive for the attack and then explained that the truth was on our side.

Ultimately, I grew immune to the incessant political attacks, yet I worried about how effective these charges would be. How could anyone believe such outlandish stories? It astounded me that, given the sliding economy, anyone would take seriously a campaign that did not seem to have a plan to help and was singularly focused on destroying the opposition. I not only did not understand it, I began to resent the implication that Americans cared more about ideological charges and political attacks than they did solutions to their problems. This could not be the reality of American politics, could it?

The answer to my philosophical inquiry was a qualified no. The frustration of the electorate led H. Ross Perot to revive his campaign. So many people were demanding change that the collective organization built around getting Perot on the ballot in all fifty states, United We Stand, managed to talk him into resuming his campaign, and he quickly chose Admiral James Stockdale as his running mate. This development, which was exciting and fascinating for me as someone who loves politics, was an uncertain element in an evolving electoral contest. Inside the campaign we tried to focus on issues and ideas, yet the attention of the larger universe of campaign coverage kept focusing on the ups and downs of news play and tracking polls. Our counterparts in Opposition Research now had to figure out how to deal with a candidate that was not directly attacking us but was diluting our focus on President Bush. Should we leak negative stories about Perot? The answer was no, but when a rumor surfaced that Mr. Perot had ordered portions of a coral reef blown up in order to move one of his yachts closer to a new home he had bought in Bermuda, some staffers wanted to confirm whether the story was true. *Time* magazine later confirmed the truth of that story, but it did not seem to reduce Perot's support. Overall, even with Perot back in the race, we knew we had to get back to our strength: issues.

The Staff and the Candidate

As connected as we were by working in the national headquarters, most of the staff rarely saw the candidate in person. When the opportunity arose, we took full advantage. In early September, the campaign received a major policy boost when Governor Clinton was endorsed by the Sierra Club. On the day that he publicly accepted the endorsement, the campaign press office arranged for an outdoor public event to emphasize that a major environmental organization supported Clinton. The word spread through headquarters that there was room for a few staffers to attend and listen to Governor Clinton speak about the endorsement and his environmental policies at Pinnacle Mountain State Park on the edge of the city. It was a bright, nearly cloud-free day, and the mountain plus the fall foliage provided the perfect backdrop for the announcement. I loved that park and had gone there a number of times growing up, so when I was asked if I wanted to attend, I jumped at the chance to go. I and four other research staffers quickly went downstairs and piled into a white van, thinking we would ride out to the park and watch the event. Instead we were driven to the governor's mansion, where we were placed in a long line of vehicles inside a security detail. It took a moment for us to realize that we were now officially riding in a presidential nominee motorcade. As we left the mansion, we noticed that all traffic in both directions had been stopped to accommodate us. When we entered Interstate 430 to head from downtown to the state park, we saw police cars and motorcycles blocking entrance and exit ramps while commuters sat in a seemingly endless traffic jam as the motorcade drove by. I rode along with a mixture of pride and incredulity: The fact that we were in a van and not an actual bullet-proof limousine did not matter at all. When we arrived at the park and watched the media set up for the press event, I mused to Kristine Zalakas, one of my fellow research staffers, that of all the things I thought might happen in this campaign, riding in a motorcade that included the presidential nominee had not even occurred to me. She smiled and said it sure would be a great story to tell, but it would not matter if we didn't win the election. The slightly surreal trappings aside, I knew she was right; our focus had to go back to winning the election.

Research and the Debates

After the Republican National Convention, the conversation about debates turned into an issue in itself. President Bush continued to resist the format and number of debates, and the resulting delay provided us with an unexpected advantage. We were ready to discuss the real problems facing the nation, and the president did not appear eager to discuss those problems. The intractable negotiations led to the cancellation of the first debate; on the night the debate had originally been scheduled, Governor Clinton showed up at Michigan State University, the debate site, stating that he was ready to discuss the problems facing the American people. The sluggishness of the debate negotiations highlighted what we believed to be the fundamental flaw with the Bush presidency: its lack of connection with ordinary people and their suffering. We emphasized that point again and again after President Bush was amazed by a supermarket scanner during a photo-op earlier in the campaign. In response to the Bush campaign's foot dragging on debates, a few Clinton volunteers began showing up at Bush campaign rallies with signs calling him "Chicken George," and one volunteer went so far as to dress up in a yellow Big Bird costume and follow the Bush campaign from rally to rally, mocking the fact that President Bush was refusing to debate. Our fearless leader, Betsey Wright, even did a mock barbecue of a guy in a chicken suit in front of our headquarters, which was of course caught by news crews.

After the cancelled first debate, negotiations quickly settled the format and number of debates, and the task for research shifted again. We prepared for the debates almost as a military unit would, preparing to have information ready to go to our people in the "Spin Rooms" on the ground at the debate site. The energy of that first debate night was palpable, as people paced the room and Betsey made sure that we had the most up-to-date statistics ready to go. As some staffers deployed around televisions watching the debate, others manned ringing office phones and stood by fax machines as they buzzed intermittently, sending notes on the issues being discussed. We sent statistics on employment and education, crime and trade issues. Whatever came up during the debates, we wanted to provide the answers the media was looking for. We tried to be as dispassionate as possible, quoting third-party analysis of Governor Clinton and his policies. We also pointed to inconsistencies between what President Bush was saying at the debate and what his policies had produced over the last four years. In 1988, President Bush told voters, "Read My Lips: No New Taxes," and that promise was broken in 1990. No matter what Bush attempted to argue, we always tried to remind voters that even as President Bush sought to portray Bill Clinton as an untrustworthy liberal, it was the incumbent who had broken his word to the American people on this core issue, and now the nation faced a severe economic downturn. Our point was that President Bush either did not understand the economic problems facing the nation or was not interested in fixing them. The instant polls after the debates showed that Governor Clinton had done well. His command of policy issues made him look presidential, and his lack of major mistakes reassured the public that he could handle the pressure of the spotlight. As we watched postdebate coverage and noted how pundits gave Governor Clinton high marks for policy detail and clarity, we knew that research had done its job; there was no devastating sound bite or major gaffe by our guy. If the media was talking about issues after the debates, we knew that regardless of instant polling results, we had won.

Research and Our Fifteen Minutes of Fame

In the last few weeks of the campaign, the everyday research work of the campaign was often interrupted by famous faces, odd video, and the just plain strange. As the campaign entered the final stretch, nearly every big name in the Democratic Party made their way to Little Rock. Democratic National Committee chairman Ron Brown, who was the first African American elected to lead a major political party (and who became secretary of commerce under President Clinton and was later killed in a tragic plane crash) came through and offered up a pep talk to the staff. Civil rights hero Ernest Green, one of nine African Americans to integrate Little Rock Central High School in 1957, came into headquarters, and I for one, as an African American graduate of Central High, admitted to being completely starstruck when I met him. The public faces of the campaign (and later stars in their own right thanks to the documentary *The War Room*), James Carville and George Stephanopoulos, popped into our office to talk to Betsey, Diane, or other senior research staff. A couple of research staffers had friends working for *Saturday Night Live,* who clued us in to some of the sketches that were coming up in the shows before the election, including Phil Hartman's classic impersonation of Bill Clinton visiting a McDonald's. We also were treated to homemade campaign ads sent in to headquarters by supporters, including one that showed grainy footage of President Bush vomiting during a dinner in Japan in 1991, then having the image morph into a picture of Vice President Dan Quayle. The tagline was simply "Remember."

These early brushes with notables, however, pale in comparison to one instance in which words failed. After spending most of one late fall morning searching for education information to prepare for the third debate, Adam, Steve, John, and I went out for a quick lunch. As we returned to the office, we noticed a small crowd from "Hillaryland" (the nickname we gave to the office that coordinated policy and scheduling for Hillary Clinton) gathered around a man standing just outside our office. We almost never had visitors on the third floor, so this person had to be either a VIP or in serious trouble. I was about to say something when I heard Steve whisper: "That's Hunter S. Thompson." We all stopped walking and stared for a second. The "gonzo journalist" himself, the man the Doonesbury character "Uncle Duke" was modeled after, and of course the author of both *Fear and Loathing in Las Vegas* and *Fear and Loathing on the Campaign Trail 1972,* was standing five feet away smoking a cigarette underneath a "No Smoking" sign, taking swigs from a silver flask that kept hitting the press pass hung around his neck, and flirting with about ten women, all of whom were at least thirty years his junior. We all looked at each other as if to say, what do we do now? We each waded in and talked to him, and I wanted to ask him something profound, not be a fan, but try and engage him. Nothing came to mind, and I settled for telling him it was an honor to meet him. He gave me a puzzled look, took a swig from the flask, and asked me if I needed a drink. I smiled and walked away. I had to walk away; what was the comeback to that question as asked by Hunter S. Thompson?

Research in the Home Stretch

After the debates ended and the essential dynamics of the race did not change, we realized that we could not just run out the clock. As an aggressive team dedicated to defense, the Research Office became a place where background and facts about the Arkansas Record could be disseminated quickly to the media office inside the campaign, who in turn gave it to reporters and to an increasingly interested public. Some voters called and requested information from our volunteers, and the volume of calls increased to the point that some calls were routed up to research. A small number of us agreed to answer some calls on days when we were not overloaded with work. It was a unique experience, dealing with policy questions about everything from tax policy to foreign debt and political questions on the response to Hurricane Andrew in Florida and the governor's decision to wear a Cleveland Indians baseball cap he received on a campaign swing through Ohio. I once spoke with a Native American activist who was upset at the governor wearing the hat and asked me if, as an African American, I would be offended by a similar caricature of black people as sports mascots. It was one of the few times in my life when I was speechless. I told him I would relay his concerns to senior staff and told him that I truly appreciated his anger. It did not matter that we were better on health care or education policy; if we could appear that clueless on ethnic imagery, we might not get the chance to implement the changes we were all working for.

As we got closer to Election Day, the need for information on Clinton and his record increased daily. Ross Perot had proven a credible candidate, and his self-financed campaign had a momentum of its own that was complicating our plans for winning the election. The idea of a razor-thin race and an unprecedented Electoral College split excited the media. Our internal polls showed the race as close, but not as close as media reports suggested. In every one of our polls, Governor Clinton was maintaining a roughly 5 percent lead, safely outside the margin of error but not enough to celebrate. We were winning, but the race had not been won. Some of the research staff decided to take advantage of the opportunity to go out into the field to work in battleground states knocking on doors, organizing rallies, and participating in get-out-the-vote efforts as the election tightened in the last few weeks before Election Day.

The idea of getting out into the field and helping to close the deal was enticing, yet I just could not see myself being anywhere else but Little Rock on election night. In the final few weeks of the campaign, we settled in to see if all the work would pay off. The pace of the campaign seemed to slow down. I was used to being up early and in campaign headquarters by 8:30 in the morning and heading home about 8:30 at night. It was exhausting and exhilarating, and the mad dash from May to November was near an end. Governor Clinton had chosen to end the campaign on a nonstop twenty-four-hour swing through several states on his way back to Arkansas. It was ending, and we were winning, and I went home the night before the election after a very emotional final War Room staff meeting feeling confident, ready, and amazingly patriotic.

Research on Election Day

On Election Day, I was unique among my colleagues in that I actually had to go and vote. Most of the research staff, who were from other states, had voted by absentee ballot, but I had been so wrapped up in the everyday life of the campaign that I had not thought about voting early. I went with my mom, and she and I stood in line for nearly an hour before I cast my vote. Then I rushed downtown to headquarters, which was empty as security swept the building after a bomb scare. A little after one o'clock in the afternoon, they began letting staff back in the building, and as I made my way into the office, the smiles all around told me all I needed to know. We pored over exit poll data from all over the country and knew that we had won. I sat at my desk for a while trying to be philosophical, and nothing came to mind. I kept hugging my fellow staffers and fielding calls from friends who wanted to be inside headquarters or on the grounds of the Old State House, where Clinton was scheduled to give his victory speech. I was told to go down to the press room and get a pass that would allow me access to the grounds when he gave his speech that night. After showing my campaign identification and getting a light blue access pass, the reality of what was happening started to sink in. The crowds outside headquarters swelled as the official watch party began in the early evening. The banners with the election night slogan, "America Coming Together," could be seen all over downtown Little Rock, and I went outside to soak up some of the energy and excitement as the hugs, smiles, and camera flashes of the gathering crowd spoke to the history being made that night. A couple of research staffers had booked rooms in the nearby Excelsior Hotel, and we went there to watch election returns and await the formal calling of the election. The sense of change was enhanced as we watched five female candidates (four Democrats and one Republican) get elected to the US Senate. A little after 10 P.M., we received the call that the governor was on his way to the Old State House to claim victory. We piled into a freight elevator, headed down to the back of the hotel, and emerged outside into a chilly, misty night. The television lights illuminated a crowd that went so far back I could not see the end of it. As we walked a couple of blocks through Riverfront Park to the Old State House, we briefly watched Andrea Mitchell of NBC News do a live report on the crowd, and we yelled at actor Woody Harrelson, who was dancing and celebrating in the middle of the street as we walked past. After a Secret Service check at the gates of the Old State House, we settled in. A wave of noise engulfed us when Senator Gore and his family emerged. Seconds later, the new president walked out and announced that the nation had voted for a "New Beginning."

Research Lessons

As much as I thought I knew about politics, the insider perspective and subtle lessons all seemed to come into focus in the hours after the election. My fellow staffers and I laughed and talked until the wee hours after the victory speech, and as I headed home that night, I realized that I had read about party platforms, but I had learned about message discipline. I understood ideology as an intellectual concept, but I began to comprehend the importance of vision as political virtue. Politics, theoretically, showcased the clash of ideas. Campaigns, however, marketed candidates in ways that I did not understand before joining the Clinton campaign but would never forget after it. Substance on issues did matter, but so did the perception of how issues affected the everyday life of voters. The Clinton campaign showed me that when you run for office, you cannot simply be the smartest kid in the class. You have to be the smart kid whom everyone else understands and likes. You have to be the candidate who represents the vision of politics that citizens have in their heads when they go to the polls.

Ten days after the election night victory, the research department had a farewell dinner. Betsey Wright handed out bright red "Arkansas Is a Natural" T-shirts to us and told us how much she appreciated all our hard work. As we posed for one last group picture, I wanted to tell her that I needed to thank her and Diane and the rest of the staff for the lessons they had taught me: lessons about campaign tactics and strategies, about passion and commitment to a cause, but most of all a lesson in why I love politics. The ideas, the people, and the promise of a better tomorrow helped me understand that Aristotle was right: Politics is the greatest of all sciences.

In the years since the campaign, I have not talked to my fellow Box Boys as much as I would like, although I do know that they are all still actively engaged in the pursuit of politics and political ideas. A few are academics, others practice law or work in the government, and one, Steve Simon, is currently a Democratic representative from the Forty-Fourth District in the Minnesota House of Representatives. That, in some ways, is the enduring lesson of my 1992 campaign experience. Today when I stand before a class lecturing on campaigns and elections, I try to impart to the students the simple truth that issues and ideas are the foundation of modern politics, but so are passion, empathy, and visions of a better tomorrow. Our modern methods of campaigning, although faster and potentially more effective than those of earlier times, are still trying to bring people together to solve the myriad problems facing us as a nation. Whenever I am asked about learning about politics, my mind often races back to the memories of that presidential campaign when I was a Clinton Box Boy. In my quest to learn even more about politics, I realized that after reading the books, analyzing the data, learning the tactics, and even getting my doctorate, the most enduring lessons came from the experience of living and working as a Box Boy inside the Clinton-Gore campaign headquarters in the spring, summer, and fall of 1992.

Acknowledgments

Thanks to Jim Bowers for the invitation to write this piece and for great editorial suggestions. I also thank my colleagues Karen Swenson, Andrew McNitt, and Richard Wandling for their comments on an earlier draft of this chapter. I dedicate this chapter to the memory of Professor Diane D. Blair (1938–2000): You made this experience unforgettable.

7

Volunteering in a State Legislative Campaign

Michael Smith

Type of campaign: State legislature (primary)

Role of author: Staff member, volunteer

Lessons to look for:

- Ambition and values are important motivators for volunteers, and not just for candidates.
- An ambitious volunteer engages in a strategic calculation to participate in a campaign, much as a candidate considers when deciding to run.
- Even for volunteers, campaigns are about taking advantage of opportunities.
- Branding a candidate and the opponent is an important component of a campaign's media strategy.
- Campaigning is a contact sport, sometimes played dirty.

In August 2002, former two-term Kansas City mayor (1976–1979) Charles Wheeler won a come-from-behind Democratic primary election victory for a seat in the Missouri State Senate. Just a few weeks earlier another campaign volunteer, a hard-boiled and cynical ex-insider, had looked at me across a barroom table and said: "You may get Charlie Wheeler elected!" The night of the election, we celebrated in Wheeler's favorite local pub while awaiting the last election returns, the ones from Grandview, the battleground where I had worked so hard. The call came at about 11 P.M., and Wheeler announced his victory to us revelers. I sat with a fellow campaign volunteer, Larry, who kept Wheeler's schedule and often drove him to events. "We did it!" I cried. Larry looked back at me, deadpan. "*You* did it," was all he said.

These are strong words of praise from fellow campaign volunteers. But what really explains the remarkable comeback victory and the eventual disappointing aftermath that followed Wheeler's election? What strengths and weaknesses did other volunteers and I bring to campaigning? And what were our motivations for volunteering to campaign for a candidate in his seventies who hadn't been in office for more than twenty years? Whatever the answers to these questions are, whatever the successes and failures of Charles Wheeler's 2002 campaign (and his subsequent single term in the Missouri Senate), one thing is clear. I bear a lot of responsibility for the success of his political campaign and, ultimately, for his election. I was one of the most motivated, consistent volunteers. I was one of a small handful of those volunteers who made certain the campaign strategically identified what we needed to do to win and kept myself and the candidate focused on those things. I was able to connect with Wheeler at a deep, personal level and keep him motivated throughout the campaign. My main role, though, was to identify a key battleground (i.e., Grandview), organize our campaign there, and keep Wheeler and his volunteers active in Grandview while other campaign volunteers attended to Wheeler's base in Kansas City's wealthier wards with a name recognition campaign. To quote the late Paul Harvey, the remainder of this chapter tells "the rest of the story."

Values, Ambition, and Volunteering

I have long had a strong interest in political action. As a rather nerdy child, I followed politics closely. By the time I was twelve, I was fixated on the 1982 midterm congressional elections, wondering how many seats the Democrats (whom I supported) would gain. I have daydreamed about seeking political office since childhood, often imagining myself making speeches in place of the actual nominees for public office that I see on television. I love to talk about politics and believe passionately in resolving problems through deliberation and action. Attitudes such as "It's not my problem" and "There's nothing we can do that will make a difference, anyway" make me very angry. I believe in being powerful, claiming that power, and acting against violations of one's values.

As an undergraduate student at Reed College, I was initially drawn to political science due to an interest in political campaigns, though I later became enamored of political philosophy, now my favorite subject to teach. Shunning law school, I instead chose graduate study in political science. Turned off by the heavily quantitative (read: number-crunching) focus of Ohio State's highly ranked program, I found myself leaving, master's degree in hand, to do my doctoral work at the University of Missouri, just two hours from my hometown. At Missouri, I chose a dissertation topic that connected me closely to "real world" politics. I focused on applying Richard Fenno's methods to the study of state representatives. Fenno's trademark research method is "soaking and poking" (more formally, it is called "participant observation"). Soaking and poking involves "shadowing" research subjects, interacting with them, and taking extensive notes while observing them act and interact with others, without any pre-established expectations. I took Fenno's qualitative research methods from his seminal book *Home Style* and applied them to my own study of state representatives in and around my hometown of Kansas City. (An edited version of my dissertation was later published as the book *Bringing Representation Home*.) During this time, I "caught the bug" to get active in politics, realizing that I would never be content to study and teach politics unless I was also an active participant. That participation also reflected my values and ambition.

Values

Why do I want to participate in politics? It is because I am angered when I see my core values violated, and I will take action to do something about it. One of these core values is democracy itself, accompanied by an honest and nondogmatic dialogue and open decisionmaking. Highly imperfect and frustrating, democracy is still (to quote Winston Churchill) "the worst system in the world except for all of the other ones." I cannot, will not, relinquish my core value of a system that encourages rational decisionmaking and honest debate within a community of informed voters. Would-be cynics mock it as an unattainable ideal, and perhaps it is. It is easy to point to the innumerable ways in which voters are manipulated, irrational fears distort elections, and voters consistently fall short in tests of elementary facts about the political systems by which they are governed. But I still believe in it. I still believe in the value of community, honest public debate, rational decisionmaking, and a system in which any and all can participate.

A second value that drives my participation is honesty and ethical behavior. I have little patience for the parsing of words, or "spin," or half-truths that cover up what is really occurring. I have even less patience with unethical or unprincipled behavior, particularly when it comes to elections and public service. In short, I participate out of a belief in democracy, clean elections, and good government. All three were factors in my decision to volunteer in Wheeler's state senate campaign.

Ambition

Values and principles drive my political participation, but so too does ambition. Concretely, my plan at the time that I joined the Wheeler campaign was to seek a seat in the Missouri House of Representatives (the lower house of the Missouri State Legislature), from a district in the wealthier, more stable, and (unfortunately) less diverse part of the city. I had lived in this area of historic houses, tree-lined streets, and close-knit neighborhoods as a young child. Just before I entered elementary school, my parents divorced and sold the house, each of them relocating to annexed parts of the city that maintained their own school districts, separate from the city schools. I had always yearned to move back to the area of my childhood, and that dovetailed nicely with my political plans. A relatively progressive Democrat and Kansas City native, I believed I would be an excellent fit with the area's liberal leanings. Now a college professor, I was also well suited to a district that included the University of Missouri–Kansas City, where some of its professors and students lived and participated in politics. In short, I wanted to seek public office, and the part of Kansas City where I had longed to return since childhood seemed a perfect fit.

My own ambition was assisted by the fact that Missouri state legislators were term limited. In 1994, Missouri voters passed an initiative imposing term limits on state representatives and senators. Statehouse members now would be limited to four two-year terms in the Missouri House of Representatives and two four-year terms in the Missouri Senate. In both cases, these limits were "lifetime," meaning that former legislators were ineligible to return to the state legislature once they met these term limits. State legislators already in office were grandfathered into the voter-approved law, so their term limit clocks did not run out until 2002.

After moving back to the area, my plan was to run for the house seat held by Democrat Marsha Campbell when she was forced from office by term limits. She was elected in 1996, so the timer on her term limits clock did not go off until 2004. Before 2004, I needed to get active and develop a major presence in area politics, which would get my name out among active voters and political insiders. The active, hard-core, "vote in every election" constituents were especially important because the district was so Democratic that voters in the primary would effectively decide the area's next state representative. Primary elections draw relatively small groups of highly dedicated, often well-informed voters. In Missouri, primaries are held in August. Once Campbell won the 2002 election, it would be her last term due to term limits. As of 2002, anything I could do to build street credibility with active, Democratic primary voters would help me win my own seat two years later. As a courtesy I spoke to Representative Campbell about my intentions. She indicated that she had no objection to my plans. So, upon returning to Kansas City, I volunteered with her 2002 primary campaign to begin building my political resume in the district.

Volunteering

Volunteering for Marsha Campbell was the obvious path to building a base for my statehouse run, two years later. Marsha did have an opponent that year in the Democratic primary. Her just-redrawn district included large portions of the district once represented by her good friend, Tim Van Zandt. Tim was gay and well connected with the city's lesbian, gay, bisexual, transgendered (LGBT) community. He was also term-limited out of office. Campbell drew a primary challenger who argued that this area, central to the city's LGBT community, needed a new gay representative now that Tim was leaving office. This type of descriptive representation is novel and would not be seen in many other Missouri districts, to say the least. It didn't work here, either. Marsha had the overwhelming advantage. She was an experienced incumbent with a very strong name recognition advantage over her Democratic primary opponent, who had never served in public office. She received an enthusiastic endorsement from Tim Van Zandt, who went door-to-door with her in the areas that used to be in his district. It was going to be an easy campaign, thanks largely to Marsha's incumbency and Tim's support. After the primary, the district was so Democratic that Republican opponents were no worry.

Helping Marsha was too easy. I needed a "hotter" campaign to fight for what I believe and make a reputation for myself. I did go door-to-door with Marsha, but it didn't take long. I found what I was looking for when my state senator, who represented the Tenth District, also was forced from office by term limits. Senator Harry Wiggins had held this seat since 1974 and was not eligible to run again. Wiggins's forced retirement created an open seat, and the turnover of the seat was huge news in local political circles. This campaign was an excellent way for me to fight for my values, help someone in whom I strongly believed, and build my own political base all at the same time. The question was, who would my candidate be? I found the answer to that question in the newspaper.

When I read in the *Kansas City Star* that Wheeler was making a political comeback by announcing for the open state senate seat in the Tenth District, I became very excited! I had childhood memories of Wheeler as a local legend. He was mayor when I grew up here, in the 1970s. He appeared regularly on local talk radio, joking with entertainer/host Mike Murphy. Even as a kid, I loved following local news and politics. Wheeler could also hold a child's attention— this child, anyway—by being so memorable and funny, even comedic. For instance, I remember that he once staged an event in his office in which he appeared to wrestle a bear! I was also drawn to Wheeler's image because both of my parents admired him. I never met Wheeler, as had so many in the community, but I was certainly aware of his reputation. I cold-called him and volunteered for his campaign. This was in February 2002—the Democratic primary, the "real" election in this heavily Democratic district, was in August. I was excited about the return of this local icon. A little Kansas City history and Wheeler's role in it will help to explain why.

A Local Icon

Charles Wheeler is a likable man and a true Kansas City icon. A pathologist who also holds a law degree, he is funny, charming, and ever-present. Wheeler is a handshaker by nature, eager to build his reputation. He likes to be in every parade. As a two-term mayor of Kansas City in the 1970s, he accomplished some remarkable things. Mayor Wheeler convinced voters to approve a tax levy needed to build a new convention hall. Just a few years later, he inspired a group of city notables to land the 1976 Republican National Convention for Kansas City, in that just-completed Bartle Hall. It did not matter that the Kansas City mayor is a nonpartisan job or that Wheeler is a Democrat at heart: The GOP Convention was a huge opportunity to showcase Kansas City to the world and advertise its new identity as "America's Most Livable City." That was quite a change from the city's reputation as a hotbed of political corruption, racial strife, and organized crime. Wheeler also spearheaded the drive to replace the city's aging (and once-segregated) two general hospitals with a new teaching hospital affiliated with the University of Missouri–Kansas City. Earlier, as a county judge (an archaic term denoting a county legislator), Wheeler was part of a successful drive to approve construction of a new sports complex for the Kansas City Chiefs and the Kansas City Royals, which is still in use and now under renovation. And still earlier, Wheeler developed a reputation as a hardworking pathologist and county coroner who was outspoken in his criticism of the city and county's decrepit medical facilities. (He once did an autopsy in a parking lot!) After serving as coroner, county judge, and mayor, Wheeler was defeated in his bid for a third mayoral term, in part due to resistance from the local firefighter's union. He returned to private life and his pathology practice. However, he continued to be very active in the community, serving on boards of community groups and so forth.

In a city known for its share of political corruption, Wheeler was well respected for his integrity. In office, he allied himself with those promoting "good government," starting with his very first election as county coroner. The city was once dominated by political machine boss Tom Pendergast. Organized crime's influence in Kansas City lasted long after its ally Pendergast went to prison. Wheeler didn't start the city's good government movement, but he joined it early in his career. Their message was this: We are *not* the old boys' network, and we are *not* the Mafia. The need for such an effort was dire. For instance, in 1970, a presumed Mafia "hit" was carried out when African American community leader Leon Jordan was gunned down at the tavern he owned. Jordan had just been elected to the Missouri General Assembly from a heavily African American district. No one was ever charged with his murder, but local lore holds that Jordan was murdered for moving onto the Mafia's political turf by winning one of the "black wards." In the 1970s, the North End establishment (read, the Mafia) even sent its own lobbyist to the Missouri General Assembly. Wars between rival Mafia families also destroyed the city's River Quay entertainment district when Wheeler was mayor. Wheeler positioned himself as a supporter of Kansas City police chief Clarence Kelly, appointed before Wheeler became mayor. Kelly was active in diminishing Mafia influence before being appointed director of the Federal Bureau of Investigation (FBI) in 1973. In short, in his early career Wheeler symbolized good government to a city that desperately needed it.

Although the Mafia added violence, embarrassment, and some panache to the city's political reputation, the old-boys' network was an even more pervasive influence. Starting shortly after Pendergast's trip to Leavenworth prison and lasting until Wheeler's election as mayor in 1976, the city's mayors were mostly corporate lawyers. Their priorities were paying off the Pendergast debt, building freeways, and annexing would-be suburbs before they incorporated as separate cities. Pendergast and his city manager, Henry McElroy, had left the city with massive debt and labyrinthine bookkeeping to hide it, so city leaders spent much of the 1950s just climbing out of this financial hole. On another front, Wheeler and other old-time Kansas Citians still lament the loss of the city's streetcar system, replaced by cheaper buses in the 1950s. This was done mostly because the streetcar lines blocked the city leaders' true priority (i.e., freeway construction). Downtown became less walkable, now surrounded with a freeway loop and its innumerable overpasses and ramps. Traffic ways were constructed to speed commuters to the growing suburbs in Johnson County, Kansas, and elsewhere. The city did nothing while its schools struggled with declining enrollment and racial strife. In 1960, a major annexation drive to the north of the city tripled Kansas City's land area. The annexation of the "northland" ensured that some suburban growth would occur within city limits. Instead of trying to keep more of the middle class in the city, planners chose to take the city limits out into suburban territory. Meanwhile, city and country infrastructure crumbled in the urban core. Wheeler was particularly incensed about the neglect of public medical facilities, which he saw firsthand as a pathologist and then county coroner.

Against this backdrop, Wheeler's status as an *icon* began during his two terms as mayor of Kansas City. The city continued to struggle in the 1970s, as did virtually all US cities outside the sunbelt. The Kansas City school district entered a precipitous decline in the 1970s, marked by racism and white flight, local refusal to pass bond issues, and an ugly strike by teachers in 1974. But in other respects, under Wheeler's leadership, Kansas City appeared to beat the odds. The city never came close to bankruptcy, unlike Cleveland. The influence of the Mafia fell apart after their infighting and literal explosions rocked the downtown River Quay entertainment district. Kansas City never requested federal loans during the 1920s, unlike New York in the 1970s. (There is a famous *New York Post* headline from this period that reads: "[President] Ford to New York: Drop Dead.") The city's annexed areas experienced significant growth, which mitigated population losses in the urban core. Certain city neighborhoods such as Brookside held fast to their reputations as vibrant, stable, close-knit communities, even in the face of competition from growing suburbs. The construction of Bartle Hall and hosting of the 1976 Republican National Convention, both spearheaded by Wheeler, brought tourist dollars and boosted public morale. Even the international artist Christo noticed Kansas City, choosing it for one of his public art projects in 1978. Christo wrapped all the walkways of stately Loose Park in yellow canvas. A marketing campaign labeled

Kansas City "America's Most Livable City" during this time, and that phrase was on every civic booster's lips for years afterward.

Wheeler's quirky, funny, sometimes tempestuous style; his distinctive nasal voice; his style of dress; and a general sense that Kansas City beat the odds for US cities in the 1970s all combined to give him a larger-than-life reputation. In his distinctive seersucker suits and bowties, topped off with the "hat of the day" from his vast collection, Wheeler shot right past the status of local celebrity and became a Kansas City icon. Like his hero, Harry Truman of neighboring Independence, Missouri, Wheeler saw time polish off the rough edges of his reputation after he left public office.

When Wheeler and a cadre of other volunteers and I staged Wheeler's political comeback in 2002, few remembered that Mayor Wheeler was defeated for reelection in 1979, due mostly to a dispute with the firefighters' union. Those that did remember often felt that city voters had made a mistake in rejecting him back then. In short, our campaign didn't have a candidate; it had an *icon*. And given the good feeling that we had about the return of Wheeler, our feelings of apprehension toward his two primary opponents were just as strong.

Opponent 1: Hardworking, Shady . . . and in the Wrong District

Our principal opponent, Henry Rizzo, was a term-limited Missouri House member whose own home had just been moved through the 2000 reapportionment from another state senate district into the Tenth District. By no means did I lack respect for Rizzo. He was well-known around Jefferson City as a hardworking state representative who would take on unglamorous issues such as the safety of petroleum storage tanks. (His district included an industrial area.) Some of my friends and political allies backed Rizzo because of his experience in the statehouse. With term limits taking effect in Missouri, some believed it was smart and necessary to preserve institutional knowledge in Jefferson City. As a term-limited state representative now seeking a state senate seat, Rizzo seemed perfect.

However, I was worried about past ethics and current political associates. The primary instance of Rizzo's ethical troubles was his time in prison for a check-kiting scheme. Check kiting is a type of financial chicanery that involves writing a bad check to cover another bad check, then writing another bad check to cover that one, and so on, in the hopes that it will never be exposed that there is no money to cover the checks, or in order to buy time until money is available to cover the balance. Rizzo had owned a car dealership at one time, and when the business faced deep financial troubles, he kited checks to keep it solvent. The dealership eventually went bankrupt, and Rizzo spent a few months in prison after his conviction.

Rizzo also was closely tied to Jackson County executive Katherine Shields. Shields spent hundreds of thousands of taxpayer dollars to redecorate her office. She also was indicted on a mortgage fraud scheme involving her own house! Rizzo was closely tied to Shields in terms of fund-raising and political connections. That history added greatly to my wariness about Rizzo.

Like his association with Shields, Rizzo's ties to political consultant Pat Gray also were a concern to me. Gray was well-known among Kansas City's political insiders for being effective, manipulative, and unethical. His signature move was to design logos for candidates that tied the candidate's name to a popular consumer product. Marsha Campbell got a design imitating a Campbell's soup can label, for example. For the Rizzo campaign, Gray designed a signature logo modeled on the Nestlé candy bar "Oh Henry!" No effort was made to secure permission from the trademark holder, Nestlé. Rizzo actually lost a few crucial days in the campaign to news coverage of swirling rumors that Nestlé would pursue trademark infringement—rumors that we helped fuel. Nestlé never sued, but the rumors alone were costly to the Rizzo campaign.

Gray also was alleged to have a manipulative, backroom-dealing side. A few years earlier, rumors abounded when Gray simultaneously managed two ballot referenda authorizing tax levies. One funded a light rail project. The second one increased funding for the city's fire department. The firefighters' union is a massive political presence in this city. The political buzz was that Gray deliberately positioned the light rail referendum as a sacrificial pawn in order to pass the firefighters' levy, the logic being that voters confronted with two tax increases would choose only the one that they thought was more important.

Gray's involvement in Rizzo's campaign helped our campaign recruit volunteers. We inherited at least one volunteer who had been involved in the light rail campaign and was embittered toward Gray. Another one of our volunteers was a longtime political consultant that had worked with Gray earlier and swore that Gray was unethical. This drive to defeat not only Henry Rizzo but also Pat Gray mobilized two of our core volunteers and reinforced our campaign's "good government" image.

Besides his ethical lapses and questionable associations, I believed that Rizzo did not understand the whole district, having originally planned before redistricting to run in a different state senate district with different demographics and different public expectations toward elected officials more aligned with Rizzo's style of politics. Rizzo's neighborhood and his old statehouse district were the historic North End mentioned earlier in this chapter, once a base for the Pendergast machine and the Mafia. Throughout the city's history, that community has been a landing pad for immigrants. (Once they came from Ireland and Italy, today from Mexico, Vietnam, Somalia, and numerous other places.) Throughout the district's history, its working-class immigrant constituents had overlooked political excesses and ethical lapses such as those Rizzo had committed in exchange for political effectiveness.

Rizzo was used to representing that kind of constituent. However, much of the Tenth District didn't reflect Rizzo's style of politics or accept unethical behavior. A good portion of the Tenth District consisted of wealthier neighborhoods and good-government, reform-minded constituents. I concluded that Rizzo wouldn't understand these constituents. Equally as important, they would not understand him. In short, Rizzo wasn't a good fit for the Tenth District.

Opponent 2: Arrogance on Display

Our second opponent was Suellen Dice. My concern with her candidacy stemmed mainly from the presumptuousness and arrogance of her campaign and its supporters. Dice had been recruited to run by pro-choice women's groups. She was a local community notable and activist, particularly on women's issues. She was closely tied to the powerful Greater Kansas City Women's Political Caucus, a formidable group. At one point in the mid-1990s, the mayors of Kansas City, Missouri, and Kansas City, Kansas; the Jackson (Missouri) and Johnson (Kansas) County Executives; and the city's representative in Congress (on the Missouri side) were all women, closely tied to the caucus. These pro-choice groups were unhappy about Rizzo's anti-abortion voting record. He was a devout Catholic. Like Dice, Wheeler was also pro-choice, but Dice's supporters dismissed him completely. Instead of backing him, they recruited a candidate with no experience in elected office whose candidacy could cost Wheeler crucial pro-choice votes.

In many ways, I was much angrier with Dice's supporters than with Rizzo and his team. Rizzo's supporters took our campaign very seriously once we gained steam, and Rizzo himself worked very hard to meet our challenge. Rizzo sweated it out by going door-to-door in Missouri's summer heat, something the nearly eighty-year-old Wheeler didn't attempt. Rizzo always treated Wheeler and his volunteers with respect, even while we subtly but sharply attacked him about the check kiting. Dice's campaign supporters, by contrast, seemed arrogant and out of touch with Kansas City, oblivious to Wheeler's iconographic status, and dismissive of his attempt at a political comeback. My anger at the way Dice's supporters treated Wheeler was one of the reasons I picked up the phone in February and called Wheeler. By Election Day, however, our biggest worry wasn't that Dice would win, but that she would be a spoiler for us. In the end, she finished a distant third and did not cost us enough votes to affect the election. I still savor that victory.

Given this contrast among the three candidates and their supporters, I could not, and would not, stand by idly or content myself simply to cast my single vote in the August primary. I was prepared to do something about it, and what I did took me to Grandview, Missouri, the ground zero of the Tenth District senate campaign.

The Tenth District: What's Up, G?

At the time of the 2007 elections, Missouri's Tenth Senate District had been deliberately gerrymandered into the shape of a capital letter "G." The district was drawn this way in order to protect the "majority-minority" Ninth District, which the Tenth District surrounds. Majority-minority districts are gerrymandered to ensure the election of a candidate of color to office. The Ninth District was drawn purposely to include Kansas City's heavily African American East Side to comply with the Voting Rights Acts Amendments of 1989, which call for enhanced efforts to draw majority-minority districts. Ironically, the Ninth District is truly gerrymandered, but as a result, the Tenth District has a contorted shape.

The best way to visualize the G is to imagine drawing it, starting in the upper right, making an arc to the left (or west), moving down (south) to make the spine, wrapping around the bottom by moving to the right, and then moving up, finishing it with a cross that makes it make a G instead of a "C." The beginning of the G, in the upper right, was Rizzo's base, the North End mentioned previously. It has a long history of political corruption. Parts of it struggle with high murder rates, and it has a nasty reputation as the city's red-light district. However, it also features spectacular historic homes, some gentrification, and the incredible diversity of a community of immigrants. Politically, voter turnout is low, partly because of sociodemographic factors. The community is mostly working class, and lower- to middle-income voters are less likely to vote than wealthier ones. The area also has a fairly high percentage of rental housing, which in turn means fewer stable, longtime residents.

The north-south spine of the G begins with downtown, just west of Rizzo's North End. The entire spine is less than two miles wide, beginning in the eclectic downtown/midtown area and moving south to encompass nearly all of the urban core's wealthier neighborhoods. The spine is bounded on the east by Troost Avenue, the city's infamous dividing line of race and class, and on the west by the wealthy suburbs of Johnson County, Kansas. Downtown Kansas City is the northernmost point of the spine. Immediately adjacent to downtown is the West Side, center of the Latino community, where community leaders split between Rizzo and Wheeler (none supported Dice). South of downtown and the West Side is the city's midtown, a diverse and eclectic area featuring older homes, many longtime residents, a bohemian/artist culture, and the bar district, Westport. Downtown and midtown were up for grabs in the campaign and were not a part of either candidate's base. However, midtown features a lot more voters than downtown. Furthermore, many midtowners are politically active, longtime Kansas Citians, likely to be familiar with both candidates. We predicted that many midtowners would make up their minds well in advance of the election.

Continuing south, the spine of the G moves through the Country Club Plaza shopping district, which is becoming a second downtown, with many office buildings and condominiums open or under construction. Wheeler's base began just south of the Plaza. These are the city's wealthiest wards, and, unfortunately, some of its least diverse ones. The area includes the celebrated, historic Brookside neighborhood, an oasis of urban stability and high property values in a changing city. Just west of Brookside, one finds the multimillion-dollar mansions along Ward Parkway, home to many of the city's elite. This is a politically plugged-in, newspaper-reading, good-government constituency. With the area's wealth and lack of diversity, one might assume it to be Republican, but several factors mitigate that, most notably a pronounced tendency for voters who choose urban living over the suburbs to be more liberal. This may in turn be related to another phenomenon that marks the area: the active and visible gay and lesbian community. Most of the area's residents are heterosexual but have an open and affirming stance toward our gay and lesbian neighbors.

Wheeler lived right at the center, between upper-middle-class Brookside and hyperelite Ward Parkway. Just south of Brookside sits Waldo. Waldo is a slightly less expensive neighborhood demographically similar to Brookside (thus answering the question, "Where's Waldo?"). This whole area of town is called the "Ward Parkway corridor." It is astonishing to realize that less than two miles of eastward travel separates Ward Parkway from the city's symbol of segregation, Troost Avenue. Immediately east of Troost (where the majority-minority Ninth District begins, surrounded by the G) sits the 64110 zip code, recently identified by the *Kansas City Star* as having Missouri's highest percentage of residents who go to prison.

The Brookside–Waldo–Ward Parkway corridor area has been Wheeler's political base since he was coroner, county judge, and mayor. Constituents in Wheeler's base are apprehensive about political hardball. Mostly middle-class or wealthy, we wanted a good-government type to represent us. As some of our signs proclaimed during the campaign, this district was "Wheeler Country." Rizzo's onetime prison sentence would not sit well with constituents here.

The bottom of the G, south and east of Wheeler's base, was the suburb of Grandview and the only part of the district outside Kansas City. The suburb includes land once farmed by Harry Truman, which he later sold to developers who created a shopping center on it in the 1950s. Suburban growth followed. More recently, Grandview has been transformed by "black flight," a phenomenon similar to white flight that occurs when African American families move to the suburbs to avoid the inner-city schools. Unfortunately, racism and fear provoked Grandview's white residents to flee to whiter outer-ring exurbs, depressing property values and straining schools along the way. Despite the resulting white flight, Grandview actually includes many stable, middle-class wards.

Not living in the Kansas City area, longtime Grandview residents never had the chance to vote for Wheeler when he was mayor. Wheeler didn't have a base there. However, Rizzo didn't have a base in Grandview either, in that Grandview was at the opposite end of the district from his base. In addition,

Grandview was the only part of the district with a substantial African American population. In this segregated city, divided by Troost Avenue, neither candidate had extensive experience cultivating black votes. Nor was Wheeler, Rizzo, or Dice known there by many voters. These factors led us to conclude that Grandview would be the real battleground in the state senate primary. A few days later, I felt vindicated when I noticed Rizzo's brand-new campaign headquarters . . . in Grandview!

The last part of the district, the cross on the G, is the Ruskin Heights neighborhood, in a part of the city known as Hickman Mills. Demographically, Hickman Mills is very similar to Grandview (i.e., working-class and racially changing). It has its own school district, separate from the city schools and experiencing the same waves of change being felt in Grandview. I grew up in Hickman Mills, right near the Grandview border, graduating from Hickman Mills public schools. I had experienced the changing neighborhood and its racial strife firsthand. My first job was in Grandview, and my high school girlfriend (later my first wife) lived there. I knew Grandview and Hickman Mills better than anyone else on our campaign. The other volunteers came mostly from midtown Kansas City. I alone was the "Grandview guy" in the campaign, even though I lived in an apartment just a few blocks from Wheeler's house, near Ward Parkway.

In short, this G district encompassed several completely different types of communities, but almost all its wards were bound together by one thing: the Democratic Party. The district was so heavily Democratic that the primary election winner would be the community's next state senator. No Republican even filed for the seat. Wheeler's base in the Ward Parkway corridor was clear, as was Rizzo's in the North End: Grandview and Hickman Mills were the only parts of the district that were up for grabs.

G Is for Grandview

In our campaign, I became responsible for delivering Grandview to Wheeler. I had some understanding of the community, more than others in the campaign, because I grew up near there. I knew the suburb's longtime mayor, Harry Wilson, who had once sold insurance to my parents. I immediately cultivated a relationship with Mayor Wilson. Wilson held a nonpartisan office, but was a Republican at heart. Politically savvy, he knew that the Democratic primary winner would be the district's next state senator. Wary of Rizzo's political past and his supporters, Wilson was a strong Wheeler supporter. We asked Wilson to refer us to others in Grandview with whom we could cultivate a relationship and good publicity. Wilson referred us to the publisher of the Jackson County *Advocate,* a family-owned newspaper covering Grandview and neighboring suburbs. This was another lucky break. The editor of the *Advocate,* a diehard

Democrat, was a strong Wheeler supporter. I took Wheeler out to the *Advocate* offices for a long chat with the editor, and they liked one another right off. After this meeting, the *Advocate* featured Wheeler's events in Grandview, including meetings with the mayor and with another supporter we discovered, John Martin, superintendent of the Grandview School District. Martin broadened our coalition in another way, too: He was a high-profile Wheeler supporter who was African American. The population of Grandview was about 40 percent African American at that time. The *Advocate* prominently featured photos of Wheeler with Mayor Wilson and Superintendent Martin, as they posed for photo-ops before and after meetings.

Despite this high-profile support in Grandview, we still had some problems. One major disadvantage in Grandview, and elsewhere in the district, was Wheeler's age. Now in his late seventies, Wheeler was not quite up to going door-to-door during a Kansas City summer, when humidity is high and daily high temperatures often exceed 100 degrees Fahrenheit (the primary was in early August). Rizzo did do so, however, working and sweating all day in the heat and knocking on doors throughout Grandview. (We heard no reports of Suellen Dice going door-to-door there.) To compensate, I became Wheeler's stand-in in Grandview, going door-to-door on his behalf. Having volunteers go door-to-door is not nearly as effective as having the candidate do so, but in our case it was a strong second-best alternative. These house visits, combined with our good publicity in the *Advocate* and strong relationships with Wilson and Martin, sent a message that the Wheeler campaign was very much present in Grandview.

I identified the precincts in Grandview with the highest voter turnout and concentrated on those, sometimes walking with a friend and fellow Wheeler supporter who was also familiar with Grandview's neighborhoods. Good voter lists are crucial to local campaigns. A good list of carefully targeted frequent voters serves as a "walking list" for door-to-door canvassing, which is the lynchpin of many campaigns. They can be sorted, for example, to target senior citizens (many lists feature birthdays or ages of voters) or voters likely to be parents. I formed our list by getting data from two sources: the Kansas City Election Board and the Jackson County Election Board. Most of Kansas City is, in fact, located in Jackson County, but the separate election boards are another legacy of the attempt to clean up Pendergast corruption. Kansas City was given its own separate election board with strict rules of bipartisan supervision, in hopes of mitigating the Pendergast influence. The institution lives on, long after Pendergast. The data for Grandview came from Jackson County. Before I joined the campaign, the other volunteers were so focused on Kansas City that no one had thought to get the Jackson County data for our list. If I hadn't changed our course, our door-to-door visits and direct mail would have completely missed Grandview voters.

I sorted the data using Microsoft Excel and isolated precincts that had high concentrations of frequent voters. Learning to use the "sort" command of Excel proved to be enormously beneficial. We also raised enough money at the last minute to do a direct mail campaign, and my list served as our mailing list. With a good printer and the right commands, data manipulated in Excel can become mailing labels. If it had not been for my efforts, our mailer also would have missed Grandview completely. But despite my good calls on getting us the data we needed to compete in Grandview, along the way I still made some mistakes.

Rookie Mistakes

I had never had a role like this in a campaign before, and I was full of energy. Sometimes, this energy got the best of me, and I became impulsive, making miscalculations that could have been politically costly, gotten me arrested, or harmed me. My first mistake was to go door-to-door alone. I sometimes went with another volunteer, but I often went alone in Grandview. This is a mistake for two reasons. First, if a candidate has mobilized enough supporters for a viable campaign, it shouldn't be necessary for the candidate or one volunteer (or, heaven forbid, the campaign manager, who has other things to do) to go door-to-door alone. There should be a strong, grassroots base of volunteers willing to take turns going door-to-door using the buddy system. The campaign looks better when teams go door-to-door instead of one lone wolf, especially when that lone wolf isn't even the candidate him- or herself. I took great risks in going door-to-door alone. The crime rate in Grandview is lower than in Kansas City's toughest neighborhoods but higher than in the Ward Parkway corridor or the outer-ring suburbs. Some of the neighborhoods were a little gritty. Luckily, I only encountered the occasional loose dog that didn't seem too happy to see me. It would have been much safer and more effective to go door-to-door in teams. I took foolish risks with my own well-being and limited the effectiveness of the campaign by going door-to-door alone.

My second rookie mistake was removing the opponent's campaign signs from unauthorized locations. Presumably, campaign yard signs were originally designed to go in yards—specifically, the yards of supporters who choose to display them. Somewhere along the way, yard signs jumped the fence and started appearing in easements, vacant lots, highway median strips, and so forth. In Kansas City, political consultants such as Pat Gray and even our own consultant, Pat O'Neill, actually pay people to go around placing yard signs in these locations. The signs are unsightly, and the law is vague on the legality of this practice. It also creates a public backlash against political yard signs. Some suburbs and subdivisions have tried to ban their display, even in a homeowner's own yard. Fortunately, these bans have been overturned by courts as a violation of free speech, though municipalities are allowed to limit how many weeks prior to an election the signs may be displayed and may also require their removal immediately after Election Day.

Pat Gray got right to work having workers place Rizzo signs in all sorts of questionable locations, including many in and near Grandview, such as vacant lots, easements, and even one in a public park! By contrast, we knew we had so many supporters who would display Wheeler signs in their yards that we had no need to put them in unauthorized places. At one campaign staff meeting, a veteran volunteer was grousing about these signs in what he called "illegal" locations. I took his comments to mean that yard signs in unauthorized locations were fair game to be removed. Working on my own, without telling anyone what I was about to do, I spent a few nights driving around Grandview, removing these signs. Of course, I never touched a sign in anyone's yard or on the property of any business. But signs in vacant lots and so forth came up and out and into the trunk of my car for a trip to the dumpster behind my apartment building, which filled up with "Oh Henry!" signs pretty quickly.

To this day, I still do not understand the laws governing yard signs in such locations, but what has become clear is that candidates and volunteers who remove their opponents' signs can get in big trouble with the news media, even if the signs are in unauthorized places. Since 2002, two separate incidents of candidates being filmed removing opponents' yard signs from locations like these have brought scandalous headlines (and many YouTube hits) in Kansas City. In hindsight, I am extremely lucky that I was not seen or videotaped removing these signs. I acted in good faith that the signs were in unauthorized, illegal locations, but I made the potentially catastrophic mistake of not discussing ideas and plans with the rest of the campaign before striking out and acting on my own. It was an incredibly foolish thing to do and could have been very costly to Wheeler, the campaign, and me.

Branding Wheeler to Mobilize Voters

If the battleground of our campaign was Grandview, our base was the Ward Parkway corridor. Demographically, these neighborhoods might be taken as Republican, being heavily white, professional, and wealthy. But these voters had spent the last several decades bucking white flight to the suburbs, and they have different values than those who left the city. They are urban, well-connected, tolerant of others (such as the LGBT community), and passionate about good government. They vote. They are not, for the most part, members of labor unions, part of Rizzo's core constituency. There is a sizable minority who are Republican or independent, but they are sophisticated enough to know that the Democratic primary often determines winners in this district, and they are not shy about requesting a Democratic primary ballot. (Missouri is an open-primary state in which voters do not register as party members. A voter may take either a Democratic or Republican primary ballot on primary election day.) The community is stable enough to include many voters that were living in Kansas City when Wheeler was mayor, and those voters love their neighbor, Charles Wheeler.

Our challenge throughout the district was the same as all campaigns: to mobilize voters. At the heart of our efforts here were the tried-and-true methods of name recognition, media coverage, and volunteers covering the polls on Election Day. In short, we branded Wheeler. In all of this effort, we were helped enormously by a brilliant political consultant, Pat O'Neill. O'Neill's father had been a consultant for Wheeler in the 1970s. Pat was happy to continue his father's legacy by backing Wheeler—this despite the fact that Wheeler's campaign had raised little money early on. We could only pay for materials. We couldn't pay O'Neill's usual consulting fees. Still, O'Neill volunteered his time and ideas out of loyalty to Wheeler. He may have also relished the chance to take on the city's most feared consultant, his sometime rival, sometime ally: Pat Gray. It was the battle of Pat versus Pat. In this election, "our" Pat got the better of the ruthless Gray.

O'Neill handled the name recognition part of our campaign, focusing on two themes, "Integrity" and "He's Back!" both of which figured prominently on our yard signs. The integrity theme contrasted Wheeler's iconic good-government reputation with Rizzo's perceived shadiness. The message "He's Back!" was designed to tell voters that the iconic Wheeler, now older and out of the spotlight for decades, was still alive and ready to reenter public life.

On this last score, O'Neill marketed Wheeler's iconographic image by keeping it simple. O'Neill designed a simple silhouette of Wheeler, a little hunched over, with trademark cap and glasses. Some of these logos featured predictable text, "Wheeler for Senate." But others relied entirely on the silhouette to summon voters' memories of our candidate, and amazingly, it worked! Soon, silhouettes of Wheeler with the words "He's Back!" or "Integrity" were appearing all over the city, and a few even sprouted up in Grandview. When going door-to-door in Grandview, I asked strong Wheeler supporters for permission to display yard signs on their property, and many agreed. In fact, placement of the yard signs was not a problem, as Wheeler's fans came out of the woodwork once they saw what we were doing, calling campaign headquarters to request signs. Some volunteers kept lists and checked off addresses that already had signs, while others drove around placing the signs. I did some of this, too, again focusing primarily on the yards of supporters I had met in Grandview.

In branding Wheeler, our single biggest challenge was convincing some voters that our candidate was still alive! Wheeler was still well-known by many, but he had been out of public life for over two decades. He was only in his fifties when he left the mayor's office, but somehow Wheeler always seemed a little older than his years. His distinctive voice and slow cadence are the likely cause. Our candidate was now in his late seventies and in reasonably good health, but voters naturally made assumptions about his long absence from public life. Some even assumed that the candidate we extolled was Wheeler's son!

But the silhouette did not hide Wheeler's senior years, and it, along with relentless word of mouth, got out the word that not only was Wheeler alive, He's Back!

Our branding of Wheeler was helped along even more when we secured the *Kansas City Star*'s endorsement. This was a huge development. Meeting with Wheeler shortly after he had been to see the *Star*'s editorial board, I felt his confidence that the meeting had gone well. The *Star* did not mention Pat Gray in its endorsement editorial, but otherwise the editorial board's reasons for backing Wheeler could have been lifted, word for word, from our campaign materials. They stressed integrity, Rizzo's checkered past and shady connections, and Wheeler's knowledge of the district and Kansas City and his successes as mayor in the 1970s. The endorsement was a huge coup for us and built support among newspaper readers, a key constituency in low-turnout elections such as this.

A second endorsement came from the *Kansas City Call,* the city's historic newspaper of the African American community. Wheeler, I, and other volunteers worked hard on the *Call* endorsement, cultivating a close relationship with the editor. Unfortunately, the *Call* is not circulated as widely in Grandview as it is in the city, but every little bit helped. We hyped the *Star* and *Call* endorsements every way we could, talking about them on door-to-door visits, putting them in our handouts, and having Wheeler mention them at campaign appearances. With little money to publicize the endorsements through direct mail, though, the best publicity was the endorsements themselves, which reached the politically active, newspaper-reading constituencies.

On Election Day we hoped our campaigning for and branding of Wheeler paid off. To give it the best possible chance, we spent Election Day working the polls. Of course, I headed out to Grandview that morning, having used the list to identify the precinct in Grandview that had the best combination of high turnout and lots of voters. I arrived before voting started and planted my folding chair at the minimum, legally required distance from the front door of the voting location (a school). I offered voters the only Wheeler literature we had, copies of the postcard that had been our single mail piece and the only one we could afford. I was gratified by positive comments from many voters. I also noticed that no Rizzo poll workers were present here. Another good sign for us!

Others worked the polls in the highest-turnout wards in Wheeler's base. One Ward Parkway church handled voting for four adjoining precincts, each precinct's voters directed to a separate part of the building. This made a great place for poll workers to target voters. After a morning and early afternoon in Grandview, I made my way to this church. Along with other Wheeler volunteers, I found an interesting phenomenon. The Rizzo poll workers were being paid for their time. They were mostly teenagers working for the money, not particularly excited about or even familiar with Rizzo. From what we could see, Rizzo had paid workers but few volunteers. Our campaign, by contrast, was entirely volunteer-based. Late that day, I watched a Rizzo supporter and local union leader pick up one of the teenage poll workers in his car. Looking at me around the big "Oh Henry!" sign in his car window, he told me, "You guys ran a great campaign. It's going to be close." That made my day.

What really made my day was us winning. I didn't deliver Grandview to Wheeler. He did win some precincts while holding Rizzo's lead down in others. Rizzo didn't win nearly enough votes there to overcome Wheeler's huge advantage in the Ward Parkway corridor, where voter turnout was far higher than in Rizzo's North End. In Grandview we held Rizzo to a slim lead: In one precinct there, the two candidates were separated by only one vote. We then crushed him in the part of town that was Wheeler's base.

As satisfying as Wheeler's victory was on election night, my own ambition, one of my main reasons for volunteering, became a casualty of the campaign. Along the way I forgot to or didn't know enough to build my own credibility for a future run for the state assembly in 2004. Instead, I let my admiration for Wheeler and other reasons for volunteering, such as my apprehensions about Rizzo, dominate my involvement in Wheeler's campaign.

Ambition Changed

In retrospect, my admiration for Wheeler's reputation proved to be a mixed blessing. On the one hand, Wheeler was the kind of candidate with whom I was comfortable, high on honesty and integrity and committed to good government. He was the perfect candidate to counter Rizzo, who hailed from the old-boys' network and had a shady reputation. Our campaign and Wheeler's victory made a definitive statement that the Tenth District senate seat did not belong to anyone but the people of the district. We upended the conventional wisdom and stuck it to the city's political establishment. I got to make my point that I would act powerfully when I saw the values of open, honest, democratic decision-making being subverted.

I grew so enamored of Wheeler, however, that I stopped thinking critically about my own ambition and how that was an equal factor in why I joined his campaign. I wrongly assumed that having one breakthrough victory as a Wheeler volunteer was all that it would take to get his endorsement, and that, in turn, is all it would take to win the state representative seat that Marsha Campbell would be vacating in 2006. But other variables interceded between Wheeler's victory and my planned run in 2004. Most notably, both houses of the state legislature turned from Democratic to Republican majorities. With the Democrats out of power, I lost the will to seek Campbell's seat. I had never seriously contemplated this happening nor had thought of what it would be like to win but serve in the minority. Instead, I focused too narrowly, first on getting

Wheeler elected, then on securing his endorsement, and then on winning the statehouse seat. I did not keep myself open to other possibilities for elected office, nor on how to build power from a minority party. Rather I became discouraged, withdrew from being politically active, and reexamined my ambition to seek elected office.

Staying in touch with Wheeler over the next four years, I found that, like me, he too had put all of his hopes and energies into winning the campaign. None of us, candidate or volunteers, had faced the "day after" question of what to do after victory, particularly victory in the minority. We had heard many rumors that 2002 would be the year that this increasingly Republican state would turn its statehouse over to the GOP, due to population growth outside of St. Louis and Kansas City, particularly in fast-growing, conservative southwestern Missouri located in and around Springfield and Branson. Despite the rumors, Wheeler, I, and other volunteers had not planned or prepared. Instead, we found ourselves frustrated. Wheeler left office after one term and didn't endorse anyone as his successor, and I still have not sought a statehouse seat. Several years later, I am just now coming to grips with this frustration and renewing my base building for an eventual run, this time as the candidate.

Since Wheeler's victory, I have worked in a few other local campaigns, but none successfully. I also withdrew from politics and now am preparing to reenter, but with a different focus. My current public life is centered around More-Squared, Kansas City's affiliate of the Gamaliel Foundation. Gamaliel is a faith-based, community-organizing group for which President Barack Obama worked when he was a community organizer in Chicago's Altgeld Gardens neighborhood. The centerpiece of Gamaliel's power building is aggressive training that forces organizers and volunteers to identify their own self-interests and the self-interests of those they seek to "move" and to act upon self-interest instead of being "do-gooders." Gamaliel's training, along with some other personal growth work, has forced me to clarify why I want to be powerful and what I am willing to do to get it. At my best, I seek power because I want to respond to violations of core values, particularly the value I place on honesty and direct, democratic decisionmaking. At my worst, I seek power because I like to be admired and because I like to do things myself instead of working with other people.

Over the next few years, I will need to decide how much I want to have political power and be honest about whether I seek this power to represent people and core values or just to be admired while I work alone. If I seek power for these latter reasons, I would do well to forgo a public life. However, I truly believe that the value I place on political action, on having a political voice over the systems that affect me, and on solving social problems through honest and direct dialogue are strong enough to propel me into a healthy public life, leading, being led by, and being in relationship with other people who share core values with me. To do so, I intend to design a comprehensive plan to build power in different circumstances, rather than just rely on a single election victory and a single endorsement to win public office. I will need to stop being the lone wolf and start building and leading teams and communities of people who share the values that drive me. I intend to do this. One day soon, people may say of *me,* "He's Back!"

8

Family as Staff
in an Amateur Campaign

Jordan McNamara

Type of campaign: District attorney (general)

Role of author: Staff member, volunteer, family member

Lessons to look for:
- Amateur campaigns make amateur mistakes (but can still win).
- Family is an important source of volunteers but not necessarily needed expertise.
- For family, friends, and other volunteers, campaigns are emotional roller-coasters not to be viewed objectively.
- The main differences between amateur and professional campaigns are resources and expertise—the emotions are the same.
- Campaigns are about taking advantage of opportunities.
- Campaigning is a contact sport, sometimes played dirty.

In 2007 my dad, Scott McNamara, ran for district attorney (DA) of Oneida County, New York. At the time he began his campaign, I was a sophomore at St. John Fisher College in Rochester. My dad, assuming that a political science major would know something about elections, made me the research director for his campaign. I thought that it sounded like something I would feel comfortable doing. I had taken some political science classes in college that I felt taught me the basics of what a job like research director might entail. I had learned the importance of opposition research and how to analyze voting trends. However, by the time I was done with my assignment as research director, I realized that I would have been better off taking a shop class and drivers' education.

Overall, what my title was in the campaign didn't matter. It was my dad running for public office. I would have helped him no matter what he asked me to do, and I wasn't the only family member involved either. The main core of volunteers in Dad's campaign ended up being mostly composed of family members. The campaign truly was "a family affair." And that's the main focus of this chapter: the role of family as campaign volunteers and how a campaign run by amateurs functions and sometimes malfunctions.

The Political Landscape in Oneida County

Politically Oneida County, New York, is a reasonably strong Republican county. In 2004 Republican president George W. Bush defeated Democratic senator John Kerry by about 13 percent (55.4 percent to 42.2 percent). Comparably in 2000, then-governor Bush beat Vice President Al Gore 49.6 percent to 45.8 percent. At the time Dad ran for DA, the Oneida County legislature was controlled by Republicans and the position of county executive was also held by a Republican. Prior to Dad's election, Oneida County had elected only two Democratic district attorneys, Michael Arcuri in 1993 and Everett Arthur in 1948. In Utica and Rome, the two largest cities in Oneida County, Republicans occupied both mayors' offices. Given the county's Republican leaning, winning a district attorney's race as a Democrat seemed to be a bit of a tall task. But in 2007 there were other factors in Oneida County that reduced the Republican advantage. First, Arcuri had been reelected three times, in 1997, 2001, and 2005.

Second, as part of their huge victory in the 2006 midterm elections, the Democratic Party picked up New York's Twenty-Fourth Congressional District, which included most of Oneida County. In 2006, the district was an open seat because incumbent Republican representative Sherwood Boehlert was retiring. Seeing an opportunity to advance politically, DA Arcuri decided to run for the seat. His opponent was Republican state senator Raymond Meier. The race attracted attention from both national parties because the Democrats saw it as crucial in gaining a majority in the House of Representatives. The Republicans, in turn, saw the Twenty-Fourth District as crucial to defending their congressional majority. As a result, money from both the Democratic Congressional Campaign Committee and the Republican National Congressional Committee flooded the district, mostly in the form of negative attacks. On Election Day, Democrat Arcuri beat his Republican opponent 54 percent to 45 percent. In Oneida County he did slightly worse, winning 53 to 46 percent.

Arcuri's 2006 victory created energy and enthusiasm among local Democrats, which were important factors in Democratic efforts in 2007 to retain the Oneida County DA's office that Arcuri was now vacating. Another important factor in the Democratic Party's fight to retain the DA's office was that my dad was the probable Democratic candidate.

At the time Arcuri was elected to Congress in November 2006, Dad was the first assistant district attorney, a position he had held since 2001. With Arcuri's impending departure to Washington, D.C., Dad was also the hands-on favorite to be appointed to fill the remainder of Arcuri's term. It wasn't surprising that he had decided, long before Arcuri's November victory, that if his boss won he would run for DA in 2007. Though Dad had no prior political or electoral experience, he had always aspired to be DA someday. That day appeared to be now.

Arcuri's four elections as district attorney had somewhat softened Oneida County's general Republican disposition. So, too, did his 2006 victory. Nevertheless, Oneida County still leaned Republican and was at best in transition. What helped Dad in all this and made him an attractive Democratic candidate was that he had strong ties to the mostly Republican rural parts of Oneida County. Dad grew up on a dairy farm in Deansboro, a hamlet in the southern part of the county. A large portion of his family still resided in rural Oneida County. Perhaps the most important family tie in the area was his mother and my grandmother, Joan, who had a diner in Deansboro. In a town with no stoplights, having strong support at the major dining and meeting establishment in the town is a tremendous advantage. Her diner gave Dad good name recognition in a typically Republican town. Throughout the campaign, my grandmother's diner would play a major role hosting several campaign meetings, a fund-raiser, and the Election Day breakfast.

Getting Organized

Soon after Arcuri's victory, the preparations for Dad's running ramped up. As the novice politician that he was, Dad bought a book about political campaigning. He read through it and came to the part about the positions needing to be filled in a campaign organization. He told me that I should take the position of research director. Not knowing what I was getting myself into, I said, "Sure, that sounds cool."

We began to assemble additional campaign staff in late 2006. Family members came first, but for my family politics was pretty foreign. We were all a bunch of rank amateurs. We had one political science major who graduated from State University of New York–Plattsburg (my aunt Cami, Dad's sister) and a sophomore political science student at St. John Fisher College (me). That pretty well summed up my family's political experience. Aunt Cami became campaign treasurer. She was tasked with the traditional duties of a treasurer, like filing campaign finance reports and managing the campaign's bank account. As the campaign began to move forward, however, her role expanded to organizing fund-raisers as well as having more control over the spending and distribution of campaign funds. In essence, she grew into a treasurer/co–campaign manager, an enormous workload for a volunteer. Our campaign manager was a political science professor from a local college who had worked on previous countywide campaigns. In addition, a couple of consultants from Congressman

Arcuri's campaign provided some invaluable guidance in the early planning stages.

The remainder of the campaign staff and volunteers were friends and community acquaintances. One of the most memorable volunteers was Dan Callan. "Pops," as he was commonly referred to, was the grandfather of murdered New Hartford police officer Joe Corr. Pops and Dad had struck up a friendship after Officer Corr was murdered. Pops walked with the help of a cane, and even though he was not in the best physical shape, his mind was tremendously sharp. In the closing days of the campaign, Pops went out driving around the county with my uncle Dan as they pulled our campaign float in the many parades we participated in. Numerous times during the day he yelled at pedestrians, telling them to make sure they voted for McNamara. Pops always had us laughing, even when the stress and pressure seemed to shut off the part of the brain that makes one laugh.

Sadly, a few weeks after the election, Pops went to the doctor because he had a spot on his chest that appeared to be growing. The doctor diagnosed a rare type of cancer that was difficult to treat and spread quickly. In July 2008, I saw him at a charity softball tournament being played in memory of his fallen grandson. Pops looked weak, and my heart sank a bit as I talked to him about the presidential campaign and the prospects of "our beloved" Barack Obama becoming the next president of the United States. Pops died a few weeks after that conversation. Even with his body under siege by cancer, he never lost the wit that made him so loved among members of our campaign.

Our First Staff Meeting

Our first campaign staff meeting was in December 2006. I was home from college, and I was excited about this adventure. At the meeting, about twenty people showed up. Most were family: my mom, my fourteen-year-old sister Rachel, Dad's brother Sean and his wife Karen, Dad's sister Cami and her husband Dan, and my grandmother Joan. A few of my dad's closest friends showed up, as well as a couple of college professors (including our campaign manager). Also attending were the two campaign consultants from Representative Arcuri's campaign. The meeting began with a general discussion about strategy and fundraising targets. The consultants had developed a list of key election districts we would need to target as well as a goal for fund-raising. The bottom line on fundraising was a daunting amount: $300,000. After pulling my jaw off the floor, I began to think this might be difficult. Dad didn't like asking anyone for money, and Oneida County didn't seem like a hotbed of interest groups willing to foot a large bill in a countywide district attorney campaign.

After a while, people started asking about some of Dad's positions on issues. Abortion came up, and Dad discussed how he supported a woman's right to choose but morally questioned the practice. Then the death penalty came up. He discussed how he supports the death penalty in extreme cases, but in order to feel right about pursuing the death penalty in a particular case, he would have to be willing to "push the button" in that case. Then he was asked about guns, and he said he supported the Second Amendment but did not think the Second Amendment allowed people to carry machine guns.

After the meeting, I rode home with Dad, Mom, and my sister. He was somewhat flustered that his stance on abortion would matter. He knew he had more experience to be DA than almost anyone else in the county. Although he was right that he did have experience oozing out of him, he didn't understand that some voters vote only according to a candidate's position on gun rights or abortion, regardless of the office. As a "raging centrist" (my characterization of Dad's politics), he did not conceive of ideological stances or partisanship determining his district attorney race, a result of being a political novice. He probably could not imagine a lot of what would come.

Two weeks later, we planned a meeting at my grandmother's diner to discuss our first fund-raiser. My family made up most of the principal actors of this meeting. We scheduled a $20-a-ticket fund-raiser for the end of January at an American Legion hall in the southernmost part of the county, the same American Legion hall Dad had played baseball for when he was a teenager. Having Dad, a Democrat, go to the southernmost, rural, and Republican tip of Oneida County to throw his first fund-raiser did not seem like the most lucrative idea to kick off a campaign. Nevertheless, my grandmother had decided to make some food for the event, and other food was being donated, so we thought we'd keep our costs down and profit margin high. We began discussing whom we would invite and ways to sell tickets. The discussion veered into whom we would invite to future fund-raisers where the price would be steeper. Rachel made one of the most memorable comments of the campaign. With a bewildered look on her face, she asked: "Why would anyone want to give money to Dad?" It must have been my aunt Cami who responded, "That is a very good question. I'm not really sure either." We all chuckled, but I wondered to myself whether we could find enough donors to raise $300,000.

Turns out offering good food is a good way to attract people to a fund-raiser, at least in rural Oneida County. On the day of the fund-raiser, I drove home from college in Rochester and arrived about an hour early. I was impressed when I walked in. The room looked immaculate. Balloons were everywhere, beautiful tablecloths covered the tables, and every table had a nice centerpiece. Members of my extended family had done most of the decorating, and I thought, if this is any indication of how the campaign would operate, we would be all right. The fund-raiser turned out to be a great success. Over two hundred people showed up, and we generated some enthusiasm and raised some cash. On my way back to school that night, I thought about how we didn't get all the people we invited and how we missed our overly optimistic fund-raising goal, but still I thought it was a success. It was right about then that I got pulled over by a state trooper. Turns out when I knocked the snow off my headlights before I left the fund-raiser, I broke the headlight. That was probably a signal to me that this campaign was not always going to be such an easy ride.

Becoming the "Incumbent"

In January 2007, when Mike Arcuri was sworn in as representative for the Twenty-Fourth District, Dad became Oneida County's acting district attorney. At the same time, New York governor Eliot Spitzer began searching for a permanent replacement for the remainder of 2007. Dad sought the permanent appointment, doing so out of his commitment to the office and his career ambition to be DA. However, I recognized the political advantage of the appointment as well. It would make Dad a quasi-incumbent and allow the campaign to say "Elect District Attorney Scott McNamara."

In February, the governor's office asked Dad to come in for an interview with some of the governor's staff. A few weeks later, I was sitting in class and got a phone call from him. Phone calls during the campaign tended to be something I didn't enjoy. Usually, they were from someone in the middle of a crisis or in need of something urgent. Fortunately, that was not the case. A few minutes later I got a text from Dad that said, "The governor just appointed me." I didn't even know that he was in Albany at the time. Turns out the governor's office had called the previous week and told Dad that he would need to come back to Albany for a second interview. Upon completing the second interview, the governor's appointment secretary asked him if he had any questions. He said no. She told him that she was going to take him down the hall to meet Governor Spitzer. It was then that the governor informed Dad he was being appointed the Oneida County district attorney.

Confronting Tragedy

Dad was now the incumbent DA of sorts, which would help the campaign. He had a full-time job to do, and we had a campaign to run. As winter turned to spring, our campaign was going relatively well, and Dad was settling in to being the DA. Then on April 12, 2007, Police Officer Thomas Lindsey pulled over a car for running a stop sign in a region of Utica known as Cornhill. Cornhill is considered the roughest part of Utica and probably the roughest part of the county. Drugs, gangs, and violence were all too common in this neighborhood. Sometime during the pull-over, things turned tragically wrong. Gunshots rang out, and Officer Lindsey fell to the ground in a bloody heap. He had been shot to death.

Officer Lindsey and Dad were friends. They had worked on many cases together. Not surprisingly, then, Lindsey's murder was hard on him. It also was tough on the community. This was the second time in fourteen months that a police officer had been murdered in Oneida County. The first was New Hartford police officer Joseph Corr, Pops's grandson. Officer Corr had been shot and killed in February 2006 after a jewelry store robbery. With this second cop killing, fear in the community ran high. The driver of the car Officer Lindsey had stopped was in custody, but no one had yet been charged with murder. The day after the murder, a press conference was held at Utica City Hall. Chief of Police C. Allen Pylman took questions from reporters about the case and gave updates on how the murder investigation was progressing. After a few questions, he turned the press conference over to Dad. Dad noted how Tom Lindsey had been a friend to many, including him, and he talked for a few minutes about the fallen officer. At one point during the press conference, Dad turned and looked directly into the camera and calmly yet forcefully said: "We will find Tom Lindsey's killer. And that person will be brought to justice. I assure you of that."

It was a moment I will remember until the day I die. I rarely have seen Dad show this kind of intensity. Here he was, the newly appointed district attorney, confidently reassuring the entire community that the murderer would be brought to justice and punished. The intensity and commitment he conveyed that day came to define him as DA. It also, I believe, provided a defining image of him as a candidate. I recognize that in times of tragedy, looking at the political benefits of that tragedy seems to be cynical, callous, and opportunistic. However, it is also the reality of politics and campaigns. Facing tragedy with a strong and coherent response can be a huge factor in the public's opinion of a candidate and politician. One only has to look at the political career of President George W. Bush to see this case in point. After the terrorist attacks of September 11, 2001, President Bush responded strongly, both in his address to the nation that night as well as during his visit to Ground Zero days later. As a result, his approval rating soared to meteoric levels above 80 percent and, at one point, 90 percent. In contrast, in 2005 when Hurricane Katrina struck the Gulf Coast and nearly leveled New Orleans, President Bush's response was weak. The federal government reacted slowly, and images of New Orleans residents stranded in the floodwaters caused public opinion to turn strongly against President Bush, beginning the slide toward approval ratings of little more than 20 percent as he left office.

The financial panic that hit during the 2008 presidential campaign provides another example. Senator John McCain's response seemed irate and impulsive. In contrast, Senator Barack Obama appeared steady, reassuring, and unflappable. These competing images of the candidates during the financial crisis may have been the defining moment of the campaign. Like it or not, Officer Lindsey's murder was going to be a similar defining moment for Dad.

Unlike me, Dad never saw Tom Lindsey's murder in political terms. For him, it was about justice, about prosecuting the murder of a police officer and friend. For him, cases like this one and others weren't about scoring points with the electorate or winning endorsements. They were simply about justice and right and wrong. But even though he did not see Officer Lindsey's murder in the context of his election, I could and did. I saw his strong response as an example of the type of leadership he would and did bring to the DA's office, to a community that had lost its second police officer in fourteen months and was afraid.

The Campaign Moves On

Our Opponent

From January through early spring, our campaign did pretty well. We were raising money and developing a strong campaign organization. We also got a Republican challenger: David Longeretta, a defense attorney based in Utica, Oneida County's biggest city. At first I felt anxious because I was concerned about our fund-raising. Dad was doing well raising money, but as the DA, he had little support from criminal defense attorneys. I was worried that these attorneys might begin donating large chunks of money to Longeretta so they could have one of their own at the helm of Oneida County's Office of the District Attorney. The more I saw of David Longeretta, however, the more I liked our chances and my anxieties subsided. Longeretta had very little criminal law experience in Oneida County. As a result, I knew that our campaign could really pound home Dad's campaign message: "Experience You Can Trust."

As the race heated up moving into the summer, Longeretta's strategy also became clear. It was to attack Dad's record or, more correctly, distort it. After all, that is what politicians do when they have no record of their own to stand on. Particularly interesting to me was Longeretta's claim that Dad was soft on crime. Longeretta must not have picked up the paper in the year when Dad was working on a methamphetamine case against Gregory "Pep" Heine, one of the highest-ranking Hells Angels in the country. Heine and a local defense attorney named Bob Moran had been transporting methamphetamine to Oneida County. In 2003 they were arrested. For the next year, Dad fought motion after motion from the defense. After almost a year, "Pep," Moran, and eight others pleaded guilty, and most were sent to state prison. During this time, threats were made against my family from people thought to be Hells Angels, and our house was placed under near-constant police surveillance. In fact, during this period not more than an hour usually passed between police cars driving by our house. Dad never told this story during his campaign (he probably should have), but it seemed highly unlikely that a defense attorney like Longeretta was going to win by attacking Dad as being soft on crime.

Longeretta's other attacks on Dad were as humorous and misguided as claiming Dad was soft on crime. Particularly entertaining was the Longeretta campaign claim that Dad was a political animal making decisions on cases just for political gain. At one point, their campaign even ran a newspaper ad trying to connect Dad to Mike Nifong, the DA of Durham County, North Carolina, who got in trouble for his handling of the Duke lacrosse team rape case. After getting past the pure audacity of the accusation, I had to stop and laugh at the desperate strategy Longeretta's campaign was using.

Walking the Campaign Trail

On June 6, 2007, Dad began walking door-to-door in the small town of Verona, New York. When we first started walking, I told my dad at least we would remember the day because it was on the anniversary of D-Day, the Allied invasion of France in 1944. My dad responded: "Yeah, I know, I worked it out this way." I was a little stunned that Dad thought about the symbolism of the day. I didn't know if he actually planned to begin walking that day or if it happened to be a coincidence. Regardless, it seemed like a good sign and we commenced our trek toward Election Day, exactly five months later.

Being the DA, though, was never far away from the campaign trail. As the sun was setting on that day of walking, Dad received a cell phone call informing him that the police had just arrested the person alleged to have murdeed Officer Lindsey. Wesley Molina-Cirino, a.k.a. "Flaco," was charged with the murder. That arrest began the fulfillment of Dad's pledge made after Officer Lindsey was murdered. Flaco was tried for first-degree murder and was convicted in March 2008, and was sentenced to life in prison without parole.

Dad's walking strategy was pretty straightforward. The campaign had figured out how many doors Dad needed to knock on per town. That number was determined in part by an analysis of how well Democratic judicial candidates had done in recent countywide elections. Arcuri's election and reelection data weren't used because since his initial reelection bid he hadn't been seriously challenged. We scheduled walks in a town during its Fields Day Parade or other festivals or holiday parades. I'm not certain of the origins of Fields Day Parades or why they were so named. Nevertheless, these parades and the weekend festivals of which they are part are held every summer throughout Oneida County as a major fund-raiser for each town's volunteer fire departments. Local politicians and candidates use these Fields Day Parades, as well as other parades, to get themselves noticed and seen by the public.

The week before Dad was scheduled to walk in a parade, he would make sure to visit the town to meet voters in the hope that these people would generate some enthusiasm at the parade the following weekend. The best example of this practice was in the town where he went to high school, Waterville, New York. Waterville sat in the southern tip of Oneida County, bordering Madison County. Waterville had a strong Republican presence, but Dad knew a lot of people there. To say that he was a hero in Waterville might be a little strong, but people there loved him, and he was one of the most notable graduates of Waterville Central School in a long time. For three straight nights in the brutal heat of summer, Dad and I pounded the streets of Waterville. We had hoped to hit at least 300 doors those three days. We didn't reach that number because Dad knew too many people. He would knock on a door, his knuckles worn from continuously knocking, and a person would answer who knew him, my uncle, my grandmother, or my grandfather, and that person would talk to Dad for what seemed like forever. Dad could never break away. But as he was talking, I heard a political bite in what he said that I had never heard from him before. The edge in his comments seemed to come from the anger he felt from Longeretta's distortions about his record and career in the DA's office. Despite Dad being a novice at the start of his campaign, I saw this bite in his campaign rhetoric as a sign of his growing political skill, or at least a willingness to engage in political fights.

One canvassing day was even a bit frightening. Usually I or someone from the campaign would accompany Dad. However, on this particular day I was unable to walk with him because I had to work early at my job at a local golf course, so another volunteer went with him. When I got home from work, my mom called me and was frantic. She told me Dad had been bitten by a dog while he was out walking. A few minutes later, Dad came through the door with one pant leg of his khakis in shreds. He told me how he had approached a house and a St. Bernard had run at him and bit his leg. Dad had a gash on his leg, and there was a good deal of blood. This incident raised a lot of concern within the campaign. Everyone proposed solutions: walking with a stick or carrying mace. Someone even suggested Dad carry a gun. Despite his family's well-meaning intentions, Dad discouraged this kind of talk and continued to pound the pavement throughout the rest of the campaign just carrying his literature—no stick, no mace, and certainly no gun. Admittedly, we overreacted to the dog bite incident, but such is the nature of family concern when the candidate is your son, brother, husband, or father.

Frankly, my concern wasn't about a dog attack but an attack from an entirely different animal. Dad made a living prosecuting people, often really bad people. In total, he had prosecuted at least 15,000 cases. The defendants he prosecuted also had families, some of whom were angry that Dad had convicted their fathers, mothers, brothers, sisters, sons, or daughters. I always worried that Dad would be confronted by one of these people when he was canvassing. Maybe it was just paranoia, but throughout our time canvassing, I often felt that we received glares from people who answered their doors, almost as if they remembered Dad prosecuting them or a loved one. Thankfully, no altercations ever occurred.

During his campaign, Dad canvassed many voters, knocking on hundreds of doors. But he didn't really have a strategy, at least not one based on anything

I had been taught. He ignored the targeted precinct analysis the consultants had provided at the start of the campaign. In fact, how Dad walked illuminates one of the major problems of having inexperienced volunteers like friends and family running a campaign. He would just start knocking on doors, introducing himself, and handing the people he met his campaign literature. There was never any recording of friendly or unfriendly responses. I look back now and shake my head about the inefficiency and waste of time and money that resulted. I also wonder why I never questioned it. I knew better. I had been taught what to do. Maybe when the candidate is your dad and the campaign is your family, it's harder to question things. Whatever the reason, scores of hours were wasted at households where no voters even lived, let alone houses where voters were registered but would not spend time voting in an off-year election or, worse, supported our opponent. Looking back, I see how this time could have been used more efficiently to better target voters and to "walk smart."

Defaced

Political commentators talk about an "October surprise," but by October, in the middle of a heated and competitive contest, nothing comes as a surprise to people within a campaign. This was true of an act of vandalism that would hit the front pages of the local paper in October 2007. One October night, vandals attacked dozens of Dad's four-foot-by-eight-foot signs that had been placed throughout the county. The next morning Dad began receiving call after call from supporters about signs being destroyed. The vandals were particularly brutal in that Dad's picture on the signs had been cut out.

The extent and nature of the vandalism frightened some within the campaign, particularly members of my family. The removal of Dad's face from the signs made Mom and others nervous. They saw that as a warning to Dad by someone who held a grudge against him. Despite my own concerns about his safety when canvassing, I saw these attacks as more of a political assault by someone who hated Dad as a candidate. The destruction of signs made me angry, not frightened. I, along with other volunteers, had spent hours building and assembling these signs and more time putting them out. Seeing them slashed and destroyed made me think of all the time now wasted in assembling and placing them. I admit, though, to being "afraid" we'd have to do that work all over again.

The vandalism made the front pages of newspapers and earned us some pretty good free media in the process, but the campaign still had to decide what to do about all the defaced signs strung across the county. Replace them? Fix them? Take them down completely? All of them seemed like legitimate options. Dad decided on a different course of action. Dad chose to leave them as they were. Whether he took this course because he wanted his campaign to focus on other activities or just out of the stubbornness that he commonly displays was unclear. It seemed great to me. I and other volunteers wouldn't need to spend time fixing the signs. And his "leave them alone" option actually may have done us some good. I came home the weekend after the defacing to go out canvassing with Dad. To our surprise, many people Dad talked to while going door-to-door told him how terrible they felt about what happened to his signs, and they assured him, "You have my vote." Though an initial distraction, the destruction of Dad's signs actually turned out to be better free media than any press release.

Election Day Jitters

After canvassing with Dad right after the defacing of his signs, I wasn't able to get home again until election eve. I drove the two hours from Rochester to my house late on Monday after my night class. Naturally, my adrenaline was pumping. I thought about the next day and about the joys of victory and the horrors of defeat. I arrived home around 11 P.M., both excited and nervous for the next day, to find my family awake. I sat down with Dad, Mom, and my sister, and we talked about my trip and, of course, the next day. I hugged and kissed my sister and mom when they went to bed and then sat watching the late-night news with Dad. After a few minutes, I noticed he was asleep on the couch. He must have known he had done all he could to win the election. He had knocked on over 7,000 doors in the five months of canvassing and walked in countless parades in every corner of the county. I did not sleep peacefully, however. I tossed and turned until well after 3 A.M., thinking about the next day, both about victory and how my family, most notably Mom, would cope with defeat.

The next morning began early. We went to vote around 8 A.M. I spent what seemed like a lifetime in the voting booth, double- and triple-checking the levers until I finally submitted my ballot. We then drove to my grandma's diner and had breakfast with my family and some close friends as local TV cameras watched. After we ate, Dad gave an interview. We then went around the county delivering baskets of food to the poll workers. Dad would get out and deliver the baskets to the poll workers as I sat in the backseat of the minivan and played Sudoku. It seemed so anticlimactic to me, and was another amateur mistake. Knowing what I know now, a much more effective use of our time would have been making phone calls as part of a get-out-the-vote (GOTV) drive.

We stopped at our house around 5 P.M. to change clothes before we went to our campaign headquarters to watch returns come in with some of our family and closest supporters. I received a phone call from my friend Fran, whom I invited to join me on election night to provide what I hoped would be sane companionship for the night. Ten months of campaigning tends to leave a person and those around him a little insane. On the phone, however, Fran told me she was nervous and felt sick, which was exactly the opposite of what I needed.

Nevertheless, I told her it was fine and that I would pick her up soon. I hugged and kissed my family and told them I would see them at headquarters.

After I picked up Fran, I drove over to headquarters, arriving shortly before the polls closed at 9 P.M. Dad's campaign manager had set up a projector to display the results on the wall. He assigned me the task of entering the results of our ten targeted election districts into a spreadsheet so we could track our progress. Before I took my seat, I walked around the room hugging family members and friends, who were all a bit nervous. I returned to my seat as Dad, Mom, and my sister arrived. We waited for what seemed like an eternity but was probably about ten minutes, to begin hearing from our poll watchers at the ten targeted districts about their results. Dad was understandably nervous. I was jittery, and Fran said she thought she was going to throw up.

A phone call broke the silence, and Dick received the news from the first targeted district: somewhere around 65 percent to 35 percent in Dad's favor. Results came flooding in: 65 percent to 35 percent, 68 percent to 32 percent, and 72 percent to 28 percent, all in Dad's favor. During this time I was also checking the countywide results on the Internet, and we saw huge margins in his favor. At one point, I turned around and saw Dad crouching behind me with his hands up to his mouth, seemingly surprised by the magnitude of his lead. When all our targeted districts came back, Dad was ahead by about a margin of 68 percent to 32 percent, with similar results reporting back countywide. After ten months of ups and downs and seemingly unending pressure, Dad had won in a landslide. When all the votes were tallied, Dad won the largest victory by a Democrat in a contested countywide election in Oneida County history.

Once we knew Dad had won, we headed over to our election night party. We held the party at Delmonico's Italian Steakhouse, where I had worked a couple of nights a week during the summer. The restaurant was packed wall to wall, and a huge roar of applause and cheers went up as we entered. I saw friends, family, and supporters. My mom, my sister, and I hugged nearly everyone in sight. It took forever to walk from one side of the room to the other. Also, I was still nearly half deaf from the roar upon Dad's entrance into the room. I escaped the crowded room out a side door to another room that was less packed to catch a breath and reflect on what had happened.

Later in the night, as we ate and relaxed with family and friends, someone asked me: "You going to follow in your dad's footsteps now?" I said unequivocally that I was stepping out of politics, only to return when Dad ran for reelection. That night I said goodbye to my dad, my mom, and my sister with celebratory hugs, dropped a relieved Fran off at her house, and drove back to college in Rochester in what felt like a state of numbness. I called roommates and friends at college and thought about the victory Dad had won. For days after Dad's victory, I had an emotional hangover. I was pretty much useless. I could not focus in class, on homework, or at work for days. It took me nearly a week to realize that the campaign was over.

Amateur and Professional Campaigns

A nearly yearlong campaign can significantly change your life, regardless if you win or lose. I had seen how much stress and strain a political campaign puts on family and friends, and I was not prepared to ever enter into something like that in the future. I remembered how we didn't eat together as a family at our kitchen table for over a year, and how when we were together there was always the stress of the campaign hanging overhead. I also remembered that my fourteen-year-old sister had spent countless hours without company at home because she had a father on the campaign trail and a mother and brother who were working regular jobs as well as doing work on the campaign. I also remembered that she was a trouper in her own right. She had spent much of her summer assembling small American flags with "Friends of Scott McNamara" stickers attached, which we passed out in the countless parades that we walked in during 2007.

However, the campaign experience did seem to make our family stronger, and definitely broadened our understanding of the world, or at least the local political world in Oneida County. One thing no one in our family really understood prior to the campaign was the true nature of politics. After the campaign, we were much more knowledgeable.

Interestingly, Dad's 2007 campaign made me begin to view politics and the 2008 presidential campaign in new ways. On Dad's election night, I said I was done with politics and would only come out of "retirement" when he needed my help. Well, I took a page out of Brett Favre's playbook and returned from my retirement about four months later, this time with the Obama campaign. I became a big supporter of the junior senator from Illinois when he was campaigning in Iowa. I was elated by his win there and distraught by his loss in New Hampshire just five days later. When Senator Obama won in South Carolina and gave his victory speech, I knew I wanted to get involved in his campaign. He spoke that night of the America that I wanted to see. It was as if Obama was trying to do for the nation what I had seen Dad do throughout his career in the Oneida DA's office: serve the public, not the politicians. I was fortunate enough to be able to go to Ohio to work on Obama's presidential campaign twice, once prior to the March 4, 2008, Ohio Democratic primary and once again the weekend before the November general election. I enjoyed my work on both trips, but my second trip really provided me with the ability to look back on Dad's campaign and evaluate it in its entirety.

Volunteering in the Obama campaign made me realize the operational weakness of an amateur campaign like my dad's campaign for DA. While working for the Obama campaign, volunteers were used almost exclusively to canvass and contact voters. The upper management of the Obama campaign was paid and had experience in their fields, which made the campaign run efficiently. When canvassing for Obama, I had specific lists of voters, identified by such things as their gender, age, and addresses. After canvassing, these lists were modified with even more specific information, particularly how those canvassed intended to vote. Undecided voters were canvassed or called again. Supporters would be targeted with reminders and GOTV information. Nonsupporters and people who had already voted were eliminated from the list. This enabled the Obama campaign to maximize their efficiency in both hours and dollars because volunteers would not be knocking on doors of unpersuadable voters or leaving literature on the porches of nonvoters.

Looking back on Dad's campaign after my experience with the Obama campaign makes me cringe at the inefficiency with which our campaign was run. It was mainly the result of our inexperience and perhaps the local nature of the race. Our volunteers spent more hours putting up lawn signs than canvassing voters. Canvassing was left solely to Dad. We should have used the methods the Obama campaign practiced in the Ohio office in which I volunteered, but we didn't know better. For people looking for lawn signs, the Obama campaign had a mock lawn sign on display that read: "I'm a lawn sign and I don't vote. Go knock on some doors." Also, our campaign's walking strategy wasn't strategic or targeted. Dad approached doors with no useful information on the voter he was canvassing. Had we applied the practices of a professional campaign, our volunteers would have been used more productively and Dad's time could have been better used raising money or contacting targeted voters. Personally, I assigned some of the amateur nature of the campaign to our campaign manager. Without question, better direction from him would have been helpful. Without other experienced staff, we didn't know any better.

Frankly, given the contrasts between the professionalism of the Obama campaign and our amateurism, I realize how lucky we were to win by the margin that we did. Nevertheless, our campaign taught us valuable lessons to apply to Dad's future races for reelection. And if I have anything to say about it, our organization will be better, our walking strategy more targeted, and our volunteers better used. Our campaigning still will be a family affair, just a more professional one.

The Emotions Are the Same

Our amateur campaign lacked the money, technology, and staff resources that the professional Obama campaign possessed. But one thing that was similar was the emotion of both campaign staffs. Both the Obama staff that I worked with and the people who worked on Dad's campaign were emotionally invested in their candidate and driven to elect him. This emotional commitment to the causes and candidates is of the utmost importance in any campaign, be it for DA or president. In Ohio in the days leading up to the general election, volunteers and campaign staff worked twenty-hour days. We slept in sleeping bags on our

GOTV staging area's floor the night before the election. At times our eyes seemed to swell and barely stay open as we worked until 5 A.M. on multiple nights. The things that kept us going were the commitment we had to our cause and the motivation of seeing our candidate elected.

It wasn't really any different in Dad's campaign, just a matter of intensity, perhaps. Family, volunteers, and friends working on his campaign were also driven by their emotional attachment and commitment to him. Like those of us in the Ohio trenches for Obama, those of us in the Oneida County trenches for Dad sacrificed time and energy to see him elected to enact his vision of law and justice in Oneida County.

At times the emotional commitment we have as volunteers can be difficult, particularly if events conspire against our candidate. I experienced this in Dad's personal and public reaction to the murder of Police Officer Lindsey. I experienced it again the night prior to the November 2008 election when Senator Obama's grandmother died. That night clips of Obama crying during a speech in North Carolina made me shed tears of my own as I saw someone I had grown so proud and fond of going through his personal pain in public. And I flashed back to Dad's reaction to Officer Lindsey's murder and their friendship. Together, the two incidents reminded me that the candidates we volunteer for, vote for, and even loathe are human despite our efforts to the contrary to make them something else. From my experience, the average person watches and listens to politicians and tends to see them in a dehumanized way. Politicians tend to be labeled as Republicans or Democrats or by their stances on issues. Their roles as fathers or mothers, sons or daughters, grandsons or granddaughters, and brothers or sisters are ignored. In my limited experience, I've observed how this dehumanizing nature of politics allows for more personal attacks and criticisms against opponents and rivals that seem to score political points but can be destructive to the general political discourse and to the candidates' families.

Such attacks were common in Dad's campaign. Between opponents distorting his record and slashing his signs, Dad seemed to experience attacks from all sides. Interestingly, though, like Obama, Dad seemed not to be bothered by them. Like Obama, he seemed unflappable. However, Mom was enraged by these attacks. Her reaction highlights an important difference between our campaign and the 2008 Obama presidential campaign. Unlike Michelle Obama, Mom was not a key public figure on the campaign trail. As a matter of fact, Mom never made a public address in support of Dad during the entire campaign. The public never saw her anger. Only family and friends saw it. That was significantly different from the presidential election, when Michelle Obama questioned, "How could Hillary Clinton expect to run the White House when she couldn't run her own house?" and Bill Clinton in defending his wife abruptly pointed out that Jesse Jackson had won South Carolina too, suggesting that Obama would also be a flash in the pan. In seeing how Mom experienced Dad's campaign, I completely understand how these gaffes by the presidential candidates' spouses occur. They're defending more than a candidate. They are defending the person they married and have spent a lifetime with.

I learned a lot about politics from campaigning for Dad, but also a lot about how to conduct myself when campaigning and in politics. The major lesson I learned about politics is that there are fewer people you can count on than you might think. When you find people who are unquestionably committed, make sure you treat them really well. At the beginning of the campaign, everyone would say, "I'll do anything I can to help," but when the time came to gather signatures, knock on doors, distribute signs, or raise money, most of them somehow had a scheduling conflict. They just couldn't find the time. I saw this trend a lot. Local Oneida County Democratic Committee members and rank-and-file Democrats alike swore up and down not to worry, that they would get a bunch of signatures, but when time came to get signatures, only a few people got an impressive number. But then there were volunteers like Pops.

Another thing I learned was that even though I was a political science major, I knew less about politics than I thought. Political science is too often about theories and other heady stuff. The reality of campaigns often escapes it in its effort to be a "science." Nor does it prepare you for the reality of doing the grunt work in a campaign, doing the seemingly menial tasks of building signs, knocking on doors, making phone calls, and collecting signatures. As a political science major, I thought that was boring. I wanted to be crafting strategy, developing ads, and writing speeches, but I was young, too inexperienced, and knew too little. Working in Dad's campaign (and the Obama campaign as well), I realized that you don't start out in politics as James Carville, David Axelrod, or Karl Rove, but rather you start as a volunteer doing the essential grunt work, even if you're the candidate's son and you've been given the lofty position of research director. You prove yourself at the bottom and then begin to rise in the organization. Having some sort of emotional connection to the campaign can usually help supply the energy and willingness to do the fundamentals. I experienced that emotional connection in two ways: because I was one candidate's family member and because I had a commitment to another candidate's policy goals and vision. For me, commitment to life in the campaign trenches came from both sources. I loved Dad, and Barack Obama inspired me. At the local level, emotional commitment may be easier to accomplish. Local candidates are simply more approachable, easier to get to know and to meet. And as it was in our case of helping Scott McNamara become district attorney of Oneida County, New York, sometimes it's a family affair.

PART 3
Being a Candidate

9

Almost Winning Missouri's Ninth Congressional District

Richard J. Hardy

Type of campaign: US House of Representatives (general)

Role of author: Candidate

Lessons to look for:

- All campaigns are basically local.
- Planning, organization, and strategy matter.
- Campaigns are about taking advantage of opportunities.
- Money matters, and it matters most to challengers.
- Incumbency, like inertia, is hard to overcome.
- Close only counts in hand grenades and horseshoes.
- Campaigns carry personal costs and sometimes personal tragedy.

What was I thinking? I should have had my head examined. In 1992 I was an associate professor of political science at the University of Missouri–Columbia and made the fateful decision to take an unpaid leave to run for the US Congress in Missouri's Ninth District. It was my first-ever race for public office. And I ran as a Republican in a historically and considerably gerrymandered Democratic congressional district against Harold L. Volkmer, a savvy, well-funded, high-profile, eight-term incumbent who had never lost an election in his thirty-two-year political career. Among the twenty-one counties in the Ninth District, seventeen could be classified as rock-solid, one-party Democratic counties. The remaining four Republican-leaning counties were relatively sparsely populated and had consistently voted for the Democratic incumbent. No Republican challenger had ever come close to beating Volkmer, although one well-heeled, highly visible, party-backed challenger came within 6 percentage points in 1984. All other Republican challengers, many of whom were seasoned political veterans, were trounced.

Compounding the absurdity was the fact that the Republican Party was seriously gasping for political air in the Show Me State in 1992, especially at the top of the ticket. Incumbent president George H. W. Bush was particularly unpopular in Missouri's economically depressed Ninth Congressional District. Many factories had closed, farmers were struggling, and President George H. W. Bush had naturally become the political lightning rod for discontent. A divisive Republican gubernatorial primary also had caused wide chasms among party leaders, which spilled over to the diminishing party faithful. The eventual GOP nominee for governor, State Attorney General Bill Webster, was facing a certain federal indictment (and subsequent conviction). As managing editor Hank Waters, writing in the November 7, 1992, edition of the *Columbia Daily Journal,* put it: "This year Nikita Khrushchev probably could have beaten Webster, whose political baggage was so heavy he couldn't even get off the ground, let alone cross the finish line." It was definitely not the year to run as a Republican in Missouri.

The problem was further exacerbated by my decision to allow former students, all political neophytes, to run my campaign. Of course, that decision was made largely out of necessity since neither the Missouri Republican Party (MRP) nor the Republican National Congressional Committee (RNCC) offered much help. Both organizations doubtless viewed me as a political gadfly who had absolutely zero chance of success. Party insiders were especially chagrined that I had not attended the GOP campaign school, refused to hire their recommended professional pollsters, and, most importantly, had many Democrats and independents on my staff. Indeed, my campaign manager and communications director were both unabashed Democrats!

Raising money was especially difficult. I entered the race very late, with absolutely no funding. Additionally, the Webster campaign had siphoned off most of the party money trickling into the state, and I had publicly eschewed political action committee (PAC) funding. I therefore relied almost exclusively upon small donations, scores of volunteers, and tons of earned media. Most disconcerting of all, I was forced to deplete my family's savings account, at a time when my two children were in college and my wife's position at the university had been eliminated. It was a recipe for disaster.

Yet, despite all the seemingly impossible obstacles, I nearly won! Although Republicans took a severe beating in the Ninth District, early returns on election night showed me running ahead of the incumbent. Indeed, the Missouri Net, a statewide news agency, had projected me as the surprise winner, and some Washington, D.C., newspapers had erroneously reported the next morning that I had pulled off a major upset. The race was nip and tuck all night long, and it was not until the early morning hours that I learned my fate. A special ten-page postelection analysis published in the November 8, 1992, edition of the *Columbia Missourian* perhaps summed it up best:

> So Close . . . When Rick Hardy stepped from the classroom to the campaign trail eight months ago, his mission to topple eight-term Democrat Harold Volkmer at

first seemed akin to Don Quixote's tilting at windmills. Instead, Hardy built a serious coalition of students, disaffected Democrats and die-hard Republicans. By the time the votes were counted early Wednesday morning, Hardy had come close to toppling the Hannibal congressman.

But close does not count in politics. It hurts to lose. Nevertheless, the experience provided me and my students with some priceless insights into the workings of American politics in a way that could never have been accomplished in a traditional classroom setting. The remainder of this chapter is an insider's account of my congressional race and how I, along with the tremendous help of past and current students, almost beat an eight-term incumbent congressman.

Political Background

It is perhaps axiomatic that a political science professor would be interested in politics. I came by my interest rather naturally. Although my parents had but high school educations and were never active in party politics, they were relatively well informed and constantly talked about current events. My father was a printer for the *Burlington Hawk Eye,* the oldest newspaper in Iowa, and read the news and political editorials each day as he cast and set lead print. Indeed, he could literally and figuratively read the day's news upside down and backward. They studied the issues carefully and were familiar with nearly every candidate's positions. Most often they voted Republican but would not hesitate to cross the partisan divide. On rare occasions my parents would split their votes. For example, my father voted for Harry Truman because of the president's straight talk and pro-union stance on Taft-Hartley, but my mother refused to vote for Truman because of his crude, salty language. My father constantly recounted how he held me when he was in a crowd in Iowa during President Truman's whistle-stop train tour in 1948.

My first recollection of politics was the presidential election of 1952. Because we had no television set at the time, my father took me to watch the election returns on a display set in a downtown store window. My first real-life political participation came in high school when I volunteered for President Lyndon Johnson's 1964 presidential campaign. A local college professor recruited me to play my guitar for local Democratic functions and to distribute campaign fliers door-to-door on behalf of the Johnson-Humphrey ticket. (I still have that "All the Way with LBJ" campaign button.) In my freshman year of college, I joined the Des Moines County Young Democrats. However, for various reasons, including the Vietnam War, I became disenchanted with the Democratic administration and changed my allegiance to the Republican Party. The fact that I was dating a beautiful young Republican (who later became my wife) may have contributed to my political conversion.

In 1978 I completed my Ph.D. and accepted my first tenure-track position at the University of Missouri–Columbia. My first practical experience in Missouri politics occurred in 1982. I volunteered to help Del Gebhardt, a fellow church member, run for the Twenty-Sixth District seat in the Missouri House of Representatives (the lower house of the Missouri State Legislature). Gebhardt was a businessman running as a Republican against a very popular and highly organized Democratic county clerk. I began by stuffing envelopes and going door-to-door but quickly found myself writing press releases, raising money, conducting opposition research, and ultimately managing the Gebhardt campaign. My candidate lost the race, but I learned a great deal from the experience. The process also brought me into contact with many key Republican leaders.

The most influential person I met was George Parker, who is often credited with transforming Missouri from a one-party Democratic state into a two-party competitive state. In 1966, Parker became the first Republican since the Civil War to be elected to the Missouri House of Representatives from Little Dixie (the Democratic counties in central Missouri). He later chaired the state GOP and helped recruit and elect John Danforth and Kit Bond to statewide offices. Parker also wrote *How to Win an Impossible Election,* a blueprint for conducting political races, and founded the National Grand Order of Pachyderms, a nationwide organization of civic clubs affiliated with the national Republican Party. George Parker became my political mentor; he encouraged me to join the local Pachyderm Club, introduced me to many civic leaders, and taught me the finer points of waging political campaigns.

During the 1980s, I became especially active in Republican politics. I was the faculty adviser to the University of Missouri College Republicans (CR). With the help of some outstanding student leaders, that club grew to over 500 members, becoming the largest student organization on campus and, arguably, the most active CR club in the entire nation. Instead of engaging in the proverbial symbolic campus activities, the CRs set out to influence elections. Over several elections, we organized student volunteers to assist in the races of John Ashcroft, Margaret Kelly, Roy Blunt, Wendell Bailey, Kit Bond, John Danforth, and, most especially, Carrie Francke.

Carrie Francke was a role model for college students and a good friend and mentor to me. In 1984, Carrie unsuccessfully challenged Harold Volkmer in Missouri's Ninth Congressional District. As an undergraduate, Carrie had majored in political science and was the first woman elected student body president of the University of Missouri–Columbia. She went on to earn a master's in public administration and a law degree and served as Senator John Danforth's press secretary. I admired her spunk, high energy, integrity, and grit. I also appreciated the knowledge she shared with me about the district and key political players.

But the College Republicans' most important contribution was in the area of voter identification, registration, and get-out-the-vote drives at the local level.

To win elections, you must identify your supporters and then get them to the polls. That is easier said than done. In Missouri, voters do not register by party; thus, in order to determine citizens' partisan leanings, it becomes necessary to conduct surveys. After obtaining voter registration lists, the CRs set up extensive telephone banks to identify voters' partisan tendencies. The process took weeks to complete, with ten to twelve volunteers working the phones each night. Once the data were collected, the volunteers telephoned identified voters to determine their support and get them to the polls on Election Day. In 1988, twenty-seven CRs became deputized registrars and helped register thousands of new voters, most of whom were Republicans. That year marked the first time two Republicans were elected commissioners in the history of Boone County.

One of those GOP commissioners elected through the help of the College Republicans was Donald Sanders, a local attorney who became one of my closest friends and political advisers. Prior to seeking public office, Don was a legislative aid to Congressman Dick Ichord (D-MO); an agent with the Federal Bureau of Investigation who was assigned to protect Martin Luther King and other civil rights marchers in Selma, Alabama, during the 1960s; and a member of the minority counsel investigating the Watergate scandal. Don was hired by Senator Howard Baker (R-TN) to be part of the Watergate inquiry and worked directly under GOP counselor Fred Thompson (later a US senator from Tennessee). It was Don who discovered the White House taping system that would lead to the eventual resignation of President Richard M. Nixon.

In the early 1990s, I became actively involved in two highly publicized statewide reform drives. The first was the "Yes for Ethics" movement. The Missouri General Assembly had experienced a series of scandals involving charges of influence peddling and illegal drug use among some of the leaders of the House of Representatives, and all efforts to create a state ethics commission had fallen on deaf ears. That is when I joined with five civic activists to organize a bipartisan movement called "Yes for Ethics." We crafted and circulated a proposal through the initiative process that would significantly revise the legislative article in the Missouri Constitution. The centerpiece of this amendment was the creation of a state ethics commission that would investigate charges of wrongdoing. After submitting over 230,000 signatures to the secretary of state, the measure was placed on the ballot for voter approval. Then, within weeks of the election, the speaker of the House filed suit, averring the Yes for Ethics measure unconstitutionally contained too many provisions. The Missouri Supreme Court ruled to strike our proposal from the ballot.

The ruling did not deter our efforts to clean up the General Assembly. Our core group next forged an alliance to start a second petition drive, "Missourians for Limited Terms." This petition drive called for limiting state legislators to eight years (four two-year terms for representatives and two four-year terms for senators). Missouri was just the third state to initiate legislative term limits, and our group had little trouble gaining the requisite signatures. Corporate mogul Sam Walton even permitted us to use the state's Wal-Marts to gather petitions. Over the course of several months, I crossed the state to speak out and debate on behalf of our cause. In the end, our reform group prevailed. Term limits passed with 72 percent of the vote. Our efforts also forced the Missouri General Assembly to establish an ethics commission. And federal authorities convicted two state legislators for drug dealing and the speaker of the House for influence peddling. Other experiences also laid the groundwork for my congressional race. In 1990, Governor Ashcroft appointed me to the Missouri Peace Officers Standards and Training Commission (POST). The POST Commission supervises the training and certification (and sometimes de-certification) of the state's 13,500-plus law enforcement authorities. I also worked closely with the Missouri Bicentennial Commission under the direction of Missouri Supreme Court chief justice Albert Rendlen. Over the course of several years, I conducted nearly two dozen workshops on the US Constitution and Bill of Rights, which brought me into contact with hundreds of social studies teachers at secondary schools.

Thus, by 1992, I had garnered significant political and civic experience. I had volunteered, consulted, and worked on dozens of races at all levels of government. I had acquired experience as a campaign manager, communications director, speechwriter, public speaker, policy adviser, volunteer coordinator, fund-raiser, political watchdog, pollster, and election analyst, to name but a few. I became knowledgeable about election laws, electoral maps, and voting patterns. I had helped lead two statewide reform drives, had served as a state commissioner, had delivered hundreds of civic speeches, and was quoted widely. Most importantly, I was expanding my network of connections, earning a reputation as a political reformer and a civic educator, and building name recognition in the Ninth Congressional District.

Decision to Run

By 1991, speculation had begun to grow that I might run for Congress. But when pressed by reporters, I responded truthfully that the time was not ripe. Here is what Rudi Keller, one of the state's top political reporters, wrote in the August 14, 1991, edition of the *Columbia Daily Tribune:* "MU political science professor Rick Hardy said today that he has ruled out running against incumbent Harold Volkmer next year. Hardy, a prominent Republican who helped lead the Yes for Ethics initiative last year, had been mentioned by several local politicians as a possible challenger to the eight-term Hannibal Democrat." I was accurately quoted as saying, "I never say never . . . But at this point, I'm pretty well set with my teaching, and I truly enjoy teaching. I would hate to give that up." Of course, that was not the only consideration. My general plan was to wait until my daughter and son were out of college or for the possibility of an open seat. Still, pressure began to build for me to run. In November 1991, a group of politicos led by Don Sanders and George Parker established a "Draft Hardy for Congress" exploratory committee and held press conferences in Columbia, St. Charles, Hannibal, and Kirksville to encourage me to enter the race. Here is what political analyst Steve Bennish reported in the November 12 edition of the *Columbia Daily Tribune:*

> Richard Hardy, come on down. The MU political science professor is the man to unseat longtime US Rep. Harold Volkmer next year, a group of prominent local Republicans said at a news conference this morning. But Hardy, who could not be reached for comment today, said in August that he had ruled out challenging Volkmer next year. An exploratory committee is not waiting for Hardy's assent and will be traveling throughout the Ninth District today to test the waters for his candidacy . . . "I have one simple message today," former county commissioner Don Sanders told a crowd of loyalists. "It's way past time for Harold Volkmer to give up his seat. If he won't do that, Rick Hardy is the man to beat him in 1992."

To further entice my reconsideration, the "Draft Hardy" committee regularly placed one-page ads in newspapers throughout the Ninth District. The ads were headlined "Citizens Urge Hardy to Run." The responses to those ads proved overwhelming. Scores of backers emerged, and the ads grew exponentially longer, listing the names of the draft supporters. Soon I was bombarded with calls from reporters and supporters. Most gratifying was the response by my former and current students. By then, I had instructed over 13,000 students, and many of those living in the Ninth District volunteered to help, including a significant number of Democrats!

I was also encouraged to run by political guru Lyn Nofziger, former campaign manager for Ronald Reagan. Nofziger and I had consulted on State Representative Craig Kilbey's race for secretary of state in 1991. After visiting my American government class, Nofziger said, "Rick, people are talking about you running for office. You have what it takes, but if you don't do it now, you may never get another chance." I received further encouragement from US senators John Danforth and Kit Bond, outgoing secretary of state Roy Blunt, State Treasurer and former US representative Wendell Bailey, and Randy Enwright, a former student who was the RNCC's southern states' coordinator. Despite this outpouring of support, I still had doubts about running.

The turning point came on November 16, 1991. On that day, my parents were visiting our home in Columbia. My father was the first to read that day's edition of the *Columbia Daily Tribune* and was pleasantly startled by the following headline: "Hardy for Congress—Time for Volkmer to Take a Walk." This was the district's leading newspaper's *official endorsement!* The endorsement was written by Henry J. Waters, the *Tribune*'s longtime publisher and managing editor, and arguably the most influential person in the entire district.

> MU political science professor Rick Hardy is considering running for US Congress as a Republican from our Ninth District. He would stand against incumbent Harold Volkmer. I have never touted a candidate this early in the proceeding, preferring usually to wait until the field is known and the candidates have had most of their campaigns behind them. In this case, however, it's easy for me to urge Rick Hardy to get into the race. . . . Hardy stands with the best. He combines an excellent academic background with a strong record of practical public experience. He understands and works the political system. He is willing to take controversial stands and seems to have the stomach for the political meat grinder. He is bright, attractive, and a good speaker.

That was it! Now it was clear that I had to run. Although the task was daunting, the time was late, and I had no funding, I took solace from the fortuitous events that had transpired. Most importantly, I had the blessings of my wife, parents, children, siblings, neighbors, friends, former students, and even most of my colleagues, all but one of whom were Democrats.

Organizing the Campaign

My first decision was to ask Don Sanders to serve as my campaign chair. He then assembled a "kitchen cabinet" to advise me on strategy and policy. The kitchen cabinet met regularly and consisted of George Parker, Cindy Beale, Sharon Lynch, and Chris Baker. Each adviser brought considerable political experience to the table. We then agreed to employ Walt Carlson, a certified public accountant, to serve as my treasurer.

One vexing problem was deciding when to file for office. The filing deadline was March 31, 1992. Filing early would enable me attend the RNCC campaign school in Washington, D.C., and start raising money. However, University of Missouri rules and regulations strictly prohibit employees from running for a full-time public office. An early filing would thus force me out of the classroom and redound in a loss of several paychecks. I therefore opted to secure an unpaid leave beginning March 30, 1992.

Teaching courses prior to my filing was especially tricky. I made sure to give the university my 110 percent effort, as I always had and continue to do. I arrived early, stayed late, was punctual, attended all meetings, maintained extended office hours, returned examinations on time, and accommodated every request. As a professor, I have never avoided discussing sensitive issues, and I have always made it a practice to discuss *both* sides of every issue, irrespective of my own personal views. To that end, I often play devil's advocate to ensure both sides are presented. But this approach also made me vulnerable. In the months preceding my filing, "strangers" would appear in my auditorium class to tape-record my lectures. I also received countless hang-up calls, I assume to determine if and when I was on the job. Additionally, there were requests by local Democrats to audit my university telephone to determine if I had made any campaign calls. The audit revealed I had not.

When I was not at the university, I was busy preparing for my race. I arose every morning by 4 A.M. to prepare for the day. I would typically meet supporters for breakfast and give civic talks at lunch. The evenings were spent on the road delivering more speeches, making courtesy calls, and cultivating political leaders throughout the district. I was lucky to be home by midnight, and I rarely slept more than four hours a night. For months on end, I worked eighteen to twenty hours per day, seven days a week.

Naturally, I was relieved when filing day arrived, because then I could concentrate solely on the campaign. The campaign kicked off with a four-stop swing through the district, accompanied by my family and members of my kitchen cabinet. I began with an early morning press conference at First Christian Church in Knox City, Missouri. That was the church my great-grandfather, Reverend George H. Nicol, helped build, and I wore the very stovepipe hat his congregation had given him. The next stop was Mark Twain's historic home in Hannibal, Missouri. That was symbolic because as a child, I had won a Tom Sawyer look-alike contest. The third stop was O'Fallon Civic Park, where I fielded questions from members of the St. Louis–area media. The final stop was Jefferson City, where I filed my candidacy with the secretary of state. This tour enabled me to reach all media outlets in the district.

Once filed, I could begin accepting campaign donations and purchasing campaign paraphernalia. The campaign theme was "No Strings Attached!" The message was simple and signified my decision not to accept PAC money. The campaign colors were reflex blue on white. Reflex blue is a universal color that requires no mixing. Using just one color (besides white) would reduce costs and ensure uniformity. All single-panel and trifold brochures were printed on recycled paper using soy ink. This satisfied environmentalists and farmers alike. In addition, my campaign decided to employ union printers. Affixing the "union bug" to brochures and posters was done both out of respect for my father and to help me avoid unnecessary union criticism.

The kickoff fund-raiser was held at a local civic center and was organized by my kitchen cabinet with the help of my family. It attracted hundreds of friends, associates, party loyalists, and college students. There was live music, great food, and excellent media coverage. When the event concluded, I counted the donations. I had many contributors, but they all gave small donations. After expenses, the event cleared only about $3,500. That was barely enough to pay for my campaign brochures. Volkmer already had 100 times that amount in his war chest, and he could match what I raised with just two PAC checks! That was depressing.

Assembling a campaign staff was a high priority, but it is obvious I could not afford to hire professionals. Out of necessity, I relied upon former students. My first campaign manager was Christopher Molendorp, a twenty-two-year-old who earned his B.A. in political science. Chris was bright, brash, and energetic and had gained some experience working on Wendell Bailey's statewide campaign. He agreed to work for a meager $400 per month. Chris immediately located a campaign office in downtown Columbia: It was within easy walking distance for students at Columbia College, Stephens College, and the University of Missouri. Office furniture was acquired at auctions, and we purchased user-friendly Macintosh desktops for the benefit of student volunteers.

The staff and volunteers grew rapidly. Chris Akers (with a B.A. in political science from St. Charles) became my finance director; R. E. Burnett (a doctoral student in political science and a Democrat from southern Missouri) became my chief strategist; Cordell Smith (a graduate student who had run for state legislature) researched my position papers; Joe Carrier (a doctoral student in political science and a veteran who supported Ross Perot) served as my office manager; Marie Bartlett (a Korean American graduate student in communications and a Clinton Democrat from Arkansas) served as my communications director; Marc Long (a political science major with broadcasting experience) was assistant communications director; George Liyeos (a political science major from St. Louis) was the project director; Jill Watskey (a political science major from Rolla) became my volunteer coordinator; and Mike Pinkston (a political science major) served as my travel aide. Two former graduate teaching assistants, Jon Hagler and Candy Young (both Democrats), served as political consultants. Other key volunteers included political science students Kristine Miller, Joe Hunter, Rick Buckman, Whitney Smiley, Chris Hayday (a leader in the Sierra Club), and Rachel Bringer (whose grandfather was Democratic chairman of Marion County). The only students I had not taught were district coordinator Cindy Beale (longtime county GOP leader), noted media consultant John Thompson (Thompson Communications), and field director Joe Huett (a politically connected insurance agent).

The District, Opponents, and Strategy

The Ninth Congressional District comprises twenty-one counties in the northeastern quadrant of Missouri. The bulk of these counties were represented by powerful Democrats Champ Clark (speaker of the House, 1911–1919) and Clarence Cannon (1923–1964). The district's population in 1990 was 568,347, of which 95 percent were white, 4 percent were African American, and just 1 percent were Hispanic. Boone (Columbia), St. Charles (suburban St. Louis), and Franklin (Washington and Union) Counties are the most populous and fastest-growing industrial areas of the district. But agricultural production is critical to the economy, especially corn, soybeans, winter wheat, cattle, and hogs. Still, there were wide differences among the counties.

The district's counties could be grouped into overlapping categories. "Little Dixie" included the counties of Audrain, Boone, Callaway, Randolph, and

Ralls. These counties were settled by farmers from Virginia and Kentucky who remained loyal to the Confederacy long after the Civil War. Many voters in these counties considered themselves "yellow dog" Democrats, meaning they would rather vote for a yellow dog than a Republican. The "northern counties" are Adair, Clark, Knox, Lewis, Macon, Scotland, and Shelby Counties. These rural counties, known for growing corn and soybeans, were economically depressed in the 1990s. Farm auctions were commonplace, and once-thriving small towns were filled with empty shops and dilapidated buildings. "Mississippi River counties" included Marion, Pike, Lincoln, and St. Charles. These counties were first settled by French and English immigrants, but German, Swedish, Italian, Irish, Czech, and Hungarian communities dot the map. They contain many factories and strong pro–labor union supporters. "The Rhineland" is the area along the Missouri River settled by German immigrants and includes the counties of Franklin, Gasconade, Montgomery, and Warren. Prior to Prohibition, the Rhineland was known for its breweries, but in later years it has gained a reputation for its excellent vineyards and wines. Citizens in these counties often voted Republican but were drawn to Volkmer's social and economic conservatism. Thus, Volkmer had the best of both worlds: Liberal Democrats voted for him because he was a Democrat, and Republicans voted for him because he was conservative.

Harold Volkmer was sixty-one in 1992. He was born in Jefferson City, attended St. Louis University, and earned his law degree from the University of Missouri. He was Catholic, was an Army veteran, and had a wife and three grown children. His political career included serving as Marion County (Hannibal) prosecutor from 1960 to 1966, state representative from 1966 to 1974, and member of Congress from 1976 on. In Congress, Volkmer had gained seniority on three committees—the Select Committee on Aging; the Science, Space and Technology Committee; and, most importantly for Missourians, the Agriculture Committee, where he chaired the subcommittee dealing with feed grains, wheat, soybeans, milk subsidies, livestock, and family farms. These committee assignments gave him considerable clout and respect among farmers in the district. However, he was best known for his opposition to gun control and had been accurately labeled "the National Rifle Association's leading House ally" for his successful efforts to kill many of the provisions of the Brady Bill. It is easy to understand why Volkmer had received thousands in campaign contributions from various agricultural and gun PACs.

But Volkmer was not my only opponent in 1992. I first had to defeat Republican Joseph Brajdich, a union worker from Washington, Missouri, in the August Republican Party primary. I won with nearly 80 percent of the vote. Brajdich was poorly organized and not much of a challenge, but his candidacy prevented me from securing party funding. There were also two minor-party candidates, Jeff Barrow and Duane Burghard. Barrow was the Green Party candidate from Boone County (Columbia). He was a thirty-six-year-old graduate of Stanford University who criticized Volkmer's votes that permitted timber harvesting in national forests. Burghard, age twenty-seven, earned his B.A. in political science from the University of Missouri and served in the US Navy. He ran as an independent but was really a liberal Democrat who opposed Volkmer primarily on social issues. Both candidates were bright and energetic but lacked sufficient organization and funding to seriously challenge the incumbent.

There were several factors that made Volkmer vulnerable in 1992. First, there was Congressman Volkmer himself. He had become increasingly unpopular among his colleagues and constituents alike. In *Politics in America 1994: The 103rd Congress, Congressional Quarterly* observed: "Winning friends has never been Volkmer's strong suit in the House. He can be surly when he disagrees with someone, which is not infrequently. And his recent elections demonstrate that his particular combination of social conservatism and pork barrel politics is showing signs of wear with a significant segment of his constituency." Second, Volkmer faced significant primary opposition in 1992. Six liberal to moderate Democrats challenged him on issue after issue. Volkmer won with 57 percent of the vote, but the divisive Democratic primary took a significant bite out of his image of invincibility. Third, Volkmer had lost favor with two key farmers' organizations in the district, the Farm Bureau and Missouri Farmers Association. Leaders of both farm groups offered me advice and support on agricultural issues they thought Volkmer had neglected. Fourth, Volkmer's votes in the fastest-growing urban and suburban areas of Boone, Franklin, and St. Charles Counties had been eroding over time. Finally, I detected a significant increase in ticket splitting in the district, particularly among rural Democrats. Although these voters overwhelmingly supported Democrats at the local level, they had grown distrustful of Bill Clinton on issues of gun control and abortion rights. Unwilling to support President George H. W. Bush, many began to turn to Ross Perot, as evidenced by the legion of Perot signs that had sprung up throughout the district.

Several weeks after filing, Chris Molendorp; his wife, Linda; and I flew to Washington, D.C., to meet with GOP leaders. Our first stop was the Republican National Campaign Committee for discussions with director Guy Vanderjagt and his assistant, Spencer Abraham. Vanderjagt was a long-term Republican congressman who had just been upset by an unknown candidate in the Michigan primary. The meetings were mainly symbolic, and the two offered little, if any, help. In actuality, I would have preferred to meet with Vanderjagt's opponent. The next stop was with Congressman Newt Gingrich. Gingrich devoted some serious time to discussing strategy and offering me assistance from the Grand Old Party Political Action Committee (GOPAC). It was used to raise and distribute money to Republican candidates. I willingly accepted Gingrich's advice but respectfully declined GOPAC money. Finally, we met individually with Missouri's Republican congressional delegation—Senators John Danforth and Kit Bond and Representatives Mel Hancock and Bill Emerson.

Senator Danforth discussed issues and was particularly interested in my plan to resolve the abortion issue, which he shared with Democratic senator Daniel Patrick Moynihan of New York. Senator Bond lived in the Ninth District but was careful to keep his distance, since he was running for reelection that year. Representative Hancock, the two-term representative from southwestern Missouri, invited me to a subcommittee meeting and offered me a great piece of advice—changing shoes often on the campaign trail will help avoid fatigue! Representative Emerson was particularly helpful. He was a two-term incumbent from the Eighth District, a traditionally conservative Democratic area in southeastern Missouri. Emerson credited much of his success to the Missouri Farm Bureau and his willingness to mirror its positions on the issues. Also helpful were periodic calls from Texas representative Dick Armey, a former college professor and close ally of Gingrich, offering analyses of Volkmer's voting record.

My strategy was simple. First, I ignored my primary opponent and the two minor-party candidates, concentrating solely on Volkmer's record. That would enable all of us to gang up on the incumbent. Second, I downplayed that I held a Ph.D. or was a college professor. Instead, I campaigned as "Rick Hardy, the schoolteacher." And whenever Representative Volkmer referred to me as "Professor Hardy" or "Dr. Hardy," I called him "Lawyer" Volkmer. Third, I neutralized Volkmer by supporting his two most salient issues—abortion rights and opposition to gun control. Although I took a pro-life stance, I proposed a plan to put the issue to the voters. Fourth, I challenged Volkmer's opposition to campaign finance reform and legislative term limits, and repeatedly pointed out that Volkmer lived in Washington, D.C., and had lost touch with the voters. However, as the campaign progressed, I found that few cared about Volkmer's domicile, and the issue of campaign finance reform was too complex for most voters to digest. Fifth, I distanced myself from the Republicans at the top of the ticket, especially Bill Webster. I needed to attract independents and disaffected Democrats to have any chance of winning. Finally, I drew upon a slogan that generated instant public recognition—"Diapers and Politicians Should Be Changed Regularly!" People readily identified me with this slogan. It was humorous, easy to remember, and, most of all, effective. It was my wedge issue.

The Campaign

My first priority was to raise more money through direct mailings, telephone calls, and personal visits. I also developed a finance committee and asked each member to seek donations from at least ten other people. I found this all distasteful but necessary. I had to make payroll; contribute to workers' compensation; cover insurance; purchase computers; lease software; order stationery; and pay for rent, utilities, telephones, signage, postage, and gasoline. Bills multiplied quickly.

Of necessity, I ran a retail campaign. My 1988 Chevy S10 pickup truck, 1987 GMC minivan, and 1983 sixteen-passenger Dodge Ram van served as "Hardy for Congress" campaign vehicles. All were professionally lettered and contained the conspicuous "Diapers and Politicians" logo. The pickup was my main mode of transportation, whereas the vans were used for transporting volunteers to parades and other events. I also relied heavily on bumper stickers, such as "Farmers for Hardy" and "Sportsmen for Hardy." Within a few short weeks, thousands of cars began displaying one or both bumper stickers. It was also not uncommon to see automobiles contain both "Hardy" and "Clinton" or "Hardy" and "Perot" bumper stickers.

Congressional campaigns require significant television advertising, but running ads was difficult for two reasons. One, there was no "natural" media outlet in the district. The media markets were at the four corners of the district (Columbia, Kirksville, Hannibal, and St. Louis), thus resulting in wasteful broadcast spillovers to other districts. For example, the Hannibal station covers western Illinois and the Kirksville station extends into Iowa. And two, it became too expensive for me to purchase ads, especially in the St. Louis area: Reaching those constituents either through television or drive-time radio would cost over a hundred thousand dollars!

Yet several things worked to my advantage. Early in the campaign, Volkmer saturated the television and radio airwaves with ads that cited my name. They were negative ads, of course. One ad, for example, stated: "Harold Volker works 14 hours a day, while Rick Hardy works just 6 hours a week." This was a reference to my teaching load, a slam that was hard to take, given my penchant for working seventy-hour weeks! Still, these ads gave me name recognition and drew the ire of many college professors, including many Democrats. I was, however, able to reach targeted television audiences by purchasing reasonable cable inserts and buying radio ads on Christian and country radio stations. Most importantly, I was able to take advantage of earned media. Virtually all my press releases were reported on radio, television, and newspaper outlets, due in large measure, I suspect, to the fact that many of those journalists were my former students. Whatever the reason, I beat Volkmer in earned media by a margin of 8 to 1.

Volkmer made good use of his congressional franking privilege. To counter his free mailings, I relied upon student volunteers to spread the word. Each day, student volunteers were organized to drive to selected communities and pass out "Diapers and Politicians" fliers. Student volunteers also canvassed at parades, county fairs, football games, and wherever people gathered. Each foray helped spread the word while building an esprit de corps among young people. I came to believe there is no substitute for experience—unless you are nineteen years old! Unlike most adults, students were not afraid to hold up signs, wear campaign T-shirts, or make telephone calls. And I was blessed to have hundreds of student volunteers. They were the lifeblood of my campaign.

New problems constantly cropped up: One day I was scheduled to meet with physicians in Columbia and attend a fund-raiser in Kirksville at the same time; another time, I missed a meeting with a key supporter in Monroe County; then I did not show up for an award because nobody told me to go; not to mention the day I was scheduled to make back-to-back appearances at opposite ends of the district. Once a phone volunteer mistakenly told a pro-life inquirer I was pro-choice. Twice thank-you letters went to the wrong contributors. It was organized chaos at best.

Aside from the difficulty of fund-raising, my biggest problem stemmed from internal conflict among campaign personnel. One problem concerned my twenty-one county coordinators—local leaders charged with finding sign locations, organizing local fund-raisers, distributing literature, marching in parades, and getting out the vote. There was no shortage of energetic volunteers to serve as county coordinators, but they were difficult to deal with, needing constant attention and reassurances. In several counties, especially Macon, Warren, and Franklin Counties, there were serious rifts among Republicans, and the county coordinators in those counties came with considerable baggage. Visits to these counties were like driving through political mine fields. I was forever putting out political fires within these counties and had to be mindful of the warring factions.

My dealings with the GOPAC and the RNCC were also stressful. As noted, I refused PAC contributions, including those from GOPAC. However, GOPAC constantly sent me unsolicited audiotapes and campaign materials that it listed as "campaign donations" on its Federal Election Commission (FEC) reports. Repeated attempts to stop the contributions were ignored, until Don Sanders got it straightened out. It was fortunate Volkmer's people did not spot this. They would have either claimed that I accepted PAC contributions or failed to report the GOPAC donations (audiotapes—no money). It shows how little things could turn into big issues. Additionally, I went round and round with the Republican National Committee (RNC) over visits by Vice President Dan Quayle. The RNC insisted that the vice president campaign with me in the Ninth District. Knowing that his involvement would not sit well with independents and Democrats, I respectfully declined the offer. There were several heated exchanges, but I held my ground.

Then there were never-ending rifts among paid personnel and between paid personnel and volunteers, often about inconsequential matters. Each evening when I returned to headquarters, I would be met with grumbling. It became a constant battle to put out fires among staff members. That is when I decided to hire a new campaign manager, replacing the young Chris Molendorp with the more seasoned R. E. Burnett. Burnett had many more life experiences. He also had great organizational abilities, excellent speaking skills, and a firm understanding of the issues. The fact that Burnett was a Democrat did not bother me, but it raised some serious doubts among Republican diehards. Still, it was my campaign, and I needed a campaign manager who could command the troops when I was on the road.

The organization kicked into gear. Marie Bartlett and Marc Long cranked out press releases and cultivated great relations with media representatives in the district. Joe Carrier developed a significant database and trained volunteers to stuff envelopes and sort mass mailings. Chris Akers lined up donors and fund-raisers, including events hosted by Roy Blunt and John Danforth. Marie Bartlett and Joe Huett organized county coordinators, who in turn recruited local volunteers, held fund-raisers, and identified sign locations. Joe Huett organized sign-painting parties. Joe Carrier screened the signs and came up with the brilliant idea to sprinkle reflective highway beads on the wet paint. We had the only signs that glowed in the dark!

But just when things began to look up, tragedy struck. It was Saturday, October 3, 1992. Early that evening I was returning to Columbia on I-70 when a rescue helicopter buzzed overhead. Unbeknownst to me at the time, Marie Bartlett was being transported to the University of Missouri Hospital after her Ford Escort collided head-on with a pickup truck on Highway 63. Marie was returning from Kirksville, where I had sent her to retrieve some campaign documents, and she was wearing her "Hardy for Congress" shirt. After being notified by hospital officials, I rushed to the hospital and was with Marie when she passed.

Marie's death rocked my world. I blamed myself for her death. Her mother did not send her to the University of Missouri to get killed on my campaign, I thought. It was my fault for sending her to Kirksville, knowing that she was exhausted from a long day's work. I became depressed and decided to suspend the campaign while my family, my staff, and I attended Marie's funeral in Clarksville, Arkansas. R. E. Burnett and Marc Long issued this press release: "Marie was a talented and vital part of our organization. She was committed to helping our campaign succeed . . . Marie was a colleague, a professional, and, most of all, our friend. Our campaign is stunned by this loss."

I seriously considered quitting the race. The cost was too high, and no electoral victory was worth a human life. But two things helped me gain some composure. Marie's mother assured me that her daughter loved the campaign and that for me to quit now would undermine everything Marie had fought to accomplish. I was also spurred on by the fact that none of my opponents bothered to contact my campaign or extend any condolences. Marie's death actually drew our campaign organization closer together.

A major campaign turning point came with the surprising and unprecedented endorsement in the October 2, 1992, edition of the *Hannibal Courier-Post,* Volkmer's hometown newspaper. It noted:

> When voters in Missouri's Ninth congressional district go to the polls on Nov. 3, the *Courier-Post* recommends that they cast their ballots for Rick Hardy. In Hardy, voters can elect a congressman that we believe is more in touch than the incumbent with the viewpoints of a great majority of average citizens . . . We urge voters to elect Rick Hardy because we believe he is the best candidate, with fresh ideas to address America's challenges.

This was the very first time in thirty-two years the *Courier-Post* had not endorsed Volkmer. The endorsement was like a shot of adrenaline. Volunteers appeared to come out of the woodwork, small donations began to pour into the campaign, and the entire campaign became energized.

The last week of the campaign was spent organizing our get-out-the-vote drive, posting signs, speaking to civic groups, returning telephone calls, writing thank-you notes, conducting media interviews, and keeping volunteers supplied with plenty of coffee and donuts. On the final weekend before the election, my brother Bob and I traveled the district one last time. We delivered hundreds of signs and stopped at coffee shops, pizza parlors, shopping malls, fast food restaurants, factories, and anyplace where people gathered to shake hands and make one last pitch for votes. I campaigned until 9 P.M. on election eve.

The Election

Election Day could not arrive fast enough. I was completely exhausted and had not slept well in over eight months. On Election Day, Linda and I drove early to our polling place. We were pleased but embarrassed to see thousands of "Hardy for Congress" signs lining both sides of the street for blocks on end. Hundreds of exuberant students had stayed out all night posting signage and bumper stickers throughout the district. Unfortunately, they had put signs along highway rights-of-way, on fenceposts, on utility poles, and every place imaginable. Naturally, I got blamed for this, but I understood the thought behind the errors.

Reporters accompanied us to the polling booth, and many voters wished us well. It was most gratifying to see my name on the ballot and to have our children cast their first-ever votes for their father. The campaign staff prepared a large election night party, replete with balloons, decorations, live music, and plenty of great food. Hundreds of students, volunteers, relatives, and well-wishers stopped by as the returns flashed on a large-screen television. I was especially grateful to have my wife, parents, children, and other family members share the evening. The evening, however, became a roller-coaster of hope and frustration.

As anticipated, Democrats swept the Show Me State that evening, winning by wide margins the races for president, governor, and most statewide offices. In the Ninth District, the votes appeared to be a microcosm of the statewide races. The votes for president were Bill Clinton, 109,995 (41 percent); George H. W. Bush, 90,669 (34 percent); and Perot, 65,032 (24 percent). The race that did not mirror the rest of the state was the Ninth Congressional District contest, where the tallies remained extremely close and seesawed all evening. Around 9 P.M., Missouri Net, the statewide media network, projected I was the likely winner. People started shouting. I was elated but realized that not all of the counties had reported. There appeared to be "computer" problems in several counties where I knew Republicans had failed to organize adequate watchdog operations. Yet I felt my campaign had done well in those counties. That was wishful thinking.

The outcome was not apparent until the early morning hours. Henry Waters, writing in the *Columbia Daily Tribune* (November 7, 1992), summed it up best: "Politics runs in cycles. Missouri voters felt the Republicans had been in state office long enough. They replaced a ubiquitous Republican presence in Jefferson City with an equally pervasive galaxy of Democrats. . . . Republican Rick Hardy almost broke the trend by nearly unseating Democrat Harold Volkmer for Congress. The vote was so close that Hardy was talking about a recount." But close was not enough. Congressman Volkmer won with 47.7 percent of the vote. I lost with 45.5 percent of the vote.

Perhaps I can take solace from the fact I went the distance and gave Volkmer a run for his money; even he conceded that. I was proud of the fact I won Boone County, the most populous county, by a margin of 2 to 1; I was the first Republican congressional candidate to carry Audrain and Callaway Counties; I came within a whisker of winning in many other Democratic counties in a year when Republicans took it on the chin. My campaign was run almost entirely by a bunch of college students who simply out-hustled the hired guns. We started, organized, and executed a campaign in just eight short months, and the campaign was run on a veritable shoestring. Volkmer raised $354,612. My campaign raised $144,157. Volkmer out-raised me 3 to 1, with over 70 percent of his money coming from PAC contributions. Excluding PAC contributions, however, I actually out-raised Volkmer by $36,555 ($144,157 to $107,602). Equally striking is the fact that I was outspent nearly 5 to 1, with Volkmer spending $511,550 to my $139,860. Note that Volkmer's campaign finished $156,938 in the red—that is more money than was raised or spent in my entire campaign. There were times "insiders" advised me to take out loans, mortgage my home, or engage in deficit spending. I refused. It would have been hypocritical of me to campaign on balancing the federal budget while engaging in deficit campaign spending. Moreover, I did not want to be tempted by special interest efforts to pay off my campaign debts. Recall the slogan "No strings attached!" Within a few weeks of the election, I had paid off all my campaign debts . . . out of my own pocket.

So close, yet so far away. It hurts to lose. With the passage of time, I have mulled over the race and raised many questions. What if I had had more time to organize the campaign? What if Republican-dominated Osage County had not been gerrymandered out of the Ninth District in 1990? What if this had not been a Democratic year? What if the Republicans had not been so fractured? What if Barrow and Burghard had not entered the race? Would I have been the recipient of those disaffected voters? What if I had waited to run until 1996? What if I had accepted PAC money? That would have enabled me to saturate the St. Louis media market. What if I had employed professional staffers to run my campaign? And what if Marie Bartlett had not died?

With the obvious exception of Marie's tragic death, I have absolutely no regrets. The campaign was the experience of a lifetime. I had the opportunity to visit nearly every school and college in the district. I toured scores of factories, farms, utilities, and corporations, gaining knowledge and respect for a variety of occupations. The campaign enabled me to meet civic leaders, interest group representatives, city council persons, mayors, city managers, county officials, state legislators, party leaders, statewide candidates, members of Congress, and presidential contenders. It forced me to become familiar with state election laws and FEC rules and taught me how to deal with reporters. Most importantly, I acquired thousands of new friends and learned more about the political system than I ever learned from the classroom.

Acknowledgments

I dedicate this chapter to the memory of three very special Americans: Donald Sanders, Marie Bartlett, and George Parker.

Postscript. The students who ran my campaign have gone on to bigger and better things. R. E. Burnett is professor and director of the Sciences and National Security Program at Virginia Military Institute; Joe Carrier is associate professor of criminal justice at Columbia College in Missouri; George Liyeos earned his master's degree in public administration at the Truman School of Public Affairs and is city administrator of Rock Hill, a suburb of St. Louis; Chris Molendorp is a successful insurance agent and a Republican state representative (123rd District) in the Missouri General Assembly; Rachel Bringer earned her law degree from the University of Missouri and is a Democratic state representative (Sixth District) in the Missouri General Assembly; Mike Pinkston and Whitney Smiley are married—Mike is a successful investment broker and Whitney teaches piano in Springfield, Missouri; Jon Hagler earned his doctorate from Washington University and is director of Missouri's Department of Agriculture; Candy Young, an award-winning professor and educational consultant at Truman State University, is married to Larry Young, renowned artist and two-time Olympic bronze medalist; Joe Hunter earned his master's degree and teaches government and social studies at Elsberry High School in Missouri; Jill Watskey earned her J.D. at Vanderbilt and is an attorney with the Coalition of Wisconsin Aging Group; Marc Long is a doctoral student and serves as vice president of marketing and communications at St. Louis College of Pharmacy; Kristine Miller served in Senator Kit Bond's office in Washington, D.C., and became the political affairs director for McDonnell Douglas Corporation; Chris Hayday is director of the Sierra Club's Global Warming and Energy Program and has appeared on national television broadcasts; Chris Akers is a successful sales executive for Harcros Chemical Corporation of Kansas City, Missouri; Cordell Smith earned his M.A. at the University of Missouri, served on the staff of Senator John Ashcroft, and is currently the president of his own Virginia-based consulting firm;

and Rick Buckman is president of the Colorado-based firm Buckman and Associates International.

Additionally, Cindy Beale remains an active leader in Missouri Republican circles, serving in numerous GOP organizations, coordinating campaigns, and attending state and national conventions. Sharon Lynch is a successful bank executive in Columbia, Missouri. Chris Baker continues to work as an executive and consultant for local media outlets. Walt and Marla Carlson have a thriving accounting firm and enjoy golfing. Joe Huett is now retired and lives in Florida but remains active inventing and serving in his local church. John Thompson of Thompson Communications remains one of the nation's preeminent media consultants. Respected Missouri statesman George Parker remained active in civic affairs until his death on May 27, 2009. And Don Sanders passed away on September 26, 1999; he will be forever known as the "Hero of the Tapes."

10

Being a Challenger in a Long-Shot City Council Campaign

James R. Bowers

Type of campaign: City council (primary)

Role of author: Candidate

Lessons to look for:
- Planning, organizing, and strategy matter.
- Campaigns are about taking advantage of opportunities.
- Incumbency, like inertia, is hard to overcome.
- Campaigns need both earned and paid media to get their message out.
- Campaigning is a contact sport, sometimes played dirty—really dirty.
- It is possible to "run well" and still lose.

I've always been intrigued by political outsiders who run against the political establishment or great political odds. I got my first lesson in "running against" around 1978 or 1980, when as a student at Sangamon State University in Springfield, Illinois, I considered running a grassroots, poor man, populist challenge against State Representative Larry Stuffle, who represented the area in Illinois where I grew up. Leo Fitzgerald, one of the great unheralded sages of Illinois politics, taught me a four-word lesson as to why my idea was naïve, foolish, and unwise: incumbency, party, organization, and money. Representative Stuffle was the incumbent and would have all of the other three. I would have nothing.

The challenges of running against are the subject of this chapter. It is the story of my 2007 primary election campaign to become the Democratic Party nominee for the Northeast District city council seat in Rochester, New York. This campaign pitted me against the Democratic Party of Monroe County, New York; a powerful African American political boss and his political organization;

an incumbent councilwoman of sorts; and a type of "candidate racial profiling" reflected in a widely held belief among Democratic Party insiders that since the Northeast District was considered an African American district, white candidates, particularly a white male, should not represent the district or even run there.

The Political Landscape

Rochester is a midsize city located in Monroe County in western New York. It is a one-party Democratic town and has been since the early 1970s. Its mayor, city council, school board, county legislators, and delegation to the New York State Assembly representing the city are all Democrats. Like the city, the Northeast City Council District is overwhelmingly Democratic. In January 2007, there were 20,833 registered voters in the Northeast District. Sixty-eight percent, or 14,164 of them, were registered Democrats.

As a one-party town, the biggest electoral hurdle a candidate faces is getting the party's designation for office. If there is no primary challenge, a designated candidate will, for all practical purposes, have won office without a single ballot being cast. With a three-to-one Democratic Party registration advantage in the city, Republicans often do not field credible candidates and never win. November general elections in the city, then, are coronations rather than exercises in representative democracy. Because of this lack of competition, incumbents basically serve as long as they choose, regardless of the overall quality of their performance. They leave office by retiring voluntarily, seeking another elected office, or occasionally dying.

Political bossism is also an important and defining characteristic of the Democratic Party in Rochester. City Democrats are part of the Monroe County Democratic Party. However, New York state assembly member David Gantt is the real (and probably the last) boss of Democratic Party politics in Rochester. Gantt has been a fixture in Rochester politics since the early 1970s. In 1982 he was elected to the New York State Assembly from a district racially gerrymandered to be a safe African American seat. With nearly thirty years in the Assembly, Gantt has never faced a serious challenger for his seat. His political clout stems from two factors. First, Gantt has built a powerful and fairly disciplined political organization that once controlled three key city party committees that designate candidates for office. Until very recently, these committees accounted for 50 percent or more of the weighted vote necessary for winning designation as the party's candidate. Generally, that meant that a candidate seeking city office would stand little chance absent Gantt's support.

Gantt's extensive political clout also stems from him being the "dean" of the Rochester delegation in the state assembly. The assembly operates on a strict seniority system, in which institutional power over local affairs rests with the member in the majority party who has served the longest in that area. This norm is executed even when issues and projects under question fall outside that member's district. The power that flows from this practice is nearly absolute. Accordingly, whoever is the dean of the local delegation exercises enormous influence over resources and revenues that flow into the area. Gantt has been a brutal master at exercising this influence to increase his power over Rochester politics and government.

Like bossism, political sponsorship also affects whom the party will designate as its candidate. In 2007 the successful party designee for the East District council seat was strongly supported by the current mayor, Robert Duffy, thereby causing at least one other highly qualified candidate to withdraw before a key designation committee meeting even began; a second chose not to run a primary challenge. The mayor also endorsed and promoted a candidate in the Northwest District who had worked on his campaign and was at the time the Democratic minority leader in the Monroe County Legislature. At least in part because of the mayor's strong backing, she was the only candidate to emerge when the incumbent council member announced his retirement. Also in 2007, assembly member Gantt was given his candidate for one of the open school board seats. Gantt was also the sponsor, mentor, and employer of Northeast District city council candidate Lovely Warren, whom I challenged.

Candidate profiling on gender, race, ethnicity, and even sexual orientation also characterizes Democratic Party politics (and is something in which I must admit to having participated). When in 2007 a white councilwoman from the East District announced her retirement, the party designated another white woman to replace her. At the same time, another candidate for this seat who was an African American woman with substantial city government experience was overlooked and reportedly discouraged by Assemblyman Gantt from running a primary because "the East Side is a white district." Similarly, the Latino community is allotted one seat each on the city council, school board, and county legislature. If any of these seats become open, the party selects another Latino candidate to replace the departing one. The choice of whom the party will designate is often left to the perceived and politically connected leaders in the Latino community. Accordingly, when in 2007 the lone Latino member of the city school board, who himself had been appointed in 2004 to the board to fill the seat of a Latino member who had resigned, announced that he would not seek another term, the established Latino leadership backed as his replacement a twenty-something, well-connected Latina political neophyte who lacked any real political experience or background in education. Neither the Democratic Party leadership nor the party's designation committees raised any objections. Nor did other candidates seeking party designation seriously challenge her head-on. She was the only Latina candidate to run. Given that and the party's use of quotas, her designation was a lock.

Candidate racial profiling and race-based ownership of legislative districts also were at play in the Northeast City Council District. Party insiders and political observers perceived the district as being a black district, meaning that white and, to a lesser degree, Latino candidates are discouraged from seeking this council seat. There are data to suggest that African Americans, though only a 46 percent plurality of the district's population, do represent a majority of those who vote in the Democratic Party primaries in the Northeast District. But more so, the political history of the district is responsible for fostering the impression of the Northeast seat as a black district where white and Latino candidates should not run. Until around 1975, the Northeast was a white-ethnic district. In that year, though, Northeast voters did something unexpected and daring for the times. They elected Rochester's first African American city council member. A supporter and longtime party maverick sent me this thumbnail sketch history of the district in an e-mail dated April 25, 2006:

> No white has seriously competed for the NE council seat since 1975. That year [African American] Ron Good, a popular county legislator . . . challenged Urban Kress (a classic white ethnic pothole and constituent service pol) and unseated him by 2 votes. The Republican drew 40% in November. Good was Rochester's first African American councilman. He was a conventional old school pol. He retired in 1980.

This e-mail further pointed out that after Good's election, party-designated candidates and even primary challengers to the designated candidates were generally all African American. Overall then, by 2007, an African American council member had represented the Northeast District for thirty-two years. Given how the party thought in terms of profiling, there was little doubt that an African American candidate, either the incumbent or a Gantt ally, would be designated again in 2007.

Despite these influences over whom the party designates, some cracks have surfaced in recent years in the Democratic Party's and the Gantt organization's ability to prevent primaries and secure electoral success for its designated candidates. Election year 2005 was particularly rough on the Democratic Party and Gantt. They were stifled when designated party mayoral candidate Council Member Wade Norwood, who was also a Gantt protégé and employee, was resoundingly defeated by former police chief Robert Duffy, who at least for the purpose of campaigning ran as a reformer. Another 2005 loss occurred when nondesignated city council candidate John Lightfoot won one of the five at-large council seats, resulting in two of the party's designated candidates battling it out for the fifth remaining at-large council seat. The loser and the odd woman out in that election, interestingly enough, was another Gantt protégé, Lovely Warren, whom I would challenge in 2007. In addition, nondesignated county legislative candidate Carrie Andrews, whom I had recruited to this race after deciding not to seek the office myself, defeated the party's designated candidate, who was perceived to be Gantt's man in the race.

The 2005 defeats underscore the fact that the Democratic Party and Gantt have been less able to discourage primary challenges since 2000, despite their efforts. During this same period, the party and Gantt also showed less ability to deliver votes consistently for its designated candidates. The combination has somewhat devalued receiving the party's designation. That in turn has fostered some increased willingness among insurgent candidates to take on the Democratic Party establishment. These recent failings have, in effect, created the perception that under the right circumstances, successfully running against need not be an impossible task. Nevertheless, would-be challengers to an incumbent or a designated candidate still have to concern themselves with the other factors, particularly the party's candidate profiling, political sponsorship, and Gantt's bossism.

Deciding to Run

Contrary to the political landscape just described, my own entry into Rochester electoral politics came from outside the Democratic Party and from an area toward which many political regulars are at best ambivalent and at worst hostile (i.e., the media). Since I joined the Political Science Department at St. John Fisher College in 1988, the media have regularly called upon me to provide political analysis and observations on US, state, and local politics. Over the years, I built a reputation as a fairly outspoken and entertaining political analyst and observer. This role granted me some limited celebrity status and opened doors that merely being Professor Jim Bowers could not.

One door was the 2001 Democratic Party designation contest for the city school board. At the time I had a son in city schools and was growing frustrated with the educational experience he was having; had grown politically close to Rochester mayor Bill Johnson, who in 1994 became the city's first African America mayor and also had won by running against; and was teaching urban politics with a focus on issues such as the relationship between sustainable public schools and sustainable cities. The nexus of those three factors convinced me to run for the school board in 2001. I announced in February of that year, and I was the only challenger to the three incumbent school board members. Employing a weighted vote convention strategy developed by Twenty-Seventh Legislative District leader Adam McFadden, who was supporting me, and with the added assistance of Mayor Johnson in flipping another important committee from a weak and vulnerable incumbent, I won the party's designation on the second ballot at the May 2001 convention, something that at the time rarely happened. Interestingly, though, a counting error found by the Monroe County Board of Elections the week after the convention but not reported to me until months later actually showed I had won on the first ballot. The actual school board election was anticlimactic, reflecting much of what I've previously noted about party and electoral politics in Rochester. Party leaders persuaded the losing incumbent not to force a primary. The two other designated Democratic school board candidates and I faced only token Republican opposition and were easily crowned the victors. I served one four-year term on the board of education, deciding early in the third year not to run again. At the end of my term in December 2005, I had no intention of running for anything else. But there is an old adage in politics, "never say never," and throughout 2006 I found myself considering a long-shot and maybe even hopeless candidacy for the Northeast District city council seat.

When I considered running for the Northeast District city council seat, the political conditions suggested from the beginning that my candidacy would be a long shot, but not without some small possibility of winning. All the factors dominating Democratic Party politics just discussed were present. First, we had to seriously consider that Council Member Ben Douglas was a sixteen-year incumbent. Second, the profiling of the Northeast District as a black district was against us. A "down-and-dirty" analysis that one key supporter did for me laid out the difficulties a "white populist candidate" would have running or challenging Douglas in the Northeast District. Using several different kinds of local elections, he documented that overall in the district, African American candidates outpaced and won over white candidates. In the 2005 mayoral primary in the part of the district we called "Davidland," in recognition of Assembly Member Gantt's control there, African American mayoral candidate Wade Norwood won 62 percent of the vote against two white mayoral candidates. Overall in the Northeast District, Norwood won 52 percent of the vote. The analysis concluded that in 2007, a probable scenario was that in those areas Gantt controlled, the primary vote there would be no less than a ratio of two to one, and probably more, for a white populist candidate running against an African American candidate. The final conclusion was "a third candidate would help."

Despite the odds appearing to be against us, there were some political conditions that might break in our favor. First, there were two substantial pockets of voters in the Northeast City Council District who appeared open to voting for white candidates (i.e., the remaining older white-ethnic and Latino voters). White ethnics still made up 31 percent of the district's population. Twenty-three percent of the population was Latino. Our analysis showed that in the 2005 mayoral primary, 57 percent of these two blocs of voters voted for the two white mayoral candidates. Fifty-two percent voted for the two white city court candidates over the African American candidate. Given those data, we were able to conclude that under the right circumstances, there remained a substantial number of voters in the Northeast still willing to consider the merits of a white candidate.

Second, Council Member Douglas had some vulnerability. In some corners of the district, concerns had emerged that Douglas was losing touch with his constituents and becoming an absentee council member. A more damaging vulnerability for Douglas was the collapse and financial failure of the city's Fast Ferry. The Fast Ferry was an innovative, meritorious economic development project advanced by Mayor Johnson and his administration to link metropolitan

Rochester to Toronto, Ontario, which was just a short two-hour boat ride across Lake Ontario. However, despite concerted city support, the private owners of the Fast Ferry enterprise never got their financial "sea legs" and the ferry operations ultimately collapsed. To save the sinking ship and its investment, the city stepped in and borrowed $40 million to purchase the ferry and its operations. At the time, Douglas chaired the city council's finance committee. In this capacity, he was appointed to and elected president of the authority board the city created to oversee the city-owned Fast Ferry enterprise. Under Douglas's "leadership," the Fast Ferry continued its financial hemorrhage and soon appeared to be approaching bankruptcy. Despite its continued financial problems, there were some reasons to believe that if the city could get another full year of ferry operations under its belt, the enterprise might begin to make a profit. Nevertheless, in 2006 incoming mayor Bob Duffy, in part to create the public impression of decisive leadership, permanently dropped anchor on the Fast Ferry and authorized its sale.

Given his leadership role in it, Douglas was politically vulnerable on the Fast Ferry issue. He could be "blamed" for its failure, whether or not he had truly caused it. At the same time, his focus on trying to save a financially sinking ship could be used to create and further fuel the perception that Douglas was growing out of touch with his district. Given the eroding conditions in the Northeast District, exploiting Douglas's efforts to save the sinking Fast Ferry as his own district continued to drown in urban blight was a real plus for a campaign that was based on running against. Though some might question Douglas's culpability in the Fast Ferry's failure, as a challenger to a long-term incumbent, we knew we had to maximize any possible vulnerability he had and exploit it to our fullest advantage, and we were fully prepared to do so.

Another factor in my favor was the real possibility that a third candidate, who was African American, would enter the race. Throughout 2006, we kept hearing that Lovely Warren would enter the race and challenge Douglas for the party's designation. Shortly after her 2005 at-large city council defeat, Warren bought a house in the Northeast District. Sources informed me that Warren moved to the district with the clear intention of running for the Northeast District city council seat. Fueling her decision to run was her narrow defeat in 2005 and Gantt's desire to have one of his own people on the council. He had lost his key person in city hall when Council Member Norwood lost his mayoral bid. Gantt also seemed willing to let Warren challenge Douglas for his council seat. Douglas had strived to be an independent voice throughout his political career and as a result was never Gantt's favorite. However, the bizarre rationale, sources informed me, for Gantt's immediate displeasure with Douglas and therefore his willingness to have Warren challenge him was Douglas's failure to support Norwood's mayoral candidacy soon enough. Douglas had waited until the end of the primary season to do so. Clearly, a political three-way would be a plus for my candidacy, and early on it seemed to be a distinct possibility. A three-way race would likely split the African American vote between Douglas and Warren. Under this scenario, our focus would be on building a winning electoral coalition consisting of older white ethnics, Latinos, and whatever percentage of African American voters we could attract.

A final factor in my favor was me. I was potentially an attractive candidate. First, I had a previous track record as a successful citywide candidate for the school board. I was known to be politically independent. Even out of office, I had maintained a reasonably good level of name recognition within the community because of my continuing role as a political analyst for local media. I was also known as a strong advocate of government accountability and fiscal responsibility. Correspondingly, I had a knowledge base regarding urban issues formed from teaching urban politics and serving on the school board. Finally, I had resided in the district for nearly twenty years and had a respectable record of neighborhood involvement. On the negative side was the profiling issue. I would be a white candidate running in a perceived black district. If I were truly a conventional politician driven mainly by ambition and need for office, I would have disqualified myself on this factor alone. Second, party leaders and insiders did not view me as a "good Democrat," because according to Joe Morelle, state assembly member and Monroe County Democratic Party chair, I "didn't go along with the Party." In addition, I had become one of Gantt's main antagonists during my tenure on the school board. Given the animosity between us and the likelihood I would be challenging his latest protégé, it was clear that Gantt would use his considerable political power and organization to defeat me. Finally, I had neither money nor an organization.

By year's end, I concluded that the pros of running still outweighed the cons. Because I neither needed to be in elected office nor sought long tenure in one, running posed no real personal or political risks. Instead, the council, I concluded, needed an independent voice on it since there currently was none. The Northeast District also needed an effective voice. Neither Douglas nor Warren would be that. There were even some reasons to believe that I had at least a long-shot chance of winning. With the decision made, my key supporters and I now began planning in earnest. We knew that in this campaign I really would be running against.

The Party Designation and a Not-So-Surprising Surprise

In structuring the campaign committee, one of the most important decisions we had to make was who should be the campaign manager. After some discussions and false starts, we selected Aaron Wicks. Wicks was a political operative who came with a decent, but not a winning, resume from other campaigns. Like me, Wicks was also a political scientist. In 2004 he had willingly managed the campaign of the Democratic Party's ill-fated state senate candidate against a widely popular Republican incumbent. In 2005, he cochaired the long-shot mayoral campaign of City Council Member Tim Mains, both in the Democratic Party primary and during Mains's third-party mayoral bid in the general elections. It was clear from his record that Wicks was not afraid of a challenge or gambling on long-shot candidates. In addition, Wicks brought to the campaign a clear sense of the unlimited role and responsibilities of a campaign manager. In recruiting Wicks, we did gain respect and acknowledgment among some party regulars and insiders. It may have been the first indication to them that I was serious about my campaign.

With Wicks on board, the first official meeting of the Bowers for City Council Campaign Committee was held on Monday, January 29, 2007. At this meeting we agreed to gear ourselves entirely toward running a primary against whomever the party designated as its candidate. Political reality forced this strategy upon us. We knew I had little chance of winning the party's designation with either Douglas or Warren seeking it as well. Two complete party legislative district committees and five election districts in a third committee would determine the designation. We thought we might be able to split the vote in one full committee. However, the second full committee, which had a substantial weighted vote, Gantt controlled. That would spell trouble for Douglas as well. In a three-way contest, with Gantt controlling a substantial bloc of votes and delivering them to Warren, Douglas could and would be denied re-designation. Accordingly, we decided to go through the designation process but not put too much effort or many resources into it. I'd make perfunctory calls to all or most committee members, focusing particularly on those who might be friendly, and ask them to attend their designation meeting and vote for me. I'd go to the three meetings, make the appropriate appeal, and then let the chips fall where they may. The real campaign for us would be the ballot access petitioning period between mid-June and early July and the primary campaign that would take place from mid-July through primary Election Day. We also decided to announce my candidacy early. By announcing first, we wanted to make clear that I intended to run, challenge Douglas for his council seat, and stay in the race regardless of any other candidates who might also announce. The actual announcement came on January 31, during one of my semiregular appearances on *The Talk Show with Bob Smith,* which aired on WXXI 1370 AM, Rochester's National Public Radio affiliate. The on-air announcement was coordinated with a press release to other media outlets.

After announcing, there was little to do until the party committees began to meet. In the meantime, we worked on developing our platform, firming up our organization, and making plans to raise money. Soon, though, events began to conspire against us. In a letter dated March 16, 2007, Douglas announced to party committee members that he was seeking reelection to his council seat and laid out his case for re-designation. However, about this same time, we began hearing from our friends in the party and on council that something was afoot, that Mayor Duffy was about to "buy off" Douglas with a job offer in the city's Law Department to get him out of the race. We were also told that the "fix" was in to appoint Warren to the vacancy created by Douglas's departure. Both proved true. On March 21, city hall announced that Douglas would be resigning from the council and taking a position in the Duffy administration. The Douglas buy-off was a hardball political maneuver most likely executed by Mayor Duffy, Gantt, and party chair Joe Morelle. The job offer was too attractive for Douglas to turn down. It saved Douglas from a tough reelection campaign, whether he would be challenged by both Warren and me or just one of us. It gave him a comfortable five-figure salary somewhere between $65,000 and $75,000 and a good pension when he retired.

Publically, the party, city council leadership, and Mayor Duffy maintained there was no buy-off of Douglas or fix for Warren. The mayor even tried to convince me of this at the April 18, 2007, designation committee meeting of the Twenty-First Legislative District Committee. Until I began my council campaign, Mayor Duffy and I had been friends of a sort and politically allied, dating back to the late 1990s when I was doing research on Mayor Johnson. After Duffy announced his candidacy and retired as police chief, I played a role in getting him a visiting fellowship at St. John Fisher College. I was also instrumental in helping Duffy gain the support of Darryl Porter, who was a well-known and politically astute African American community leader with whom I served on the school board at a time when few high-profile black leaders supported Duffy. In addition, I talked with Duffy regularly during the mayoral primary season, providing him with analysis and other advice. Given this history, Duffy apparently felt he owed me some explanation regarding the Douglas buy-off and Warren's impending appointment. Seeing me in the hallway of the building in which we were meeting, Duffy asked if we could talk. We moved over to a secluded corner of the hallway and in a hushed tone he said, "Jim, I want to assure you there was no conspiracy here [to hire Douglas and appoint Warren]." To which I replied: "Yeah, right, Bob."

The Douglas buy-off was an early indicator of the hardball politics and uphill battle that my campaign would face. However, Douglas's departure from the race didn't change my decision to run. It just guaranteed that Warren would be the party's designated candidate for the Northeast seat, which she eventually did become. In addition, Douglas's departure meant we lost our three-way and turned it into a two-way campaign with the one scenario we least desired. It now would be a more difficult race, but again, not impossible, so we weren't too disheartened. When we did an analysis of Warren's 2005 at-large council campaign and how she ran in the Northeast, we saw some reason for hope. She didn't run as strong as we thought someone with support from the Gantt organization should have, including in areas where Gantt's candidates usually do well. In the Northeast District in 2005, Warren ran fourth in a field of nine candidates. That was good enough to win one of the five at-large seats, but she ran substantially behind the first-place finisher: Her percentage of votes cast was 38 percent lower than his. We concluded that her numbers hardly reflected great strength, particularly when the Gantt machine was so engaged. In addition, our early opposition research suggested Warren had her own vulnerabilities, including a possible residency issue.

Douglas's departure also meant that we had to contend with the issue of Warren being slipped into his vacant council seat without the party leadership or the council giving serious consideration to other contenders for the vacancy, especially me. Still, we went through the process much as we had the designation process. We submitted a letter of interest to party chair Morelle, asked for an interview from council, tried to reach out to those council members who might even be remotely supportive of my appointment, and sent out the necessary press releases indicating my interest in the appointment and my readiness to serve the people of the Northeast District. We also took the position and recommended to some on council that a "caretaker" council member be appointed, someone who could represent the district in the short term but who would not be an active candidate for the position in the September primary. We took this position in part because of the relative certainty that I would not be appointed and because we were hearing from a couple of friendly council members that the leadership was having some difficulty finding the fifth vote it needed to guarantee Warren's appointment. In the end, the fifth vote wasn't a problem. Warren was chosen, and no one else was seriously considered because Gantt didn't want anyone else appointed. That was confirmed in a meeting I had with Joe Morelle at Democratic Party headquarters, in which Morelle informed me that the party was recommending Warren over me because "that's what David [Gantt] wants."

The changing dynamics of the race did have one major plus for us. Douglas's departure from the race opened the door for me to invite former Rochester mayor Bill Johnson to be my campaign chair, a largely ceremonial yet highly symbolic position. Bringing Johnson on board was something I had wanted to do from the beginning. Johnson was my friend and unofficial mentor; he maintained the allure of an outsider even after being mayor for twelve years; his brand of politics stood in sharp contrast to Gantt's bossism; and he was still a major figure in the African American community and viewed very favorably by it. But despite these reasons, If Douglas had been in the race I could not have secured his help. As noted earlier, Douglas's main political vulnerability was the poor performance of the Fast Ferry under his presidency of the Fast Ferry board. However, since the Fast Ferry had been one of Mayor Johnson's major economic development initiatives, I couldn't very well attack Douglas on the Fast Ferry issue with Johnson as my campaign chair. In fact, because of our relationship, I already had decided to target any attacks on the Fast Ferry at Douglas and the council and not mention Johnson or his administration at all. Now with Douglas out of the race, the Fast Ferry was a moot point, and it opened the door to bring Mayor Johnson on board the campaign.

Johnson's selection was important and a big boon to the campaign since he was the city's first African American mayor. Johnson's support held the promise of legitimizing my campaign among African American voters. Some "leaders" within the black community did privately criticize Johnson for supporting a white candidate over an African American candidate. Johnson's selection energized my committee and gained us some credibility among party insiders who were beginning to take our campaign seriously. Some in the media began to cast the election in terms of a contest between Gantt and Johnson, a comparison which we did not mind them making. However, the first real test for our fledgling and untested campaign organization was about to come in the petitioning stage, when we found out whether we could secure ballot access for the September primary.

500 Good Signatures

Under New York state election law, all candidates for public office, even those designated by the political parties, have to petition, or collect, a certain number or percentage of signatures from the registered voters of their party living in the district in which they intend to run. Thus we needed to collect around 500 "good" signatures from registered Democrats living in the Northeast City Council District. Good here meant that the signatures were legal, not forged; they were recorded at the correct address; and the forms on which they recorded were properly completed and witnessed. We had approximately five weeks to do this, from June 12 through July 19. As the designated candidate, Warren would have assistance from the party, her own campaign organization, and the Gantt organization in collecting her signatures. We would have only our own volunteers, who had yet to be recruited and trained.

Fortunately for my campaign, both Wicks and some other senior staffers were very knowledgeable on petitioning from start to finish. A simple and straightforward petitioning strategy was put together to minimize the number of volunteers needed to complete petitioning in a timely fashion. Our goal was to secure between 600 and 650 good signatures to buffer us and ensure that we had the 500 valid signatures necessary to force a September primary. That meant we needed to gather 800 to 850 signatures. We completed our petitioning in three weeks, by June 30. This deadline was set for two reasons. First, it gave our campaign committee time to verify every signature we collected and to tell exactly how many valid signatures we had. When we turned our petitions in to the board of elections, we already knew we had secured a place on the ballot and that the petitions would hold up to review and challenges by Warren's campaign. Second, the sooner we completed the petitioning, the sooner I could get back on the actual campaign trail and, more importantly, start raising money. However, despite the early completion date, we also decided not to turn the petition in to the board of elections until the latest possible time and date to minimize the opportunity that Warren's campaign would have to scrutinize our petitions and try to mount a challenge to them.

Because we would be relying on many volunteers who were not familiar with petition carrying, we also conducted training sessions for them to minimize the number of invalid signatures collected. The training made certain they understood what not to do with their petition sheets. Two important items concerned signature dates and the petition form itself. In regard to the first, it was pounded into the heads of the volunteers that the date someone signs mattered. As Wicks told the volunteer, "If someone signs our petition and one for Lovely Warren, the one that will count is the one that was signed on the earlier date. . . . This is why we MUST get as many *early* signatures as we can." In addition, they were instructed "not to do anything to your petitions that will make them look 'unusual.' . . . Use the same pen. Have them sign sequentially . . . to ensure that the dates run in order down the left-hand side. These are . . . best practices to minimize the chance that someone will see our petition and think maybe it's fishy and should be examined more carefully."

We eventually hit the street with about twenty volunteers signed up to collect signatures at various times during the petitioning period. As the candidate, I was out nearly every day during the petitioning stage, collecting signatures and meeting potential voters. Because the district has a substantial Latino population, we also walked with Spanish-language speakers whenever possible. Generally, we tried to walk up to three hours a night, from six to nine o'clock, and double that on weekends. We tried to walk one to two election districts on weeknights and three to six on weekends. Most Friday nights we didn't walk because so few people are home then.

Though it was an intense three-week period, petitioning for us was anticlimactic. We had few, if any, real problems or issues in securing our signatures. For us the petitioning process was a triumph of sorts. We reached our goal of 850 signatures, and following our plan, we stopped collecting signatures after that. Our internal review of our petitions showed we also had reached our safe signature range of between 600 and 650 good signatures, 607 to be precise. We turned them in to the board of elections knowing we had secured ballot access and forced a September primary. Our successful petitioning effort also showed the party and Gantt that we could build an organization and recruit committed volunteers, giving them another reason to take my challenge seriously.

One petitioning story warrants retelling here. Our champion petition carrier was Charlie Eber, who up until 2000 had represented the Twenty-Ninth County Legislative District, which was part of the Northeast City Council District. Eber, now out of office and a Democrat turned Republican toward the end of his legislative career, gathered 100 signatures, or nearly 12 percent of our total signatures. Eber even walked in raging downpours when the rest of us stayed home. Being the pro that he is, Eber knew what we first ignored: When it rains, people are home. After hearing what he had done, throughout the rest of the campaign, we never let anything but truly severe weather interfere with campaigning. An added bonus was that Eber petitioning for us really got under Gantt's skin. Eber had been brought into a petitioning process through back channels by some friends of mine in the Republican Party. Eber and Gantt had at one time been politically close and retained some relationship even after Eber became a Republican. Almost as soon as we turned in our petitions, the Democratic Office of the Board of Elections made certain Gantt had copies of them. (We had to wait most of a day to get copies of Warren's petitions.) Upon seeing Eber's name on several pages of our petitions, Gantt hurriedly and agitatedly called him to complain and ask why he had done it. A source close enough to Eber to know told me that Eber replied something like this: "David, people tell me Jim's a good guy and has lived in his neighborhood a long time. He's also from [St. John] Fisher [Eber was an alum of the college]. The Fisher family sticks together. Besides David, hasn't Warren only lived in the district a short time?"

Our Primary Campaign Strategy

Among our most important decisions were how to portray me and my opponent to potential primary voters. For my presentation, we decided to focus on my lengthy residence in the Northeast District, my record as an outsider and an independent who wasn't afraid to challenge the status quo, and my plan to bring about meaningful and real change for Northeast District neighborhoods. Our overall message was captured in our main campaign slogan: "Because Every Neighborhood Counts." Our secondary slogan was "The Only Candidate with a Real Plan for Change." Together, both slogans became important tools in branding and marketing me as a candidate. In contrast, we decided to aggressively present Warren as negatively as possible while staying factually correct. Our aim was to brand her as a carpetbagger because of her less-than-two-years' residence in the Northeast District, question her independence and present her as a puppet to Gantt, and highlight the complete absence of any substantive plan to help the residents of the Northeast District. Most of these efforts to define Warren and myself would be carried out through an aggressive direct mail campaign that took place during the last three weeks before the primary.

Having decided on how to contrast me to Warren, we next had to consider which primary voters would respond best to these branding efforts. First, we had to consider probable voter turnout for the primary election. We knew that primary election turnout in local races is notoriously low, except in some highly visible cases such as the mayoral race, so we anticipated that turnout would range from 10 to 15 percent. That meant between 1,400 and 2,200 Democratic registered voters would decide the outcome in the Northeast District. Somewhere between 800 and 1,100 votes could actually win the primary election. Next, we considered who likely "Bowers voters" were. As did the Warren campaign, we assumed that race would likely be a dominant factor in how people voted. We knew we would have to use race to some degree but not run a race-baiting campaign. We were, however, relatively confident that the Warren and Gantt organizations would in one way or the other engage in race baiting. Generally, we considered probable Bowers voters to be older white ethnics, Latinos, and middle-class African Americans. Latinos were a particular emphasis of ours, given the lingering tensions between the Puerto Rican and African American communities in Rochester and evidence to suggest that without the opportunity to vote for a Latino candidate, Latinos will vote for a white candidate over an African American candidate.

Next, we analyzed primary election results in the fifty-five election districts making up the Northeast City Council District, focusing on elections in which white candidates ran well and the kinds of elections in which they ran. We also matched the election districts with census data to obtain an approximate demographic profile of them. From this analysis we determined that there were nineteen high-opportunity election districts, twenty-five moderate-opportunity election districts, and eleven election districts we labeled the "Lost EDs." They were election districts that made up the center of "Davidland," that more often than not consisted of race-based voters, and where white candidates almost always ran poorly. Finally, because all primary voters are not equal, we also identified the probable "Prime Dems" (those who voted with consistency in Democratic primaries) in the different categories of election districts whom we would need to contact and win over. In regard to the high-opportunity election districts, we concluded that we needed to focus on any Democrat who voted in any of the Democratic primaries in 2004, 2005, or 2006. In the moderate-opportunity election districts, we decided to focus only on Democrats who had voted in either the 2004 or 2006 Democratic primaries. We also decided not to contact voters and "go dark" in the eleven Lost EDs. We didn't want to fire up Warren's base. Instead, our goal was to maximize our possible turnout and do what we could to suppress voter interest and turnout among possible Warren supporters. This same reasoning was applied in dropping 2005 primary voters from the moderate-opportunity election districts. The 2005 primary was a hotly contested mayoral campaign where the candidates' race was a significant factor. By disregarding voters in the moderate-opportunity election districts who had only voted in the 2005 primary, we hoped to suppress interest among African Americans who were race-based voters and who likely had turned out that year principally to vote for the African American candidate for mayor and against the white mayoral candidates. Given what we suspected would be the race-baiting overtones coming from Warren and Gantt organizations, we didn't want to encourage those voters to turn out.

Those people we saw as our voters and those we did not defined our walking and canvassing and our direct mail strategies. We concluded that high-opportunity election districts would be walked and canvassed twice. (I walked most of them three times by the end of the campaign.) Moderate-opportunity election districts would be canvassed at least once. (By the end of the campaign, I had walked most of them twice.) In the eleven Lost EDs, we would go dark as planned, neither canvassing nor even petitioning in them, if it could be avoided. With regard to walking and canvassing, we began in May and didn't stop until the week before the primary, when we began phone banking. On average, we walked five to six days a week, carrying a brief key card and a longer platform piece in both English and Spanish versions. Walking also meant comfortable shoes, a lot of bottled water, and all kinds of weather, from 90-degree-plus temperatures and high-humidity days to rain, drizzle, and wind. When walking in predominantly Latino areas, we tried to have one or two Spanish-speaking walkers as well, preferably Puerto Ricans because they constituted the dominant Latino population in Rochester. As we walked, we recorded probable supporters and opponents on our canvassing lists to use in our get-out-the-vote (GOTV) effort.

Our direct mail campaign paralleled the walking strategy, with one important exception. Given our hopes of trying to attract as many Latino voters as possible, we decided that bilingual direct mail would be sent to every Latino Democrat who had voted in any of the 2004, 2005, or 2006 primaries, including those living in the eleven Lost EDs. Our direct mail consisted of seven professionally designed and printed pieces that were mailed twice per week in rapid succession between August 27, 2007, and September 17, 2007, the day before the primary. The first two pieces were positive and designed to introduce me to the voters and to build a favorable impression of me. They were colorful and heavily laden with pictures of me with people representing the rich racial and ethnic diversity of the district. The pictures also had me out in the district. The first piece also had an endorsement from former mayor Bill Johnson and his picture.

The next four mailings were fact-based negative attack pieces about my opponent that always ended with a positive about me. For example, the first of these was a bi-fold asking on the front: "When Political Boss David Gantt Needs a Vote on City Council, Who Does He Call?" On the inside was the answer: "Political Boss David Gantt Calls Lovely Warren!" On the back it closed with: "Jim Bowers, an Independent Voice Fighting for Us!" Also in this piece, we used a very unflattering picture of Warren that her campaign had used on an earlier piece handed out during the designation process. The next piece, entitled "Look Who Just Moved In," described Warren as a carpetbagger who moved into the district less than two years before the 2007 primary for the purpose of running for the council seat after losing her 2005 council race. The third piece called Warren out for a council vote that gave wealthy individuals tax breaks for buying luxury condos in downtown Rochester. The visual on the front comprised two pictures, one of a clearly rich couple drinking champagne and the other a working-class or middle-class African American family. The text accompanying the pictures read: "Who Do You Think Should Get a Tax Break?"

The narrative on the reverse side read: "Lovely Warren voted to give a HUGE tax break to wealthy people for buying expensive upscale condos in downtown Rochester for the next nine years!" It then asked: "Who will foot the bill for these tax breaks? The working families of Northeast Rochester, many of whom are struggling to buy their first home." It closed with a positive on me promising to "fight for tax breaks for low and middle income . . . families buying their first home."

And on it went. The last negative piece was an aggressive comparison piece entitled "Decide for Yourself." Here we laid out my plan for change, compared to her lack of a plan and complete absence of any substantive proposals during the campaign. We also used another unflattering photo of Warren and Gantt together that we had taken by a campaign photographer at a press conference they both attended. The picture captures Warren and Gantt side by side, looking as if they are scowling and angry. It was used to reinforce Warren's ties to Gantt and her lack of independence. After this piece, the seventh mailing closed on a positive note, reminiscent of the first two and stressing my plan for change and the endorsement by Mayor Johnson.

Some Serious Mud

While we were campaigning, Warren was doing the same. There was one major difference, though. We took all our shots in public. However, Warren, Gantt, and their allies did not. They engaged in a campaign of character assassination through blogs, e-mails, and the black churches that was difficult for us to counteract. In a nutshell, the campaign of character assassination claimed I was a racist, a "known" atheist, and a pedophile who likes young boys and that I had knowingly allowed thousands of dollars to be stolen from the school district. Several of those allegations were posted on a community blog on the website of the *Democrat and Chronicle,* Rochester's only daily newspaper. For example, on August 25, 2007, a Warren surrogate accused me of being an atheist, specifically noting: "You know what I also found out, I saved the best for last, the candidate that you support is a known ATHEIST." On August 26, 2007, this same blogger threw out the "red meat" that I was a pedophile: "He's a big boy that likes young boys. Ask me how I know that one! Research 101 . . . Documentation, pictures, and all."

Our African American supporters also let us know that Gantt, who escorted Warren around to the black churches, engaged firsthand in the character assault, including telling church members I was a racist. In addition, we were told of phone calls he made to our African American supporters and contributors, challenging their support for me. In a robocall recorded and made the weekend before the primary, Gantt accused me of looking the other way as others stole money from the school district. Specifically, Gantt ranted: "Her opponent failed our children when he was at the school district. . . . When he was chair of the Finance Committee, he allowed hundreds of thousands of dollars to be stolen on his watch." As a final illustration, on the day of the primary, a Warren and Gantt operative sent out the following e-mail: LET'S BRING THE BEEF . . . HOME!!! LET'S DO this!!! Hopefully, we all know the potential for resistance to more BROWN faces on city council . . . we witnessed that YESTERDAY!!" The "that yesterday" to which the e-mail refers is unclear. The only event besides phone banking in which my campaign engaged the day before the primary was a press conference conducted by my campaign manager and deputy campaign manager addressing a fair campaign practice complaint we filed against Gantt's robocall for its lies and distortion. The local fair campaign practice committee ruled in our favor later that day. (However, I should point out that early in the campaign, this same committee issued a ruling against our campaign as well.)

Gantt and the Warren campaign's goal in assassinating my character was simple. They wanted and needed to scare African Americans into voting black, much the same as Republicans tried to scare rural and small town white voters into voting white against Obama in 2008. To do this, they used race-baiting tactics designed to stir up racial fear and animosity. For example, religion is very important within the African American community, and the black churches are its cornerstone. Therefore, to make me "scary" to African Americans, Gantt and the Warren campaign needed to make me out to be an atheist or not a Christian, just as some Republicans sought to cast Obama as a Muslim. Similarly, homophobia is rampant in the African American community, particularly among black males. Accordingly, turning my record of supporting and advocating gay rights into an accusation that I was a pedophile was just a more notorious way of calling me a homosexual and was an effort to heighten suspicions about me among blacks and particularly among black males. Finally, the false claim that I allowed hundreds of thousands of dollars to be stolen from the school district and twisting my record as a board member, though more subtle, was meant to reinforce African Americans' rightful frustration and anger over the state of public education in Rochester. It was also Gantt's way of trying to assert his often-stated opinion that white people don't and can't care for black kids. In the final analysis, the attempted character assassination was nothing more than overt racial bigotry, which is vastly different than merely using race as a voting cue.

GOTV

Everything in our campaign, as in all campaigns, came down to whether we could get our voters out on Election Day. Our GOTV effort began seven days out from the September 18 primary, with several consecutive nights of phone banking to targeted voters. Overall, we identified 1,600 potential voters to call.

Among the targeted voters were 600 Latinos, 500 seniors, 200 voters with whom I had personally spoken and who indicated their support for me, and 300 other general contacts whose support seemed probable. A good portion of these targeted voters had been identified during our walking and canvassing efforts, particularly from the notes and comments we kept on them on our walking sheets. On a typical night, we had five to six volunteers making calls from 6 P.M. to 9 P.M., averaging twenty-two calls per person per hour. As with our walking and direct mail, we also relied on Spanish speakers to call Latino households. The basic goal of the phone banking was to even more precisely identify supporters who would be called again on primary day, reminded to vote, and offered a ride. The results of the phone banking were encouraging. Most of the calls were running in our favor. Though the phone banking was not meant to be a scientific poll of any sort, the broad support demonstrated in those calls seemed to suggest that if on Election Day our voters turned out, we just might make a real contest of the primary.

Our GOTV effort on primary day was a more intense continuation of what had occurred the previous nights. We also sent out robocalls with a recorded message from Bill Johnson. We tried to reach as many targeted voters as possible before the polls opened at noon. If they weren't home, our phone bankers left a message encouraging them to vote and to let us know if they needed a ride to the polling place. I spent the morning canvassing a 500-unit high-rise apartment building (so big it was its own election district) that we had reason to believe we could carry. We had active supporters in the building and had even hosted a spaghetti dinner fund-raiser there for the tenants. Other volunteers were sent out as poll watchers. A "secret friend" at the Monroe County Board of Elections had flagged seven election district polling sites with a history of Election Day shenanigans by Gantt and his organization. Accordingly, our volunteer poll watchers were sent to those sites. We were as organized and ready as we could be, but in the end it wasn't enough.

Voter turnout was in the middle range of what we anticipated. One thousand eight hundred and ninety-one voters, or around 13 percent of registered Democrats, decided the outcome of the primary. Warren won 73 percent of the vote. I got 27 percent. One explanation for such a lopsided loss is that despite running well, in the end we couldn't effectively compete with the Gantt organization on GOTV. Twenty-five percent of all the votes cast in the primary came from the eleven Lost EDs that were the heart of Davidland. Those votes alone nearly equaled my entire vote total and overwhelmingly went to Warren. Votes from the eleven Lost EDs accounted for around 30 percent of her primary votes.

In contrast, our targeted voters didn't turn out. One indirect indication of this is a soft measurement of Latino voting. Election returns in the 2007 school board primary taking place that same day strongly suggest that voter turnout among Latinos was lower than usual, as evidenced in the third-place finish in the Northeast District of the Latina school board candidate designated by the

Democratic Party. When given the chance, Latino voters often bullet-vote for only the Latino candidate in at-large elections such as school board and city council. In Rochester, that regularly results in the Latino or Latina candidate finishing first. That did not happen in the 2007 school board primary. The Latina candidate finished third in the Northeast District, including heavily Latino areas. Her poor showing strongly suggested that Latino turnout was lower than usual. If true, given the emphasis we place on Latino voters and the resources committed to this voting bloc, this lower-than-anticipated turnout was disastrous for us.

Running Well and Losing

Turnout was clearly a factor in my loss. The perception of the Northeast District as a black district and the racial profiling of candidates also were a factor. Another plausible explanation is that we lost because we ran too well to win. I know that sounds counterintuitive, but it isn't. My outsider challenge to the Democratic Party establishment and the Gantt organization was a well-executed, well-organized, and well-financed campaign. We had an ongoing presence in the district through our walking and canvassing, conducted a hard-hitting and professionally done direct mail campaign, and had plenty of money. In short, we ran too well, were too visible, and became too real of a threat, particularly to Gantt and his influence over Rochester politics. In retrospect, being less visible and conducting an "off the radar" campaign may have resulted in a closer race. However, it would not have fit my political personality.

Gantt also had vastly more to lose in this race than just seeing his protégé defeated for a second time. To lose the Northeast District city council seat, which he and most others saw as a black seat, to any white candidate would be too much. To lose this particular seat that had been held for thirty-two years by an African American to one of his political critics and nemeses, especially to me, would be unacceptable. And, to lose the council seat that sat in the center of Gantt's political base to any candidate other than a Gantt candidate was totally unacceptable. If Gantt lost here, he would be seen as politically vulnerable, much as he had been seen in 2005 after suffering a number of political losses (the mayoral primary defeat of his protégé Wade Norwood to a white ex–police chief, Warren's first council loss, and the loss of another Gantt-backed candidate in the Twenty-First County Legislative District). In the ensuing two years, Gantt filled the 2005 cracks in his political power through his position as dean of the Rochester Assembly delegation and through the assistance of a newly elected mayor, Robert Duffy, who appeared more than willing to be co-opted. He emerged from these efforts once again as the "boss."

In effect, then, it seems plausible that Gantt internalized the 2007 Northeast District city council primary as a challenge less to Warren and more to himself.

For Gantt, the race wasn't against Warren and me; it was between Gantt and me. Warren was just a proxy. She had to win so Gantt wouldn't lose. Anecdotal evidence supports this explanation. We got occasional reports from individuals close to Gantt that noted he was given to saying not that Warren had to win this race but that "I [Gantt] have to win this thing." It was also seen in phone calls Gantt made to our African American supporters and contributors, challenging them on their support for me. My candidacy and, more importantly, the success of my campaign galvanized Gantt. He had too much to lose for me to win. I, however, had nothing to lose. Still don't: nothing to lose, no apologies, and no regrets.

Acknowledgments

This chapter is dedicated to the memory of Steve Minarik, whose advice and counsel in 2007 were indispensible and who was just beginning to see the possibilities in teaching.

11

Running for Governor as a Third-Party Candidate

Michael Munger

Type of campaign: Governor (general)

Role of author: Candidate

Lessons to look for:
- The rules and procedures under which campaigns operate matter.
- Money matters and it matters most to challengers.
- Campaigns need both earned and paid media to get their message out.
- Minor parties and minor candidates get minor attention.

Morning, June 30, 2008. Five North Carolina Libertarian Party operatives and candidates gather in the parking lot at the State Board of Elections (SBOE) annex building for a meeting with Johnnie McLean, the deputy director for administration of the SBOE. It was already hot, and traffic had been miserable. But we were all there, on time, at 10 A.M., just as we had agreed in making the appointment. We were there because we had problems, and five complicated queries, involving the timetable for putting together a slate of candidates for the November election, filing fees, informing counties of our newly acquired ballot status, revising registration forms, and letting voters know that "Libertarian" was once again an option.

The party and the people interested in it were in this position because we had spent three years, and nearly a quarter of a million dollars' worth of money and volunteer resources, collecting nearly 110,000 signatures to resurrect the party as an option for voters. Now we had to switch gears and move from collecting signatures to attracting votes. Because of North Carolina ballot access law, which most scholars agree is among the most restrictive in the nation, the Libertarian Party had collected signatures to get on the ballot eight separate times, only to be thrown back off the ballot each time, leaving our registered voters to accept an "unaffiliated" designation because it was impossible to organize, get signatures, and then get votes in the same election cycle.

In the most restrictive states, including Oklahoma, Alabama, and North Carolina, ballot access laws work a cruel hardship on voters and candidates alike. Two parts of the law work together like a pair of scissors, slicing away the liberty of expression and choice guaranteed in any constitutional democracy. Signature requirements sap all the resources of so-called third or independent parties, requiring volunteers and fund-raisers to use up all their resources and energy just to get on the ballot. And then the "new" (in our case, "new" for the eighth time!) party must begin the race. But they are forced to arrive breathless at the starting line. The Democratic and Republican candidates arrive at the starting line fresh, well funded, and having had the electoral equivalent of a good night's sleep. Third-party candidates have to run the race already exhausted, having just run a marathon to just get on the ballot. That is no accident. It is an intended consequence of the law.

Still, as we walked in the annex building that humid morning in June, we were hopeful. We had done it. We had collected the signatures, and the signatures had been certified as valid. That meant that the Libertarians were a "qualified" party under North Carolina law. Except that both the state and the counties were dragging their feet. The state had refused to print up new registration forms, so newcomers to the state were unaware that "Libertarian" was an option. The counties had not been formally notified that we had qualified for ballot access, and so many were refusing to accept attempts by our nominees to register as candidates and pay filing fees. In at least five cases, county clerks had flatly refused any attempt to get them to contact the State Board of Elections to verify our ballot status.

The deadline for filing was upon us. If our candidates were not registered and filing fees paid by the close of business on the following day, Tuesday, July 1, all our efforts to get on the ballot would be wasted. After all, if we couldn't get actual candidates on the ballot, what good would ballot access be? If we couldn't get our party name on registration forms, how could anyone know that we had qualified as a viable party?

We needed answers, right away. Our appointment with the deputy director had been scheduled for 10 A.M., and we were all nervous and fretful. We waited in the drab conference room. Ten minutes, then fifteen minutes, passed. At 10:18, the door opened, and State Board of Elections deputy director Johnnie McLean came in. We shuffled our papers, eager to get to work. But McLean stood at the head of the table, looked at her watch, and then told us, "I do have to tell you, I have a real meeting at 10:30." Rather than answering, or even listening to, any of our questions, she just said, in the same soothing voice you might use to talk to a child, "Our office will work on these problems, to try to help you. But we are awfully busy right now. All of the candidates for office are trying to file, and there is a lot of paperwork."

The Libertarians all looked at each other, eyebrows and blood pressure headed for the ceiling. Well, yes, exactly. It is that paperwork we want to get the county offices to accept; accepted for *our* candidates, in addition to the two state-sponsored parties. Further, we had gotten an informal advisory opinion from a lawyer at the attorney general's office that we should not have to pay the filing fee for any office. The reason is that by obtaining the signatures we had satisfied the requirements of the law, and filing fees were for established parties who were going to conduct primaries. As a new party, we nominated candidates at a convention and so should not have to pay for primaries we weren't even holding. Nevertheless, McLean waved her hand airily. "Oh, yes, we checked with the governor's office. You do have to pay the filing fee. If you want to sue, you would probably win, and you can get your money back that way. But for now you have to pay. I don't have any choice; we have to collect the fees." And, with that, Deputy Director Johnnie McLean left the room, at 10:34. She didn't want to be any later for her "real" meeting.

That's a snapshot of the way third parties and their candidates are treated in many states throughout the country. Both the state legislatures and state boards of elections are very clearly focused on protecting the two major parties, regardless of the consequences for voters' desire to vote for the party of their choice. On its website, the North Carolina State Board of Elections admits as much: "The State Board of Elections is the state agency charged with overall responsibility for administration of the elections process and campaign finance disclosure in North Carolina. It is the only statutory bi-partisan, quasi-judicial supervisory board in North Carolina State government."

Did you get that? Not *non*partisan, not neutral in terms of party. *Bi*partisan—with fair and equal representation for *both* the Democratic and Republican Parties. Third parties? Their appointments with the deputy director are not real meetings. What are the consequences of this system for voter choice and electoral competition? What is it like to run for office as a third-party candidate? And what, if anything, should be done to change the system to make it more responsive? In this chapter, I will offer some answers that come from the political science literature, and some answers that come from my own experience running for governor of North Carolina as the Libertarian Party candidate in 2008.

Why Run? Third Parties in the States

The first question for most third-party candidates is, "Why are you running? What do you hope to accomplish?" And the prospects are even worse for candidates for statewide office. I was running for governor of North Carolina, a state of 9 million people scattered over 100 counties in a state 500 miles wide, from Murphy in the mountains to Manteo on the coast. In a local race, third-party candidates can devote extra effort to walking the district, going door-to-door. Not so in a statewide race. The monumental task of running statewide as a third-party candidate leaves many to wonder: "Isn't it just hopeless?"

Well, no. At least, not necessarily. Third-party candidates can have a big impact on elections, even sometimes on statewide races. In 1998, Independent Angus King beat both the Democrat and the Republican to win the office of governor of Maine. In the same year, Reform Party candidate Jesse Ventura beat the Republican and Democratic candidates to become governor of Minnesota. In fact, over the last six election cycles (1998–2008) with 141 governors' races contested, nearly 60 percent of the time third-party candidates got 2 percent of the total vote and received enough votes to affect the outcome in nearly 10 percent of all races.

Of course, it is still a fair question to ask why *I* ran. The Libertarian Party that nominated me was not nearly as strong or as well funded as the third-party operations that elected two governors in 1998. Also, traditional motivations for running that characterize Republican and Democratic Party candidates, such as personal ambition and a desire to affect public policy, were absent. As a third-party candidate I was unlikely to win, so ambition wasn't a factor. Further, without winning, there would be no opportunity to influence policy directly. In fact, the issues that many third-party candidates like me want to talk about almost never even come up in the mainstream media in the campaign. Therein lies my reason for running. I ran because I could raise issues that I thought might otherwise be ignored. I knew that if I could wrangle my way into the televised debates, I would have a forum to talk about my issues and my party, a forum that we could never afford if we had to buy commercials in the traditional way.

Finally, I had personal reasons for wanting to run. I had been a political science professor, at the University of Texas, the University of North Carolina, and then at Duke, for more than twenty years. I had written four books and over 100 articles on campaigns and the effect of money on politics. Also, in 2000 I had testified in the US Senate before the Rules and Administration Committee on the McCain-Feingold bill. I had written about strategy, but I had never conceived and executed a strategy. I had written about spending money on ads and buying radio time, but I had never done either. And I had written about the problems third-party candidates faced in getting ballot access, but I had never actually fought for ballot access myself. In short, despite all this knowledge I had never put myself out there as a candidate.

So, when I was approached in the late fall of 2003 by the Libertarian Party (to which I had recently switched my registration), I considered it. Except that it turned out that North Carolina state law required that candidates had to have been registered as a member of the party in which they were running a full six months before the filing deadline. So I was not eligible. Talking to party leaders and to my friends and family, I decided that I would start to explore a run in 2008, first seeking my party's nomination and then contesting the general election.

I did get quite a few incredulous or skeptical reactions when I told my people of my intentions. But the reaction of my wife of twenty-two years summed up the general sentiment pretty well. I told her I was going to run for governor, and she looked at me, raising one eyebrow. "You aren't going to *win,* are you?" she asked. Shaking my head ruefully, I said, "Thanks for your support, dear. Thanks for your support." Of course, she did support my efforts in dozens of ways and with hundreds of hours of effort and extra time away from her busy schedule as an attorney for the US Treasury Department in Raleigh, North Carolina. I owe her a great deal. But I'm still not sure she understands just what I was out to accomplish or what I had managed to prove by all that effort when it was over.

Ballot Access

As was discussed earlier, North Carolina has extremely restrictive ballot access laws, compared with other US states. There are two states that are even worse, Alabama and Oklahoma. In Alabama, valid signatures from 3 percent of the total votes cast in the previous election are required for access, with a 20 percent retention requirement. That is, the "third"-party candidate has to gather at least 50,000 signatures in a relatively small, rural state and then somehow garner 20 percent of the vote in the general election. Oklahoma requires "third" parties to collect a number of signatures equal to 5 percent of the previous gubernatorial vote, and candidates have to receive 10 percent of the votes in the general election to remain ballot qualified. Further, Oklahoma law strictly prohibits anyone but Oklahoma residents from collecting signatures, and no one can be paid to collect signatures.

North Carolina's law is a little less restrictive. To qualify for ballot access, a party has to collect a number of signatures equal to 2 percent of the vote in the previous gubernatorial election. To remain on the ballot, the law for many years required a 10 percent vote total in the general election. In August 2006, however, the 10 percent retention requirement was reduced to 2 percent. That is still four times the national average requirement for retention (with many states having effectively no burden for retention whatsoever), but at least it seemed possible to get there.

And so that is what I resolved. I would attempt for the first time in North Carolina history to secure ballot retention for my party by running for governor and winning the 2 percent or more of the total vote. To be fair, a previous Libertarian candidate, Scott McLaughlin, had collected more than 100,000 votes in 1992, for a share just over 4 percent. But turnout had not been nearly as high as it would be in this race, and the law then had required 10 percent, so McLaughlin had failed because it was essentially impossible under the old law to obtain enough votes to keep the party on the ballot. It was not clear how many votes would be required, but given the large increase in North Carolina's population from 1992 to 2008, I would have to attract well over 100,000 votes, and probably more than 120,000, far more than any other candidate had ever received.

Access Campaigns

Imagine if Coke and Pepsi got to decide how many different brands of soft drinks "needed" to be on the shelves. Two would be plenty. The same would be true if General Motors, Ford, and Chrysler got to decide if any foreign car company would be allowed to sell cars in the United States. Three would be enough. Coke, Pepsi, GM, Ford, and Chrysler don't get to write their own rules of competition. They have to play by the (more or less) fair market rules of competition, ensuring that consumers get choices. It is true that consumers may not *choose* to buy Smitty's Wonder Cola or the new Jonesycar rolled out of a factory in Missouri. The point is that the choice of "how many competitors" is, and should be, made by consumers, not by producers. Producers always have the incentive to restrict competition, but the law prevents them from doing so.

However, in politics the Democratic and Republican Parties do get to make their own laws regarding competition. They have exactly the same incentives as Coke and Pepsi to restrict choices for drinks, and the same as GM, Ford, and Chrysler to restrict choices for cars. And they do it. The difference is that the Democrats and the Republicans also have the ability to deny choices to citizens. And in states like North Carolina, they have shown that they will write whatever laws they have to write to block new parties from having a chance.

Given North Carolina's restrictive ballot access laws, the main thing that the Libertarian Party needed to get on the ballot was money. We needed 69,733 signatures, or 2 percent of the total vote in the 2004 governor's race. That had to be the "hard" verified count. Since the clerks of the 100 counties in North Carolina have to check each signature, at a cost to taxpayers of well over $100,000, we would need at least 30 percent more signatures than the hard figure of nearly 70,000.

We also needed volunteers to go out and get the signatures needed. That's no easy task. I remember one steamy day in the "Brickyard," the central quad of North Carolina State University in Raleigh, in 2007. I had bought several dozen donuts, and we had a nice shady spot under a large oak tree. We had a table, and I worked for five hours, with three young men who were representing the North Carolina state chapter of the College Libertarian Party. We talked to hundreds of people and sweated gallons. We asked each person who walked by, "Would you sign our petition? We aren't asking for your vote. We just want a chance to compete for it!" Most people wouldn't stop, and of those who would, many refused to put down all their information. The state requires that we ask for name, address, and birth date plus a full and legible signature. If any part of these requirements is not satisfied, the clerk of that county will disallow the signature. And many people told us that if they gave a random person with a clipboard their name, address, date of birth, and a copy of their signature . . . well, it felt like we were really just asking for help in stealing their identity. So they were not going to sign, thank you very much.

This attitude may be reasonable. In fact, the state is likely counting on it as a way of keeping third parties off the ballot. Even people who support the idea of another party are likely to shy away from the extreme disclosure requirements. So, after five hours in the July heat, working with three other people, we had collected only seventy-four signatures. At that rate of less than four signatures per hour, we would have the 69,733 signatures in another 18,500 hours, assuming they were 100 percent valid. Allowing for leakage for invalidated signatures, we were really looking at more like 24,000 signatures. If we assumed our volunteers were going to work eight-hour days, that translates into more than 3,000 days of work to collect those signatures. Clearly we needed more help. More help meant paid canvassers who were more skilled at collecting more signatures per hour and who could travel the state and work full-time.

Fortunately, North Carolina election law does not harass paid canvassers collecting signatures, but it doesn't really help them either. The law requires that the signatures be submitted well before the deadline, and the counties are then supposed to return the signatures within two weeks. The reason that this is important is that "new" parties need to know how many of the signatures are valid so they can get an accurate idea of how many more signatures they need to meet the hard count total. The problem is that some counties take this requirement much more seriously than others. Some counties like Durham go out of their way to reject signatures so that the failure rate is excessively high. For instance, invalid signature collection in Durham County is 45 percent or higher, compared to a statewide average of 30 percent. Other counties drag their feet in processing the signatures, making it impossible for the new party to be able to use the signatures toward the required total. In this past election cycle, the Libertarian Party submitted several sheets of signatures to Nash County in North Carolina in February. The deadline for filing the signatures is in May. The signature sheets were finally processed and returned to the Nash County Libertarian Party chair in August. So these signatures did not count toward the total needed for ballot access, and all the expense and effort required to collect them were simply ignored by the county and therefore the state as well. Further, we had no way of knowing why the processing was so delayed. In fact, the Nash County Clerk first denied the delay, then acknowledged it, said an explanation would be provided, and then stopped communicating with or returning phone calls from party officials. But regardless of whether the signatures were misplaced by accident or maliciously held up on purpose, the simple fact is that third parties who try to follow the law are often still prevented by states from obtaining ballot access.

In the end, the Libertarian Party of North Carolina spent $130,000 in donated funds and an additional $130,000 in volunteer time, travel expenses, and in-kind contributions to meet the signature requirement. The signature forms were received back from the counties and were determined by the state to have satisfied the additional requirement that petitions "must be signed by at least 200 registered voters from each of four congressional districts in North Carolina" (North Carolina General Statutes, Chapter 163, Subchapter 9, Section 96). The signatures, already certified individually by the counties, were collectively certified on May 22, 2008, to be on the ballot for the general election and established the Libertarian Party as "qualified." It had taken nearly three years and a quarter of a million dollars of money and volunteer time and resources. But we were back on the ballot, for the eighth time, as a "new" party.

Voter Registration Problems

So, at this point, the story has caught up to the beginning. Our meeting (if you can call it that) with the State Board of Elections took place fully forty days after the state had formally certified the party as qualified. Yet the counties' board of election chairs had not received notification that the party was qualified, and so many of them were refusing filing fees or voter registration forms. The registration forms themselves had not been modified; new voters or people who had just moved to the state had no way of knowing the Libertarian Party was a registration and voting option. That is perhaps understandable in the case of paper forms, which take a little time and expense to reprint. But at this point none of the counties had changed the online forms, the PDF files that were available over the Internet to download. That would take only a click or two of a computer mouse.

In some elections, it might not have mattered all that much. But the 2008 election was different. Between 2006 and 2008, more than half a million new voters were registered, a number equal to nearly 10 percent of the state's voting-age population. In many cases, the registration was done by volunteer workers or hired canvassers paid by organizations such as Moveon.org or Acorn. It may not be obvious how important these groups were to affecting Libertarian registration until you think about it. I made it a habit of approaching groups of registration canvassers whenever I saw them and asking them some questions. Many, interestingly, were paid operatives from out of state, looking to register Democratic voters for the election. Now, don't get me wrong; that's fine. And I did see them willingly register people who wanted to file as Republicans. But you could hear them laughing about it afterward: "Ah, should have ducked that guy. Another Republican. That won't help my total!" What did bother me and still bothers me is that the registration forms they were handing would-be voters had one checkbox for Democrat, another for Republican, and then a blank space that said "Other," where you could write in a party name as long as it qualified under North Carolina law. So, I engaged every canvasser I saw in a little test that summer (and I saw hundreds, as I drove around to different cities and waited around for events in coffee shops or farmers' markets or restaurants). I asked, "Can I register 'Green'? Can I register for the Green Party?" Almost every one of these workers said, helpfully: "Sure! Just write down 'Green' under 'Other' space there."

Now, that is completely wrong, of course, yet almost none of the canvassers for Moveon.org or Acorn ever said "No." At most, I got a few "I'm not sure" responses. To which, of course, I gave two responses. First, the Greens were not qualified, according to the admittedly overly restrictive laws of North Carolina. The Libertarians were, however, qualified. So the answer "Yes" to the question about "Can I register 'Green'?" was simply wrong. People who "registered" Green would actually be placed into an "Unaffiliated" registration, against their intent, because Moveon.org and Acorn gave them bad information. Second, a potential registrant would have to know the name of the Libertarian Party and know to write it down under "Other" to qualify as having registered. The workers would not write it for them. However, an illiterate citizen who wanted to register "Democrat" or "Republican" would be shown where to mark their party choice, because those names were written out for them on the form itself. And then the worker would fill out the rest of the form! When I pointed this out, the workers usually just shrugged and said that it really didn't matter. Their instructions were to offer no "leading" advice and no direction to avoid biasing the process.

How many citizens, how many of the more than half a million new voters, would have registered Libertarian if they had been presented a proper form, as should have been the case under state law, fully two months or more after the Libertarian Party had qualified? We have no way of knowing. But that's not the point. The point is that citizens were systematically denied even having "Libertarian" as an option, even though the party had climbed over all the very difficult hurdles set up by state law.

The Campaign, Debates, and Free Media

Having won the ballot access campaign, my attention now turned to my gubernatorial campaign. Despite the long odds, I believed in the campaign and my candidacy. I was well qualified to serve as governor in terms of education, experience, and leadership in a variety of public and private institutions. I wanted the job. But given the constraints we faced, our immediate goal was party survival. We needed to stay recognized as a qualified third party. To do that, we had to get at least 2 percent of the total vote cast in the gubernatorial election. If we couldn't, it was unlikely that we would be able to put together the money and volunteer effort to collect the 120,000 signatures that would be necessary to get back on the ballot. Remaining on the ballot by satisfying the retention requirement was our only chance. Given that we had used up most of our funding possibilities on the signature drive, the strategy of the campaign to do that had to focus on free, or "earned," media opportunities.

There are many chances for the candidates from the state-sponsored parties to use earned media. A campaign appearance or a press release has a decent chance of being used by television and newspapers. But minor-party candidates cannot rely on the mainstream media to use appearances or releases in the same way. The main goal, the real prize, for minor-party candidates is to be included in televised debates. This is true for any office, but for statewide offices such as governor, appearing in the debates on the same stage and with the same status as the major-party opponents can decide whether a third-party campaign will have any impact at all. But the first hurdle is to be considered.

The North Carolina gubernatorial debate schedule, announced in May, looked like this:

- June 21: North Carolina Bar Association
- August 19: WTVD (ABC), Durham–Capital Broadcasting
- September 9: WRAL (CBS), Raleigh
- September 19: Public School Forum/Education: Everybody's Business Coalition
- September 24: WUNC-TV
- October 8: WUNC-TV, Research Triangle Park
- October 15: WSOC, Charlotte-Mecklenburg League of Women Voters

The problem was that the schedule was announced as being the set of dates that "both" the Democratic and Republican candidates could work into their schedules. Since no one had even contacted me or my campaign, I assumed that meant I was not invited. Not good at all.

It became clear that to get to the debates we needed a three-part strategy: First, I had to run a campaign in June as if it were November and get the poll numbers up into at least the 5 percent range. That way my chances of being invited to one or more of the debates would be better. To do that, I had to raise money fast and spend it even faster. Radio spots, road signs, and lots of appearances all had to take place long before the traditional beginning of the campaign. Second, I had to press the debate sponsors to include me using letters, news releases, whatever we could manage. And third, I would use the debates (if the first two parts of the strategy worked) as a platform to get out my message.

The fund-raising strategy would be based on personal phone calls to try for at least a few large contributions and also a "money grenade." The idea for the money grenade was along the lines of the Ron Paul campaign's highly successful "money bombs," which by this time had brought in several million dollars for Paul's Republican primary campaign via the Internet. We ran the money grenade over the July 3–5 weekend as a way of celebrating our independence from the major parties. Of course, that also meant lots of people were away from their computers over the holiday weekend, so it's hard to know if the attempt at a tie-in was a good idea.

The result of the fund-raising campaign, however, was nearly $10,000, enough to run two weeks of radio ads in the Charlotte, Greensboro, and Raleigh media markets, which are three of the biggest in the state. The theme of the ads was simple: "If you hear my ideas, consider my views, and decide not to vote for me, then I have lost a vote. But if you don't even get to hear different views, then you have lost a choice. The Libertarians are on the ballot, and now I am hoping for a chance to appear before voters." We were not able to saturate the airwaves, but several newspapers picked up the story because they found the "David versus Goliath" aspect appealing. The media blast seemed to have the desired effect. The poll numbers started to creep up. We were at 4 percent in early July, and in several polls we were between 5 and 6 percent.

With my confidence buoyed by these rising numbers, I submitted a packet of materials to all the remaining debate event sponsors (the North Carolina Bar Association event was already past) and waited for an answer. We heard back from WUNC (public television) almost immediately. They invited me to both of the station's debates, scheduled for September 24 and October 8. More important, the station gave two other pieces of information. First, the reason they had invited me was that I was a credible candidate, in terms of background, and I was on the ballot. The station was not applying *any* polling percentage threshold, an important precedent for the future. Second, the station's cover letter noted that WUNC would provide airtime to whatever group of candidates showed up. So, if all three candidates agreed to participate, there would be a debate. If just two candidates agreed, there would be a smaller debate. And if neither major-party candidate showed up, I would still be given fifteen minutes to present my position. Again, that was very good news, not just because it meant the campaign would get some earned airtime but also because it seemed to bode well for the future of the party as having secured a level of credibility with an important media outlet in the state. The letter also noted that the Republican candidate for governor, Charlotte mayor Pat McCrory, had tentatively agreed to participate, but there was as yet no response from Lieutenant Governor Beverly Perdue, the Democratic candidate.

About two weeks later, I heard back from the League of Women Voters, in Charlotte. Now, this debate was the big enchilada, the real prize. It was the last debate before the election, it was televised statewide, and it would be broadcast on radio as well. I was expecting bad news because the league had never allowed a Libertarian to participate in any debate in the state before, even with poll numbers well over the supposed 5 percent magic number. So, I was already angry when I tore open the envelope and then saw to my delight a letter affirming that

I would be invited to the debate, that the other candidates had already accepted, and that I would receive full equal treatment. I looked down at the signature, and there it was: Amanda "Boo" Raymond, president, Charlotte-Mecklenburg LWV. It was official. We had done it. With the opening of that letter, an era of North Carolina politics ended because a third party would, for the first time, be contesting an election on a more or less level playing field, at least in terms of televised debates, with the Republican and Democratic Parties' candidates. Hundreds of thousands of people in North Carolina would see, for the first time ever, three podiums with three candidates, all having a chance to answer questions and argue about issues.

The other three debate sponsors never even bothered to respond. Instead, the two television stations, WTVD (ABC) and WRAL (CBS), both made persistent efforts to get me to record something they could put on their website and even put up blank pages to try to shame me into complying. I actually used this in a radio ad, attacking their duplicity for denying me my rightful place in the debates but then placing a link on their websites saying that I had refused to provide a video clip. The links disappeared pretty soon after that. I was never told why the "Public School Forum" didn't invite me. Presumably, as a college professor, I didn't know anything about education, or something like that.

The debates themselves were exciting and interesting. I appeared first in the two WUNC debates with Pat McCrory. I did my best to give Mayor McCrory credit for showing up, since he certainly didn't stand to gain much by debating me. He mentioned in his opening statement for the first debate that he just wanted to show respect for me as an opposing candidate. I corrected him in my own opening statement, saying that I thought he was showing more respect for the voters by giving them the chance to make a more informed choice. We ended up agreeing about many of the issues that we were questioned on, just because most of the points raised focused on education and the economy.

The second debate was a bit sharper, focusing more on areas of difference: same-sex marriage, immigration, capital punishment. We still agreed on many things, and we both made a real effort to answer the questions. However, at one point we had a pretty testy back-and-forth about a complex issue. I accused him of trying to score debate points and explained my own position. In response, Mayor McCrory paused and said, "I see. Well, if that is what you meant, then I stand corrected. You are right." The camera crew stared at him, and so did I. It was a real debate, an intellectual discussion in which two people were actually trying to wrestle with issues and understand each other. For several days afterward, people mentioned that moment to me. They said that it really made them think more of the debate process in general and more of Pat McCrory in particular. And I agreed. Whatever our disagreements, Pat McCrory had gone out on a limb to appear in those debates with me, and he did it with a style and dignity that made me admire him, then and now.

The final debate, in Charlotte on October 15, was of an entirely different sort. Each candidate had been allowed to invite up to ten people, and my folks were pretty pumped up. I half expected them to start doing the "wave" in the seating area since none of us had ever seen a Libertarian at a real debate before. The format was bizarre, with one minute to answer and thirty seconds for the other candidates to rebut. This was the first time I had really had a chance to meet, and talk with, the Democratic candidate, Lieutenant Governor Perdue. Pat McCrory and I were like old pals, though, and even sat together with our staffs in the same green room talking about Charlotte and its many restaurants.

Each candidate could use up to three "challenges" against the other candidates, or at least that is what we were told. But the event went long, partly because the debate moderators took time to challenge Bev Perdue on one of her answers. After she answered the first time, the moderator asked Perdue if she could answer again, but this time give some specifics. Her eyes widened, and then, unbelievably, she gave nearly the same answer again, verbatim. As I said later, I guess the answer to the question, "Can you provide more specifics?" was "No." I used one of my challenges, after Lieutenant Governor Perdue said that her response to the drought in North Carolina was to have a bucket in her shower, to catch the cold water before the water turned warm. I raised my hand, turned to her, and said, "You have been lieutenant governor of this state and president of the Senate for the last eight years. In all that time, your contribution to solving the drought problem is to have a bucket in your shower?" Having a studio audience of only thirty was a help, because most of the ten Munger supporters and ten McCrory supporters laughed audibly. Perdue sputtered a little and talked about her experience working with city leaders and her service on several different committees that had the word "water" in their titles. That got even more laughs, I'm afraid. It was a fairly embarrassing moment, though not for me.

After the debate, with just less than three weeks to go before the election, it had become clear that the election would go down to the wire. Most polls showed Perdue with a slight lead, and had me with numbers between 4 and 5 percent. If that held up, it would be enough to guarantee automatic ballot access for the Libertarian Party and would probably put me in a position of having received more votes than the margin between the winner and whoever finished second, a common metric for "success" among third-party candidates.

Attack of the Straight-Ticket Zombies: EV Sites

This election was the first in North Carolina history that allowed no-fault "early voting." The early voting (EV) sites were scattered all over the state and opened fully two weeks before Election Day, on November 4. The rules for registration were relaxed. To vote in person on Election Day, one had to have registered by

October 1, but to vote *before* Election Day, at an EV site, one could register and vote on the same day!

And as I drove around the state campaigning, it became clear that many of the "new" voters were doing three things: (1) registering, (2) voting early, and (3) voting straight-ticket Democratic. These trends are clearly reflected in the final vote totals: 63 percent of Democrat Bev Perdue's votes came at EV sites. Nearly 60 percent of Perdue's votes overall were straight-ticket Democratic Party votes, but 73 percent of the EV ballots were straight Democratic ticket. These three trends were very bad news for me. A huge turnout increased the denominator of the vote percent totals, making my 2 percent goal harder to reach. A huge turnout with straight-ticket voting also meant few or no split-ticket voters for me. (On the plus side, it turned out that nearly 20,000 people voted for the Libertarian Party down the ballot, nearly double the previous record high number of straight-ticket votes for my party.)

Watching the attack of the straight-ticket zombies was a little frightening. Buses pulled up, and elderly people, people who didn't speak English very well, and people who didn't appear to have much idea of how to vote would slowly file out. Democratic Party operatives would then hand out sheets of paper describing the procedure for voting a straight Democratic ticket as the group headed to the EV site.

What became clear in all this was the level of organization and commitment the Democratic Party possessed in North Carolina. On the plus side, there is no question that many people who hadn't voted before or hadn't voted for a long time were going to the polls and making their voices heard. On the minus side, they didn't appear to have much information about any of the down-ballot races, including governor. I talked to dozens of people, usually as they were coming back out of the EVs, and asked them if they were excited about the election. Their entire interest and focus was on the presidential race. I asked who they liked for governor and expected them to say that it was none of my business. But many were quite honest: "I didn't really look at those other races. I just wanted to vote for Obama."

Lest this section sound critical, let me note that this is how politics works, and in fact this is the only way it can work. Political science widely acknowledges that the mobilization of interest and turnout in the electorate is the core function of the mass-level political organization. It may sound like sour grapes for me to criticize the 2008 turnout efforts of the Democrats in North Carolina, but I also know that many people who had lost interest in politics and had lost faith in the leadership in Washington were rejuvenated and given a new sense of hope and purpose. Although one might wish that they had studied C-SPAN and the daily newspapers to know more about each office and each candidate, the fact is that the enthusiastic, early GOTV effort of the Democrats produced the desired results. The Democrats are to be congratulated, for they won a great victory against enormous odds.

The US 64 Campaign: Old-Fashioned, Handshaking, Backroads Campaigning

With the EV voting occurring, we still needed to make some kind of last push, a last attempt to capture the voters who may have either seen the debates or heard the radio ads we were running in seven different media markets around the state. To that end, on the last Thursday before the election, my campaign manager Barbara Howe and I drove out to Murphy, a beautiful little mountain town very close to the North Carolina–Tennessee border. Murphy also is the North Carolina terminus of US Highway 64, the main east-west road through the state before Interstate 40 was opened.

The North Carolina segment of US 64 is almost exactly 600 miles long, passing through 22 of the state's 100 counties. The highway passes directly through the cities of Hendersonville, Statesville, Lexington, Asheboro, Siler City, Raleigh, Rocky Mount, Tarboro, and Manteo, as well as more than fifty smaller towns and named crossroads. We had scheduled at least eight stops every day for the next four days, ending with a visit to the beach at Whalebone, east of the town of Manteo.

My voice was nearly gone at the outset. I had had a pretty bad cough, a fever, and bronchitis for several days. The travel and constant appearances now made the cough almost constant. We traveled in a large conversion van, with me trying to rest in the back while Barbara wrestled down the twisting mountain roads as we paralleled the wild Nantahala River through Cherokee, Macon, and Jackson, three huge counties whose combined population is fewer than 100,000 very poor people. We stopped at restaurants and EV sites and talked to everyone we could stop. I kept a terse diary of the trip; here are some excerpts:

Day 1: October 31

- Up at 6, working on emails. Lots of good news on media coverage; people are giving us good coverage on the "Back Roads and Small Towns" tour.
- 8:10 A.M.: We head for the "early voting" site beside the Courthouse (Murphy is the seat for Cherokee County). No action at the EV site, so we plant a sign and head on.
- 10:20 A.M.: We had been on US 64 about five minutes before getting lost, and ended up on US 74. Took NC 141 to get back on track and arrive in Franklin about 20 minutes late. I talk to the owner and her terrific kid Cole at the Main Street Coffee Shop. Talk to two other guys, who gladly take cards and talk for a moment. Then we head over to the EV site, but no one is early voting. Still a little cold in Franklin. Back in the LPV and on to Brevard.
- 12:50: Getting into Brevard, late. Wow! US 64 was a snaky road between Franklin and Brevard. The LPV is a 7k lb E150 conversion van, with the suspension of a dirigible. Poor Barbara was often having to fight off trucks to the left and rocks to the right. Beautiful, though. Just beautiful. Several large waterfalls and lakes. What a great state, unless you are driving.

- We go to the EV site, and talk to quite a few folks. Some take the literature, some walk by, and several stop to chat and ask questions. A beautiful day. . . .
- Finally to the Day's Inn. The clerk lady was very excited to meet a Gov candidate, and demanded an immediate stump speech. I was tempted to say, "We stand for more regulation of hotels!" but instead tried to give her a decent performance. She promised a 6:30 wake-up call, which did NOT happen.

Day 2: November 1

- 7:32 A.M.: Some darned fool is knocking on my door, hard. HOLY KAPOWSKI! It's 7:32 A.M. We are supposed to LEAVE at 7:30. I didn't get my wake-up call. Yikes! Shower/shave/etc. in 7 minutes, outside in 12 minutes, coughing like a fool from this cold I can't shake.
- 8:48 A.M.: Barbara has made up some time, since US 64 in this area is flatter and straighter. BUT . . . there is a 5k race going on. And Bertha (our GPS) is telling us to take a route that is blocked.
- 10:30 A.M.: Mocksville, the EV site. Lots of people coming in to exercise their right to vote and doing it early, too. A very nice guy, a Marine vet, is there stumping for McCain. And a nice lady is there for Obama and the Dems. We all talk to the good citizens of Davie County, and a lot of them stop to talk to us for a minute which is nice. Several say they are Libertarians and several more say they were impressed with the debate. We hand out rack cards until we have gone through the fistful we brought with us from the van.
- 12 noon: Lexington Barbecue, Lexington. A visit to Yumtown. I hand out a few rack cards, and the manager comes out and very nicely asks me not to bother the customers. Not a problem at all; this is private property, and I am confident he would tell ANYONE to stop bothering the customers. Then, the OWNER comes out and tells me he voted a straight L ticket.
- 4:30 P.M.: Pittsboro. By the time you get 20 miles west of Siler City, and then for a very long way, US 64 has gone all corporate and refined. We resolve to take the local "alternate" 64 on Sunday. We talk to some Obamaniacs at the Pittsboro courthouse roundabout, and they say they have gotten a couple of "you should be shot!" or "I'd rather shoot myself than vote for Obama," but that most people are at least polite. And I would say they are more than polite. While I am talking to them, 20 cars pass, and at least 15 of them blow their horns and/or yell, "Yay!" or some such. We hit the EV site, and the entire Pittsboro power structure is out there in its machine-like glory. The mayor, two councilpersons, and several other folks, all Dems. They jump on people who get out of cars like (friendly) vultures, giving them the information that they will need to vote correctly. All part of the service. I talk to three or four voters, who are (like elsewhere) surprised and pleased to see a Gov candidate in person.
- 7 P.M.: A barbecue dinner at the BBQ Lodge. Another visit to Yumtown. I have the catfish, since I had pork for lunch. Then I made a speech to the assembled faithful. Thanks, folks, for coming out. We had a good 20 people there ready to make things happen for the cause of Liberty in NC and the US. They have really done a lot of good work in this campaign, and my thank you is heartfelt. I hope

they know how special they are. Then, home to sleep in my own little-used bed. Still can't shake this cold. I'm coughing like a nut. Very disturbing.

Day 3: November 2

- 6:45 A.M.: Poor Barbara pulls into my driveway.
- 8:00 A.M., Cracker Barrel: John and Sophie, our newest BFFs, have been there since 7 A.M. A little mix-up about the time change. But they are steadfast. I have the "Mama's Pancakes" breakfast: coffee, two eggs, two sausage patties, and three big pancakes with maple syrup.
- 10:30 A.M., Princeville and Tarboro: No particular place to stop. Tarboro is a very cool little city, with lots of well-preserved ante-Bellum charm. Beautiful. Princeville, on the other side of the Tar River, is an almost all-black community founded by escaped and freed slaves.
- 11:30, Williamston: We stop at the Shamrock Cafe, on US 64 Alternate. Very friendly wait staff, and they let us have a table for quite a while. I get hot tea (this cold is killing me . . .) and peach cobbler; Barbara gets coffee and cheesecake. They are setting up the (as we say in these parts) BUFF-ay for lunch. Fried things of many shapes. A good crowd, mostly the after church crowd. Fine folks.
- 12:30, Plymouth: The Golden Skillet: An absolute archetype. If you want to get in touch with eastern NC, drop by the Golden Skillet at 12:30 on a Sunday morning.
- 3:15 P.M.: Arrived Manteo, after travelling through a whole lot of empty swamp and pine forest, for hours. Boy, is the eastern part of NC big, and unoccupied. Manteo is nice, though. And, the folks at the Front Porch were sure nice, once we found it. (Directions were of the "go to the old Simpson place, though of course that's been torn down, I don't recall the name of the road now, but anyway turn left there, and. . . .")

And, then, it was time for my appointment with destiny: the end of the campaign.

Go Jump in the Ocean: Campaign's End

My plan from the outset had been to jump in the ocean at the end of US 64, at Whalebone. Barbara set up the camera, I put up the "Munger for Governor" sign just for a little extra production value, and we did it. We had to do it in one take. It was windy and 50 degrees in the air and 53 degrees in the water. Brrr. Here is the approximate text of the video we shot, which got picked up by a number of news stations and was later used in more than a few political science classes around the country:

> Hi! I'm Mike Munger, Libertarian candidate for governor here in North Carolina. It's been a long campaign, and I know we are all glad it's almost over. My campaign manager Barbara Howe and I started in Murphy, North

Carolina, and covered every inch of US 64 all across the state. There are two reasons for what I'm about to do. First, we've been travelling a long time, more than three full days, and I'm glad we made it. But more important, third-party candidates in North Carolina have to resort to stunts and begging just to get attention from the media. In particular, two Triangle television stations, WRAL and WTVD, ought to be ashamed of themselves. They denied me the chance to participate in the debates, debates I was qualified for, both legally and professionally. So, it's to make up for the lack of commitment to public service, at WRAL and WTVD, that I am about to take this cold bath. Sure, it's silly, but until the media serve the people, instead of special interests, this is all we've got.

And, then, my appointment with destiny! After I got dried off, and changed clothes, in an utterly deserted beach shower room, we drove the two hours up to Roanoke Rapids for a final dinner at Buffalo Wings and Rings, owned by a supporter and friend. I was coughing as if I had advanced emphysema, and I was more tired than I had ever felt, but it was essentially over. There was still Monday before the election to go, but I had classes to teach and work to catch up on, so the campaign ended here. What a long, strange trip it had been.

Results and Impact

Before dawn on Tuesday, November 4, 2008, several things had become clear. First, the race in North Carolina for both president and governor would be very close. Each race turned out to be the closest in the nation, for any state. Second, the new EV provisions in state law had had a huge effect on the nature of the election, according to the North Carolina State Board of Elections. EV totals reached nearly 75 percent of the *total* votes cast. In terms of partisan affiliation, 51 percent of early voters were registered Democrats, and only 30 percent were registered Republicans. Women comprised 56 percent of early voters, and nearly 27 percent of all early voters were African American in a state in which they comprised 21 percent of the population, many of whom had voted only rarely in the past. All said, then, when the sun rose on November 4, Election Day, 2.6 million North Carolinians had already voted. And, finally, the sun wasn't really going to rise. It was pouring rain when the polls opened at 6:30 A.M., and the rain would continue until nearly the time that polls closed at 7:30 P.M.

It was a long wait until the polls closed. The North Carolina Libertarian Party had arranged a nice spot for the "Victory Party," with music and a projection television for watching the results. We also had a nice spread of food and expected the party to get started about seven that evening. No actual results would be broadcast until after the polls closed, of course, but we kept hoping for rumors. I was edgy and tired, hoping that the late polls showing my totals of 4.5 percent or higher, with one poll as high as 7 percent, might hold up. On the downside, I was worried (terrified is more like it) that I would fail to reach the 2 percent threshold we desperately needed to reach to retain our qualified party status. It was almost inconceivable that the party could again muster the resources to do a signature drive. And given the tsunami of turnout we could all see gathering around us, the signature total in 2012 might well be more than 150,000 gross signatures. We had to get that 2 percent, tonight, or it might well be the end of third parties in North Carolina for the foreseeable future.

My wife (who looked lovely in what she laughingly called her "First Lady" suit) and I (who looked grouchy, because I was) went to the Victory Party about 7:30, arriving after many of the rest of the good folks had already showed up and had a beer or two. We had a small program with a few speeches, thanks, and congratulations, but of course we didn't know if congratulations were really in order yet. About the thanks there can be no doubt. At least a dozen of the people in the room had sacrificed 100 hours or more just in the last stages of the campaign. My thanks to them was heartfelt, nearly tearful. Then we stopped even pretending and just watched the returns slowly roll in from across the state.

From the outset, it was obvious that the late polls showing that Democrat Bev Perdue had pulled slightly ahead were being borne out. She was ahead of Republican Pat McCrory by a small margin as the large urban counties reported in, and the television station reported the third line as "Libertarian Michael Munger—2 percent." Obviously, they were rounding, because it made no sense to carry the figure out to one or two decimals before even half of the precincts were tabulated. But that enigmatic 2 percent was driving me nuts. Was it 1.8 percent? Or 2.4 percent? Unlike the television station, the state board of elections would not round up, not even if the total were 1.999 percent; the law said 2 percent of the total, and one vote less than that would mean all our hopes were dashed, our efforts wasted. As it turned out, the governor's race was in fact the closest in the nation, decided by 140,000 votes. So, too, was the presidential race. It was decided by fewer than 15,000 votes.

Perdue won with just a little more than 50 percent of the vote. But I won too, getting 2.85 percent of the vote. I was disappointed with the results but was still able to take some satisfaction from the fact that the 2 percent goal had been achieved. For the first time, a third-party candidate had participated in televised debates and had won enough votes in a North Carolina governor's race to win the party a confirmed place on the ballot for the next four years. By Sunday of that week, I was coughing so hard and had such a persistent fever that I went to the doctor. She listened to my chest for several minutes, much longer than I had ever seen a doctor use a stethoscope before. Then she went back to write on her pad. I asked, "Do I need some antibiotics?" She looked up, surprised. "Of course you need antibiotics. The only thing I'm trying to decide is whether you should be admitted to the hospital. You don't quite have pneumonia, but you could easily develop it within the next few hours. If you go home, do you promise to rest?" I didn't have to think about it very long. "Yes, I promise. I'll rest."

12

The Perils of
Multicandidate Mayoral Primaries

Aaron Wicks

Type of campaign: Mayoral (primary)

Role of author: Campaign manager

Lessons to look for:

• The rules and procedures under which campaigns operate matter.

• Money matters, and it matters most to challengers.

• Campaigns need both earned and paid media to get their message out.

• Minor parties and minor candidates get minor attention.

Running against a political party's institutional strengths is always an uphill battle. Whether a full-fledged "machine" or simply a haphazard coalition of interests, parties wield powers that individuals simply do not have. They have a brand that is known to the public and the ability to marshal the people, money, and word of mouth needed to assemble voters. And perhaps most important, they possess institutional wisdom—they know the systems and rules of the political game because, quite often, it is the parties who wrote the rules.

But when the party is split and the loyalties of insiders are divided, these powers become greatly diminished. The brand is defined differently by different factions. The activists needed to collect petition signatures and to staff phone banks are pressured by leaders of different factions to support their side. With resources split among the warring factions, the party becomes vulnerable to an insurgent campaign from candidates not usually considered part of the party's leadership group. As a political scientist with experience in local politics, I see situations like these as those rare chances for independent-minded candidates with deep knowledge of the political process to outplay the players and defeat a divided party machine. And as a political scientist who cannot resist a chance to try to out-strategize the insiders, an invitation to join the fray is irresistible.

Such was the case in 2005, when I was invited to join one of three mayoral campaigns then under way in Rochester, New York. That year, Rochester held its first open mayoral election (no incumbent running) in twelve years. With no incumbent for party leaders to back and no heir apparent identified by the outgoing mayor, a struggle for control of the local Democratic Party emerged. Tim Mains, a longtime member of the Rochester City Council, saw it as an opportunity for a "nonaligned" Democrat to win a divided contest. The 2005 mayoral race introduced a tantalizing set of variables for a practicing political scientist: a divided party machine, a charismatic political newcomer, and a local media corps that found itself caught up in the narrative of the very story they were covering. How to manage these variables became a problem that occupied me throughout Mains's long, hard-fought, but ultimately unsuccessful mayoral campaign.

The End of the Johnson Era

To understand the nature of the political divide in 2005, it is important to understand the historic mayoralty that was coming to a close. In 1993, Rochester elected its first-ever African American mayor, William A. Johnson, Jr. Less than thirty years before his election, the city Johnson would govern had been the location of some of the worst urban riots of the civil rights era. And due to its low rate of population turnover, Rochester in 1993 still had a number of people who personally recalled those more troubled times. Johnson's election was therefore viewed by many as a break from the past and an opportunity for the city to heal some old wounds.

Johnson's victory in 1993 was due largely to his ideological moderation and ability to work with business leaders. Both qualities earned him the respect of local elites and a surprising last-minute endorsement of the city's major newspaper prior to the critical Democratic primary. Ironically, Johnson's victory over a crowded field of party insiders was probably his finest moment of political strategy. His governing style was low-key, and he was often faulted by party insiders for being aloof and disengaged from party activities. Johnson served three terms, producing a mixed record of results. Overall, the city retained good fiscal health during Johnson's tenure. However, there were some highly public economic development "failures," including a fast ferry connecting Rochester with Toronto, Ontario. Due to a number of mishaps, Johnson found that by late 2004, the ferry had become not his crowning achievement, but an albatross around his neck.

It was in this setting that community leaders began to look to Johnson to indicate his preferred successor. Many were certain it would be City Council

Member Wade Norwood. An African American one generation younger than Johnson, Norwood had many things going for him. First elected to the Rochester City Council in 1989 at the age of twenty-five, Norwood had clearly demonstrated his electability in several citywide elections. In those sixteen years in office, he had matured into an engaging speaker and someone who would willingly participate in political coalitions (though detractors would point to this as "me too"–ism).

Norwood had an Achilles' heel, however. He was employed in the office of New York state assembly member David Gantt. Although all three men shared prominent positions in the local African American leadership group, Gantt was the political opposite of the other two. Where Johnson and Norwood practiced accommodation, Gantt flourished in confrontation. Where they earned the respect of business and other community leaders, Gantt earned respect of a more "street" variety: the respect that comes from fear of the political reprisals he had the power to pursue if you crossed him. To many white Norwood supporters, the Gantt relationship was a serious concern. On the one hand, it offered a connection to power in Albany that Rochester desperately needed. On the other, it tarnished Norwood's clean image and raised questions about his political independence. In short, his relationship with Gantt risked alienating the support of liberal whites who still wielded a significant amount of influence in the city and whose votes would be needed to win the inevitable mayoral primary.

As some Norwood supporters wrung their hands over his liabilities, an alternative candidacy was emerging. Police Chief Robert Duffy had announced his retirement from the Rochester Police Department and had subtly begun dropping hints about future public service. Duffy supporters even formed a "Draft Duffy for Mayor" committee to build momentum for his impending decision to run. Duffy was a potential candidate straight out of central casting: tall, handsome, and looking like the chief's uniform was custom tailored for him. Duffy had led his department out of a corruption scandal by diligently working to regain public trust. In many ways, he possessed the political skills that outgoing mayor Johnson lacked. He attended virtually every funeral of victims of violence and assiduously courted neighborhood leaders with a personal touch.

It was in this setting that many Rochesterians anticipated a Johnson endorsement of Norwood in late 2004. Yet confounding the party establishment's expectations once again, Johnson pointedly declined to name a successor, instead saying in a newspaper interview that he saw a number of quality candidates and did not feel any particular impulse to interfere in the developing campaign. The race was on.

It became clear by late 2004 and early 2005 that Rochester was going to have a contested race for mayor. Norwood had not yet formally announced his campaign, but he had long ago locked up commitments from several elected officials, party leaders, and other prominent community members. His candidacy was the worst-kept secret in town. The second worst-kept secret was the impending candidacy of Bob Duffy. Although he was going through the motions of "testing the waters," going so far as to send a letter to members of the Monroe County Democratic Committee members asking for their thoughts about a potential candidacy, he was actively raising commitments for support and money and lining up potential endorsements. What became more and more clear throughout this process was that this contest was not simply over the office of mayor. It was also a battle royal for control of the local Democratic Party: On one side was Gantt and his political allies, and on the other side was a coalition dedicated to wresting control of the party from Gantt and putting him and his cronies on the outside for the first time in recent memory.

A third option loomed as well, which had the potential to wreak havoc on the well-laid strategies of the party factions. Veteran city council member Tim Mains was also considering a run for mayor, seeing an opportunity to take advantage of a split between the Gantt and the Duffy/reform factions in the party. Anyone who relishes a challenge and an opportunity to beat the pros at their game would have jumped at the opportunity. And when Mains confided that he was considering entering the race and was asking for my support, I jumped.

And Mains Makes It Three

Although he was not considered the favorite by any of the local prognosticators, Tim Mains had a resume that clearly placed him on the same field as Norwood and Duffy. When he was first elected to Rochester City Council in 1985, Mains became the first openly gay elected official in New York state history and only one of a very small handful nationwide. In his years on council, he earned a reputation as a fiscal watchdog and an advocate for progressive local ordinances, such as a living wage ordinance for city contracts and a lead ordinance to protect children from lead poisoning. As a result, Mains had a reputation for being incredibly strong on matters of public policy and tenacious in his pursuit of his positions.

Mains also had a significant liability. During his current term in office, some party leaders, including some of his own colleagues on city council, claimed a conflict of interest in his service on city council while also working for the city school district (he is an elementary school principal). Council went so far as to pass a local ordinance outlawing joint service as an elected city official and as an employee of the school district. Because the new law affected not only Mains but the tens of thousands of employees of the Rochester City School District, effectively barring them from public service in the city in which they work and live, Mains fought it in the courts. He won, but the victory was a costly one, both financially and politically. Much of the political establishment resented Mains for resisting the law and doing so successfully. He had made it clear to party leaders he would not be easily manipulated by them or go away quietly, as some hoped. Despite his twenty years of demonstrated electoral success and support for party candidates of all stripes, party leaders saw little to gain in backing Mains's mayoral bid. Without their support, it was likely to be a campaign without many operatives who best knew the political process.

Absent support from most party regulars, who were lining up behind Norwood or Duffy, Mains went looking for a team of his own. He approached me at a monthly meeting of the local Democratic Committee but said nothing about the race for mayor, only that he wanted to meet with me over coffee. (I have since learned that all political plans, great and small, start with a meeting over coffee.) At our meeting, Mains asked if I was considering running for office. Having helped manage an insurgent state senate campaign in 2004 and being involved in party activities for a few years, I had developed relationships with several party leaders. Mains suggested I consider the race for city council, but my employment situation at the time made that race—or any such campaign—impossible. We then turned to his political plans: Would he run for city council one more time or make the leap into the mayor's race? It was not his first conversation on the subject. Indeed, I was one of the last of his "inner circle" recruited into the conversation. He had been mulling the issue for some time, getting votes of support and notes of opposition from his friends and advisers. Virtually all agreed that a run for mayor would be a long shot and that it would mean relinquishing his seat on city council. However, city council had become an increasingly unfriendly environment and held few challenges for the long-term incumbent. And, as Mains would say more than once over the course of the campaign, "I *love* a challenge!"

Two Campaigns Before Election Day

Once Mains's inner circle agreed that a race for mayor was challenging but winnable, Mains announced that he needed people to volunteer for some key campaign positions—at least for the purposes of getting an organization in place. As I looked around the room, I saw several people who had experience and knowledge comparable to or exceeding my own, but I also noticed that none of them indicated they could make an open-ended commitment of their time. I saw this as an opportunity to play a major leadership role in a high-profile campaign, and I had to jump at the chance. I approached Tim after the meeting and told him I would be interested in managing the effort. Despite my relative youth, I had detailed knowledge of the process, and I also had a good reputation with some of the key party personnel we would need on our side. Mains later told me that he had hoped I would step forward as I did—though neither of us knew just how big a job it would become. Our early strategy meetings focused on broad campaign planning. The details could wait for later—

the first thing we needed to do was develop a rough plan to navigate the process successfully.

Process matters in politics because all processes are designed and implemented by people. If you know the process and you know the people, you stand at least a fair chance of finding a way to get the outcome you want. Without that knowledge, candidates are vulnerable to the machinations of insiders who will chew them up and spit them out every single time. In this particular contest, the process consisted of three phases: the designation phase, the primary campaign, and the general election campaign. Because Rochester is dominated by the Democratic Party, the general election campaign was of virtually no consequence. Whoever won the Democratic primary would almost certainly win the general election in November. That left us two separate "campaigns" to focus on: the designation campaign, culminating in the party's local designating convention in May; and the primary campaign, culminating in the September primary that would essentially determine Rochester's next mayor.

In New York, political parties are permitted to "designate" their preferred candidates, but other party members can force a closed primary (where only registered party members can vote) to choose the party's candidate for the November general election. Designation is significant because the party's designee has an enormous advantage in support from party members engaging in door-to-door canvassing, collecting signatures for nominating petitions, and just generally talking up the designated candidate. Earning the designation is not necessary, but it sure does help. Designation was determined by a small number of party members (a few hundred) who were members of local Democratic committees. A mix of insiders and activists, this party electorate was small but very plugged in to local politics. They expected to see and hear directly from the candidates. Many of them had already chosen their candidate before the formal announcements, but we knew that a chunk of them might still be persuadable. They were the target of the first campaign.

The second campaign was the primary campaign. A completely different type of campaign from designation, it meant mobilizing several thousand voters and competing for media attention to reach as many voters as possible at the lowest cost. In the 2003 primary contest for city school board, the winner received under 5,000 votes. Even with the unusually heightened interest and participation in this mayoral primary, we anticipated the winner would need fewer than 15,000 votes. The lynchpin in this relatively small electorate was a group of faithful Democratic primary voters. These voters, known as "prime Dems," numbered about 5,000 (depending on how you defined them). More difficult to predict was the larger group of less committed voters whose loyalties were likely to be more fluid and who could just as easily choose not to vote at all. This electorate would be much more focused on themes and attitudes, not the party insiderism and factional issues that would dominate the designation campaign.

We knew immediately that these two campaigns required two very different strategies. The only question was, How could we navigate both successfully as the underdog?

The Underdog Strategy—Divide and Conquer

In strategizing about these two campaigns, we realized two things: (1) Of the three candidates, we trailed the other two in popular support and funding (at least initially); and (2) our competitors and their supporters were on two sides of a divide that split the party in several ways. This latter fact is what helped convince us a come-from-behind win could be possible—if we managed the process effectively.

There were two main party divisions that would shape the race, and we had to plan for both. The first had to do with the political power of Assembly Member David Gantt, which was reinforced by the issue of race. The split between supporters and opponents of Gantt was known to all but seldom discussed. Due to Rochester's painful history of racial division, Gantt's polarizing role was impossible to disentangle from broader racial issues. Gantt's candidate, Wade Norwood, had significant African American support but also a number of powerful white establishment supporters. Duffy, by contrast, drew significant support from working-class white ethnics (the Irish, Germans, and Italians), political reformers, and elites, especially economic and business elites both inside and outside the city. (Indeed, polls would later show that Duffy was actually most strongly supported by a group of people who were ineligible to vote for him—residents of Rochester's largely white suburbs.) Latinos, an increasingly powerful voting bloc in the city, did not have a clear candidate early on, but there were indications that many Latinos were leaning toward Duffy, in part due to long-simmering tensions between the Latino and African American communities in Rochester.

We thought this divide provided Mains with an opportunity. Though white, Mains had successfully been elected citywide four times, so his electoral viability in a diverse electorate was already proven. As an elementary school principal serving a largely Latino and African American neighborhood, Mains had also developed connections with both communities. But we knew the real source of the divide was Gantt. To Gantt supporters, Norwood was the first and only choice—but to opponents (and there were many of them), the question was, Who would be the better leader of the anti-Gantt forces? Mains had conversations with a number of party leaders on this subject, and the news was encouraging: Few would say so publicly, but many were afraid of what would happen if Gantt's handpicked protégé controlled city hall. There was clearly a large "stop Norwood" movement. They acknowledged that Mains was more intelligent and experienced than Bob Duffy, but they also habitually added a statement that would haunt us throughout the campaign: "I like Bob—he's a good guy." They thought he could win.

The second divide was an unusually fractured gay community. Mains needed all the support he could get. Rochester's gay community was an important part of his electoral base; divisions in that community would be even more of a strategic challenge than Gantt and his organization. Since Mains's first election twenty years previously, the gay community in Rochester had matured into a broad political force with money, institutional knowledge, and a tightly integrated social network. Although Mains was the first, he was not to be the last openly gay elected official in Rochester. And many unelected but important and influential party members also belonged to this constituency. The problem for us was those gay leaders wanted to win, and they simply did not believe Mains could defeat both Norwood and Duffy. As a result, those gay leaders ended up supporting the highly popular Duffy. But those who read the strategic landscape as we did supported Mains.

So, our strategy was clear. We would use the designation phase to stay alive and earn credibility. We would appeal to insiders by emphasizing Mains's experience, knowledge, and reputation for being an honest broker. With a divided party emerging from this designation phase, we would then compete in the primary, rising above the partisan disputes to promote Mains as the candidate of experience, humor, and a deep and solid policy portfolio. It was a risky strategy because it relied on an ugly campaign between the Norwood and Duffy forces— a public airing of the party's dirty laundry that would permit the clean candidate to rise above the others.

We soon discovered that even a brilliant strategy can fall victim to a phenomenon.

The Designation Campaign

Step 1: Filling Committee Spots

We knew that winning the designation was a virtual impossibility, but we also knew that it would be our best chance to demonstrate our organizational power and therefore our potential to be a competitive force in the September primary. The Duffy team also knew that designation would be difficult, though not impossible. The advantage they had was one of very low expectations. Wade Norwood was the odds-on favorite to win designation, particularly among the insiders. All Duffy had to do was make a respectable showing. For Mains, expectations were even lower. We found, though, that low expectations or not, the Duffy and Norwood campaigns were taking the designation phase as seriously as we were. We all had a great deal to gain from a good showing in May.

As we approached the designation phase, we pored over maps and committee lists to plot our strategy. The city of Rochester is broken into ten committees known by the number of county legislative districts that they incorporate. Due to variation in size in these legislative districts (LDs), some committees were small and others were quite large. For example, LD6 and LD7 together formed one committee with less than 20 members. By contrast, LD21 had over 100 members. Altogether, these committees contained close to 700 active Democrats who would cast a vote at the May convention. Those votes would determine the party's designation.

The vote in May was a "weighted" vote. That meant that each committee member cast not one vote per person, but a "weight" that was assigned to the district they represented on their committee. Weights were determined by a formula that factored in the turnout of Democratic voters in the most recent gubernatorial election. Areas with high Democratic turnout had higher weights; areas with lower turnout had lower weights. That was an important factor, because the Democratic candidate for governor in 2002 had been H. Carl McCall, the first African American to run for the highest office in New York state. His candidacy was not particularly energetic statewide, but it did generate significant turnout in the African American parts of the city of Rochester. As a result, those districts had a much higher weighted vote relative to other parts of the city in the 2005 designation contest for mayor. Also, the LDs consisting of those areas were more likely to be under Gantt's influence.

Luckily for the candidates, many seats on those committees were vacant in early 2005. If we could fill committees with supporters, we could count on their votes. And if we put supporters on committees with higher-weighted seats, we could magnify our vote even further. These vacancies were the low-hanging fruit of the designation campaign, so we focused on them right from the start.

Filling a vacant seat on a committee required only that the applicant be a registered Democrat and live in the state assembly district that contained the seat (you can see how having some insider knowledge of rules and process can help in the early stages of a campaign—details like these matter!). Generally speaking, people could be added to a committee by simply providing their information to that committee's leader and having that leader add the person at the monthly meeting of all county committee leaders. As usual, there were some catches. Some leaders, because of their declared allegiances or the way they ran their committees, were not approachable. Most leaders, however, were caught in the crossfire of a potential intraparty war and had little interest in alienating one side or another. Thus six or seven committees had real opportunities to add supporters.

For about two weeks, I became obsessed with the party registration of every single person I knew. I thought about friends, fellow firefighters from the firehouse where I volunteered, work colleagues, neighbors, and anyone else I could potentially approach to make my unusual request. If people I knew were registered Democrats and resided in areas that made them useful to us, I asked if they would be willing to be appointed to a Democratic committee in order to vote for Tim Mains during designation season and again at the May convention. The request always received a confused look and a request to repeat the information. No real surprise: It turns out very few people follow politics at this level of detail. Our campaign team did the same. We maintained a central database into which we entered names and addresses and potential committee assignments. We even identified the specific seat we would request on those committees—obviously, the seats with the highest weighted vote. As you might imagine, it was precisely the strategy of the Duffy and Norwood campaigns as well.

To succeed in our effort, we had to factor in the varying personalities of Democratic committee leaders. Two leaders—Calvin Lee of LD25 and Ronnie Thomas of LD22, were almost completely unapproachable. They were solid allies of Gantt and solid supporters of Norwood. We made a salutary effort with them but did not put much hope in it. By contrast, the leader of LD24 was a longtime party activist named Sue Gerling, the leader of my committee and someone with whom I had worked closely. Although I later found out that she supported Duffy, she believed in running an open committee. If our campaign got names to her first, she would do her best to place our friends on the committee. Her committee was one of our most successful in terms of placing new members. Overall, we felt cheered by our efforts. Our information regarding new appointees indicated that we were placing new members at a rate that made us very much competitive with Norwood and Duffy. We were still in the game, and Duffy and Norwood could see it. Their knowledge of our strength was important because part of our credibility would rest on the members of their campaigns acknowledging the threat we posed and, in moments of inattention perhaps, sending that information to the media.

With the project to fill committee seats nearing completion, the campaign turned to the actual business of the designation phase: locking down commitments from committee members to support us, both at their designation caucus meeting as well as at the May convention. The designation caucus meetings that each committee held a month before the convention were very important to us. In order to be nominated at the convention, a candidate had to win 15 percent of the total vote in these designation caucus meetings. (Oddly, this vote was *not* weighted; it was one person, one vote.) Without clearing that threshold, we would be shut out from the convention, and the hill we had to climb would become infinitely steeper. We divided our efforts in two at this point. The candidate focused on identifying our campaign themes, developing our branding, and calling committee members personally, while the campaign staff worked to develop literature, raise money, and coordinate the candidate's appearances during designation season. This division was not as clean-cut as a campaign manager would like. I found out that managing a candidate like Tim Mains was both an exceptional honor and an energy-draining chore. Because Mains was so experienced, having run every aspect of various local campaigns in the past twenty years (including his own), he had a knowledge base that none of us had. It would have been foolish not to tap into it. But as most candidates find, simply allowing a group of volunteers to package you like laundry soap and talk about you like a product is not easy. You want to be involved; you want to have some control over how people are planning to present you to the public. And when those calls to committee members grow dreary, you find as a candidate that talking strategy is much more interesting.

Mains also had a propensity for graphic design, having previously designed his own campaign literature. He was fond of a blue-green color that had been his trademark in previous campaigns. For this race, we advised him to select a color that had a bit more gravitas, a maroon hue that had a stately, serious quality to it. (Yes, campaigns actually do debate issues as minute as these!) Mains was not completely sold but acquiesced to the will of his advisers. When the campaign literature arrived one afternoon and the elegant maroon we picked out looked a little darker than we expected, Mains let loose with a rare expletive: "It's f—ing brown! I can't believe this . . . it's f—ing brown." At the time, it seemed the campaign could not sustain another frustration. Mains was tired from a full-time work schedule as a school principal and a full-time evening and weekend job as a candidate. The ups and downs of personal commitments of support (some of which would never materialize) and concerns about keeping plans on track for the primary were extremely trying. If I had one strength as a manager, it was that I tended to be a little more even-tempered than the candidate. My comanager at the time (he took care of issues during the day when I was unable to due to my work schedule) spoke with the printer and smoothed things over. We were able to laugh about it later, but only after the printer grudgingly agreed to a reprint of the letterhead order.

This "literature affair" illustrates the challenge of managing a campaign when the candidate is himself an excellent campaign manager. Drawing clear lines of responsibility and keeping everyone focused on their task become much more difficult. Although campaign staff were very respectful of my efforts, they also knew that the candidate was the ultimate court of last appeal. Mains did a good job of not creating organizational chaos around this point, but it came at a cost. His efforts to maintain constant contact with his management team kept us all on the same page but also took valuable time away from those tasks that only a candidate could perform (i.e., asking committee members for votes and asking donors for money). How Mains found time to do both was a testament to the incredible stamina he needed to juggle these activities.

Step 2: The Caucus Meeting Traveling Road Show

One benefit of the designation phase was its very small, easily accessible electorate. Not only did we have the names, addresses, and phone numbers of every person who would be voting, but also we knew we would see almost every one of them personally at a designation caucus in the month preceding the convention. March and April therefore became a veritable concert tour for candidates, who appeared before one committee one week and another the next. In that way, committee members could see and hear from all three candidates at once and take their measure side by side, in person. We felt good about these meetings. Norwood would do well, but we knew Duffy might get a mixed reception because some longtime Democrats might not welcome his "Johnny-come-lately" entry into the Democratic Party. Until 1992, Duffy had been a registered Republican. He didn't register as a Democrat until 1993. Nor was Duffy ever active on the Democratic Committee.

As noted previously, committees varied dramatically in size, composition, and culture. The Northwest Democrats (a group of three committees in northwestern Rochester) tended to be more conservative, working-class, and white. They met at a local bar, and their meetings were notoriously noisy and somewhat chaotic. By contrast, the Southeast Democrats, a larger assemblage of three committees in Rochester's southern and eastern neighborhoods, were also largely white but tended to be a bit more middle-class and professional in orientation and more liberal than their northwestern peers. The Southeast Democrats met in an old fraternal organization's meeting room with only a small cash bar down the hall. The remaining four committees were led by some of the city's most prominent African American and Latino leaders and had membership that drew heavily from those communities. These committees varied greatly in their style. In the LD27 Committee, headed by city council member Adam McFadden, members expected their leader to guide them, but they also showed independence in their voting, providing an opening for candidates to compete for and win votes there. By contrast, in LD22, headed by an extremely close ally of Assembly Member David Gantt, there was a tradition of listening to candidate presentations in stony silence and then voting unanimously for one or more candidates of Gantt's choice. If you did not have Gantt's support going into the meeting of the LD22 Committee, you could expect that even the most eloquent speech would not be able to earn you a single vote.

For a budding political operative like me, the caucus meetings were absolute heaven. They were nerve-wracking and stomach-churning, but they were also everything you could ask of politics. For two hours, in a small room, a who's who of city politics would gather: candidates, party activists, members of the media, and a number of past and present elected officials. Where national politics can sometimes seem like a cynical and money-driven pursuit, politics at the local level still has that back-slapping, unpolished quality that makes it somewhat endearing. If you ever want to see, hear, and feel politics in action, this is the place to do it. Committee meetings are almost a zoological ideal: political animals in their natural habitat.

For the Mains campaign, these designation meetings proved to be a bit of a cliffhanger. We did well in the committees we expected to, particularly in the southeastern committees, and we were completely shut out in the dreaded

LD22. But when it was all over and the votes were cast in these designation meetings, we had reached our goal. We just cleared the 15 percent threshold and would be able to go to the convention.

Step 3: The Convention

Given the prominence of the mayoral contest and the number of people expected to attend, the local party elders decided to rent out the downtown arena, the War Memorial, for the convention. As a representative of the campaign, I joined two of my peers from the other campaigns to tour the facility and get briefed on the ground rules: Balloons were prohibited (they are almost impossible to remove from the cavernous ceiling), tables would be set up for campaign volunteers to greet their supporters, and banner positions in the arena would be awarded through random draw. This random draw was one of our few early victories. We used it to place our campaign banner over the main entrance to the arena. People would not see it when entering the arena but would see it as they exited, and it was squarely in the line of sight of the stage, something we thought might just stick it to the other campaigns. Campaigns definitely look for little things like this to make their competitors feel off-balance and slighted.

Like national party conventions, this local convention was little more than a scripted coronation. All three campaigns knew going into the event that Norwood would win the designation, Duffy would finish second, and Mains would finish third. What was not fully known, at least not to the members of our campaign, was just how many votes each candidate would get. It was like a political party taking a controversial bill to the floor of a legislature. We had an estimate of the vote based on commitments, but whether those commitments would materialize was anyone's guess.

When the votes were in, the news was good for Duffy and for Norwood but bracing for our team. Norwood had indeed won the designation, but only with a bare majority of the vote. Duffy finished a very strong second, only about ten points behind, proving he was organized and running well among party loyalists. Mains finished a distant third, farther behind than we had hoped. Although we knew we could not win at the convention, we had hoped to finish a stronger third or maybe even second. Instead, Norwood would win the headline as the party's designee, Duffy would be the subheadline, and our candidate would get a mention in the story's closing paragraph.

We were still alive, but it was not an encouraging end to the first phase of a tough campaign season.

Petitioning Season

Between the designating convention and the September primary lay a political purgatory of sorts (i.e., the petitioning season). All candidates, even party-designated ones, had to gather petition signatures to gain ballot access. Nominating petitions, though, are nothing like those petitions you often see people passing around at large public gatherings for some political cause. In New York state, nominating petitions have to be signed by a registered Democrat who lives in the jurisdiction. They have to be witnessed personally by the person passing them, and they must be the only petition signed by that particular person. If someone signed a Norwood or Duffy petition and then signed one for Mains a week later, our signature would be ruled invalid and would not count. Even worse, if one of our volunteers made an error in witnessing their petition sheet or not signing and dating it properly, the whole sheet of signatures could be ruled invalid. In this part of the campaign, organization and detail mattered. Most of all, getting people out on the streets day after day to get those signatures was of critical importance. The bottom line was this: New York state election law required 1,000 valid signatures for a citywide office. Without those 1,000 signatures, the campaign would be over.

In reality, we knew we needed well over 1,000, perhaps 1,200 to 1,500, signatures in order to be confident we would make the ballot. Why the extra signatures? Because the other campaigns and any citizen had the right to scrutinize every signature and challenge its validity. Even an experienced petitioner could expect that some percentage of his or her signatures would be ruled invalid for any number of reasons. That meant the one-month window for collecting signatures would demand at least 400 signatures a week, a tall order for a campaign that had a limited number of foot soldiers. Norwood's designation meant he had a huge asset in the designation period. Most of the Democratic Committee members would be taking nominating petitions door-to-door for him and other designated candidates throughout the city of Rochester to gain the requisite 1,000 signatures to qualify for the ballot. As for us, we had to recruit and educate our own volunteers on the process of collecting petition signatures.

The logistics of petition season were extremely complex, but I was fortunate to have the help of an experienced hand, Rochester school board commissioner Shirley Thompson. Thompson's participation in and later comanagement of the campaign were an interesting twist in my political life. When I first became active in politics, I knew Thompson only from a distance and had been led to believe by others that she was a bit aloof and part of an uncooperative party faction that was obstructing school board business. To the contrary, she was warm, genuine, and perhaps the hardest-working member of the campaign, other than the candidate himself and his partner. That proved to be an important lesson in my political education: Always make your own judgments about people, because what others would have you believe about them is always going to be slanted by their own preferences and political goals. Without Thompson's upbeat attitude and tireless efforts, we might not have reached our petition goal.

We opened petition season following a classic strategy: Hit the high-rise buildings, particularly the ones with a high concentration of elderly residents.

Remember, the key to petitioning is getting to people where they live and when they're home. High-rise apartments with a large senior population are a petitioner's dream. It also carries a pitfall: Management often discourages "solicitors," including petitioners (this is of dubious constitutional merit, but an angry landlord does not usually entertain constitutional arguments). Needless to say, we sent our most assertive—and stealthy—volunteers to these locations to gather as many signatures as they could before they got chased out.

As the petition season approached its end, we realized we were falling short of our goal. Even the most dedicated volunteers have lives to lead—lives that tend to get a little busy during June and July. Fortunately, we had been monitoring our progress closely and knew how much of a last-minute push was needed. The candidate, his partner, and a handful of key volunteers grabbed stacks of lists of voter names and neighborhood maps and fanned out across the city for those last few signatures. In the end, we submitted just over 1,200 petitions, fewer than we wanted but enough to feel comfortable that we would make the ballot. Not surprisingly, the Duffy and Norwood campaigns also submitted more than enough signatures. All three of us had survived this phase and would move on to the primary in September.

Or so we thought. The three campaigns made a judgment error that would come back to haunt all of us. A previously unknown candidate, a young man named Christopher Maj, had also submitted petitions in sufficient numbers to make the primary ballot. Under normal circumstances, one or more of the campaigns would have targeted Maj's petitions for scrutiny, hoping to knock him off the ballot. But in this case, the campaigns were either too tired, too fixed on one another, or too dismissive of Maj's chances to do so. If no one formally challenges those signatures, they stand, even if all 1,000 are from Mickey Mouse. No one challenged Maj, and he made the ballot. It was now technically a four-person race, meaning more competition for media and a lot less predictability with this unknown number of people now in the race. Our campaign did not need that challenge. We messed up.

The Campaign's Dirty War: Third-Party Nominations

While designation and petition activities were in full swing, a dirty battle was raging in the background, one that the media did not follow but that could have blown the lid off the campaign had they done their job. In New York state, unlike most states, candidates are permitted to receive the endorsement of more than one party in an election. For Democrats, that usually means trying to gain the endorsement from the Working Families Party (a party largely supported by labor unions) and the Independence Party (a third party founded by billionaire Tom Golisano that tends to be fairly moderate in its endorsements, supporting Democrats and Republicans at about equal rates). Neither of these third parties would draw a huge number of votes in November, but securing their endorsement would be an indication of strength going into the Democratic primary in September. They were an endorsement of credibility. But even more than that, gaining their endorsement meant a candidate would be on the ballot in the November election. The early word had been that the Independence Party was already in the bag for Duffy. Nevertheless, we decided to pursue it anyway, if only in the hope that perhaps our information was incorrect. It was not. Duffy won the nomination.

The Working Families Party proved to be the epicenter of a battle royal that sent shockwaves all the way to the state capitol in Albany. Mains had long been a friend of labor and drew many supporters from the labor movement. When the local Working Families Party caucus met and voted for Mains, we were elated. We planned to tout the endorsement as a signal of our strength and our commitment to the race. Some political wags, most of them doing so on behalf of the other campaigns, had been openly speculating about whether Mains was "really" going to run all the way through the primary. We knew this was an effort to reduce our credibility, and it took its toll. We thought the Working Families endorsement could be a game-changer for us.

But just as we were beginning to plan the press event, we received word that the party's Albany leaders had asked the local party to reconsider its vote. Our hearts sank, and we guessed what had happened. The Norwood campaign had used its most powerful weapon, Assembly Member David Gantt, to call in some favors from Albany. Given Gantt's seniority in the state legislature and the tendency of unions to stay on the good side of the powerful and connected, the Albany leadership decided that perhaps Norwood was the safer bet. After several days of back-and-forth discussions, we eventually got the good news: The local party was standing firm, and the state leadership was grudgingly yielding to its decision.

After this episode, the victory felt somewhat hollow. The endorsement made the local news, and it also meant that Duffy and Mains would be on the ballot for certain in November. For Norwood, the primary was his one and only shot at winning. But in reality, that was the case for all of us. No one expected a third-party candidate to win in November. The primary was going to be the whole ball of wax.

The Primary Campaign

With the primary phase under way, we reviewed where we were and our strategy. The designation phase had not been as successful as we needed it to be. We had survived and were still considered credible, but there was clearly a "buzz" around Duffy, and Norwood was seen as the man to beat. Mains was still too often the final sentence of each news story, as in, "Also running for the Democratic nomination is Councilman Tim Mains."

We were also dismayed that the war we witnessed in the party during the designation phase had not emerged publicly. It was clear to us that the Duffy camp was extremely disciplined. They said nothing negative about anyone in public. Even though their operatives seethed when they thought about city hall machinery under the control of Gantt and his minions, they kept these comments to themselves. And Duffy was the master of positive messaging. He never once strayed from his script. It was simply impossible to paint him as a proxy warrior in a battle for control of the party. No one would believe it.

That created a huge problem for our campaign. Duffy was an irrepressibly optimistic candidate. If you presented bad news, like Rochester's 40 percent child poverty rate, he tilted his head to the side and talked about his hope for the future. Even Rochester's unusually high murder rate, a rate that often made it the most violent city in New York state, and something you would think would make the former police chief vulnerable, did not reduce Duffy's popularity. Again, he talked about attending too many funerals and wiping away too many tears. Suburbanites saw Duffy as sharing their disgust with urban crime, and many city residents saw Duffy as a compassionate healer on these issues. Plus, Norwood and Mains, both twenty-year veterans in city council, were easily seen as political insiders. Duffy was the fresh outsider with boundless energy and hope.

At one point, we even lamented the fact that Duffy was significantly taller than Mains, yet another factor we could not overcome. In fact, I once joked that if Duffy wanted to seal his victory over Mains, all he had to do was pat Mains on the head as one would pet a dog. It would endear Duffy even further as a happy jokester, and it would completely marginalize Mains. Thankfully, Duffy resisted this temptation.

So the challenge was this: How do you run against someone with inexplicably wild, but not firmly established, popularity? It is a classic question for political challengers taking on incumbents and for any underdog taking on a better-known, better-funded candidate. In our case, the Mains team agreed on the following:

1. Despite Norwood's designation, the real challenge was Duffy. He soaked up the media attention, and we had to move our candidate into his spot to grab some of the media spotlight.
2. Negative attacks were not going to work for us. Most people would not believe that Duffy would do anything underhanded, and negative attacks on his policy statements would be deflected by his ebullient optimism.
3. A traditional policy-oriented campaign would not break through in the media. They loved the Duffy story. The only thing that could compete would be something else new and compelling.
4. Our strength was still Mains's experience, class, and integrity. We had to find a way to leverage that in the final days leading to the primary.
5. And finally, without a significant amount of free media, we were going to be utterly lost in the shuffle between Norwood and Duffy. Lacking the

money to compete on television and radio, we needed the news media to carry our message for free (and given number 3 above, it wouldn't be easy).

With these five concepts providing the boundaries for our planning, we plotted strategy around two areas: a series of debates that would lead up to the September primary and a series of policy announcements that would gain us some media attention and hopefully allow us to steer the conversation to our strength: policy.

The Debates

Points 1 and 2 made debate strategizing difficult. Although we believed Duffy was the candidate to beat, Norwood was no slouch. He was intelligent, articulate, and a solid debater. We knew Norwood would also be targeting Duffy, but we also suspected that he had a similar reluctance to be overtly negative. So, how do two candidates take on one foe in a debate without coming off as ganging up on him and sounding shrill? And, since we knew policy alone would not carry the day, we struggled trying to find the right tone, themes, and facts that would make Mains look like a leader striding ahead, while the others trailed far behind. Our best bet was for the debates to contain something that Duffy could not control or predict—a variable that might catch him unprepared or that might throw him off his game. When that happened, Duffy would repeat himself, talk in circles, and come across as tired. With the right surprises, Duffy could finish a debate looking defeated—an image we needed to contrast with Mains's knowledge, persistence, and experience. Our bet was a long shot, but it was all we had.

In any normal election year, the Republican candidate for mayor would receive little or no attention. Republicans have not held a citywide elective office in Rochester in years, and no one genuinely expected 2005 to be different. Nevertheless, Republicans made a spirited effort by nominating local defense attorney John Parrinello. Parrinello is perhaps the most well-known defense attorney in Rochester, in part because of his courtroom skills, but also because of his ability to draw media attention to his causes. Of the Democratic candidates, Duffy was likely the one who had the most to lose with Parrinello in the race. Parrinello harbored a deep, visceral antipathy for Duffy due to the prosecution of some Rochester Police Department officers that Parrinello had defended in which Duffy earlier in his police career had played a major role. In Parrinello's eyes, they had been railroaded by a Rochester Police Department administration intent on finding a scapegoat, and Duffy was complicit in the episode. For my part, I had no idea whether Parrinello had a valid beef with Duffy, but I was happy to have him turn his fire on Duffy and not my candidate. In politics, this is true: The enemy of my enemy is my friend.

In joint appearances at several community meetings, Parrinello was sharp and loud in his attacks on Duffy. At first we thought they might dent Duffy's polished image by giving people doubts about his character and a campaign that offered little in the way of substantive policy. Failing that, we hoped Parrinello might throw Duffy off balance and lead to a blowup. Duffy's big advantage was his calm, upbeat demeanor. If Parrinello could show him to be thin-skinned and irritable, Duffy might start to look mortal—and beatable.

Given these calculations, our campaign and the Norwood campaign both argued for including Parrinello in televised debates leading up to the September primary. But since Parrinello was a Republican candidate and not a Democrat, it created an interesting dilemma for the local media. Parrinello would not appear on the ballot until November; the "real" election would be in September when Democrats selected their candidate. As local news stations began to plan candidate debates, the big question was this: Should Parrinello be included or not?

Unfortunately for us, most stations opted to include only the Democratic candidates in their September debates. Though they knew very well that the September election was the only one that mattered, they reasoned that the debates prior to the Democratic primary should include only Democrats. The Duffy campaign was also promoting that argument—and although it certainly had internal logic, it simply did not reflect political reality. Several local organizations had held candidate forums that included all candidates, based on the logic that public attention was at its height prior to the Democratic primary and that all the candidates should debate each other at once so voters could compare them with one another.

The local public television station, to its credit, took the approach that all candidates on the ballot should participate in their debate. Although this included long-shot Chris Maj, it also meant Parrinello would be at the table to get under Duffy's skin. But what started out as a plus for us quickly fell flat. The format also called for "average citizens" to sit at the table with the candidates. The idea was to simulate a sort of "conversation" among voters and candidates, with minimal moderation. This took time away from the candidates and also made Parrinello slightly less willing to savage Duffy as much as we expected. Worse than that, the format ended up playing right into Duffy's hands. While Parrinello launched muted attacks on Duffy and Mains tried to answer voters' questions directly, Duffy went into full schmooze mode. Duffy danced around substance as he sounded his upbeat themes—never responding with any specifics to the voters. And it worked like a charm. The voters at the table—all selected because they claimed to be undecided—seemed impressed with Duffy's platitudes (or so it seemed to me, having witnessed the same phenomenon countless times). By the end of that debate, it was clear: Parrinello or no Parrinello, the only debate format that could possibly work would be one with a moderator with a spine of steel who would call Duffy on his vague answers and make him take a position. It was not likely that our local media were going to morph into Mike Wallace or Chris Matthews anytime soon. That meant the debates would be a total wash—no gloves would be landed on Duffy in these settings.

Great Ideas: Too Bad No One Heard About Them

Perhaps the most frustrating period of the campaign came in the later stages of the primary. Seeking some free media, we decided to unveil some policy proposals that would show the depth of our candidate relative to the others, as well as his ability to go against the grain and take bold positions. As noted previously, we knew traditional policy pronouncements would not be enough. We needed to be bold and throw down the gauntlet to the other candidates. With a little luck, the media coverage would be favorable, and our campaign would be driving the news cycle.

The first of them was a proposal called the Rochester Children's Initiative. Building on an existing program in the area (and a model that had been successfully implemented in several small communities across the country), we proposed an ambitious antipoverty strategy that would connect every single baby born in the city limits with a visiting nurse for the first three years of its life. Poverty in Rochester is an enormous problem. Approximately 30 percent of all residents live below the poverty line, including 40 percent of children under eighteen. It was and remains one of the highest rates of child poverty in the nation. On top of that, the city of Rochester has had a notoriously low high school graduation rate and periodic bursts of youth violence. The Rochester Children's Initiative would speak directly to these statistics in a way the other Democrats were not.

We unveiled the children's plan at a press conference at a neighborhood recreation center on a rainy day. The media turnout was low, and the coverage was superficial. A few weeks later, we tried again with a tax proposal, the Pioneer Tax Plan. On the surface it was a policy only a tax policy wonk would love, but we soon found that when people took a moment to understand it, virtually everyone stood back and said, "Wow, that's a really good idea. That could actually work!" The plan was designed to spur economic development within the city. It was based on a quirk in the city tax code that taxes commercial property at twice the rate of residential property (which is taxed at the "Homestead rate"). We proposed that any significant investment in a commercial property in the city would be taxed at the lower, residential rate for twenty years, thus providing an incentive for commercial growth in the city at no cost to the taxpayers. Unfortunately, the media did not give the Pioneer Tax Plan nearly the attention it needed to catch on. One two-minute story would not do it justice. And when the competing candidates failed to engage the policy, the media assumed it was now old news and moved on to other stories.

Looking back, the major mistake we made was not properly preparing the press for these stories. We hadn't cultivated any of the local reporters in any consistent way, feeding them information and giving them a regular narrative to help them frame their coverage. What I have since learned about the media is that they tend to be fairly lazy and, with only a few exceptions, are not terribly curious. Instead, reporters and their producers and editors liked "easy-to-gather news." The easy story was the upstart, optimistic Duffy against the party favorite Norwood. It was the story the media covered. To derail this narrative, we would have had to present an alternative and equally easy story. But what narrative would be credible? A Duffy scandal? Not likely. Catching Duffy in a contradiction? The Norwood campaign tried that by subtly pushing the fact that Duffy, the big booster of the city, sent his own children to a private school. But the story went nowhere. The school was a parochial school, and Duffy explained his children's attendance there as part of a "family and faith tradition." Who would begrudge a family their faith and their traditions? Late in the campaign Norwood attempted a harder edge, blaming Duffy's administration of the police department for the city's recent high homicide rate. But this effort appeared to backfire. The Norwood campaign seemed desperate. Duffy brushed off the criticism without much effort.

An obvious media narrative for us could have been the potential of Rochester electing its first openly gay mayor. This was not a story we considered very seriously. First, Mains was not an "identity politics" practitioner. Yes, he was open about his sexual identity, but he was much more interested in the problems of the city. Indeed, his strength compared to the other candidates was that he knew the city's finances, economic issues, and educational issues better than anyone else. Why not play to those strengths? Equally compelling was the fact that it was known by us early on that the gay community was fractured. And although we and our supporters made appeals to unity, the gay community would not unify in this election. Thus, the obvious alternative narrative—the historic candidacy—would not play politically and would not draw much media attention to our cause.

Given our struggle to find an accessible narrative for the media, it is easy to see why our policy press conferences were flops. The press had no idea where these stories fit into the narrative of the campaign, how they should cover them, or how they would change the horserace they had been covering for so long. To the media, these policy pronouncements were not "game changers," nor were they easy to report, and therefore they did not merit anything more than passing reference.

The horserace, as it turns out, was not close. Of the 20,000 Democrats voting in the city's September primary, Duffy fell just short of a majority in a competitive field, receiving 48 percent of the vote. Norwood was 10 percentage points behind with 38.6 percent. Mains was a very distant third, with just 10 percent of the vote. Although we were congratulated by a number of party insiders for having run a very competitive campaign under difficult circumstances, the loss was still difficult to take. Mains was magnanimous in defeat but clearly stung by the loss. He was someone who thrived on public service and was well versed in both the policy and politics of public life. Some say that there is no shame in losing a well-fought race, but the circumstances involved, including the media inattention, the fawning coverage of Duffy, and the dirty tricks of some party insiders, made the loss feel that much worse. The rejection of voters is something you can only appreciate after you have put your own name or your time and reputation on the line.

Conclusion

Putting together a strategy for a high-profile campaign, even a local one, provides an education on politics that exists in no textbook. Managing volunteers, raising money, developing a communications strategy, organizing voter mobilization, and keeping all these elements together on schedule are monumental tasks. I was fortunate to have several volunteers who gave the better part of their free time for about nine months to help manage a campaign we all believed in.

The experience is difficult to describe. Seeing politics up close is fascinating. Despite the stereotypes of cigar-chewing political bosses and backroom deal making, a great deal of political theater occurs in the open and is fairly accessible for a citizen with some time to give. The vast majority of campaign volunteers are not cynical political operatives who believe in winning at all costs. They are instead friends and colleagues of the candidate, neighbors, students, retirees, and others from the community who, for whatever reason, have decided this candidate is someone they believe in. That genuine desire to give one's time and effort for a candidate is necessary for a democracy to survive and flourish.

But there is also the disappointing side of the process. Invariably, more candidates lose than win, and as I described, losing is painful, no matter the circumstances. And whether you win or lose, the media coverage always feels biased. But the bias is a very human bias, understandable, if not totally excusable. Reporters have deadlines, they have limited understanding of the ins and outs of the people and the policies they report on, and they also cannot help but inject their own perceptions into their stories. If you expect the media to be objective documentarians when it comes to politics, be prepared for perpetual disappointment.

In the end, though, no unsuccessful campaign can legitimately blame the media for its loss. Winning and losing are clear in democracy. It depends on nothing more and nothing less than a simple count of votes. We developed a strategy that we hoped would translate into more votes for our candidate than for the others. Knowing the process—the twisted path from announcing, through the party designation process, through petition season, and then to the September primary—was critical for our campaign's survival. But knowing a process and being able to completely manage it are two very different things.

PART 4
Conclusion

13

The Next Step:
Get Involved in a Campaign

James R. Bowers and Stephen Daniels

That's indeed the question: Where do you go from here? You've vicariously experienced life inside campaigns through these chronicles. You've gone inside all sorts of campaigns, from presidential to local. You've witnessed successful campaigns, along with ones that failed. You've experienced life as a candidate and life as an overworked and underappreciated volunteer. You've seen how money is raised and mud is slung. You've been introduced to a number of important lessons. No doubt you've come up with some of your own. But there's still so much more to learn. Campaigns are a never-ending education—there's always something new to learn.

Every campaign presents new experiences and new lessons that can—and should—be applied to the next one. Stephen Daniels's chronicle in Chapter 3—with its story of a citizen group's activities over a series of elections—reflects that very well. It is a story of learning from success, from failure, and even from opponents and then applying those lessons to advance the group's goals. Chapman Rackaway's chronicle (Chapter 2) is a similar story of learning. He always applied what he learned in one campaign to the next and jettisoned what didn't work. Over the years, he developed tried-and-true campaign methods that he employed for the benefit of his candidates. Richard Hardy's story in Chapter 9 shows how his rich electoral background helped in his run for Congress, especially his experience in running statewide ballot initiative campaigns.

Michael Smith's account (Chapter 7) of volunteering also shows how lessons in one campaign are carried over to the next. Recall that he learned that volunteers, just like candidates, have to stay conscious of and know why they are involved. They have to "keep their eyes on the prize." In his current work at the Kansas City, Missouri, affiliate of the Gameliel Foundation, Smith is doing just that. James Bowers (Chapter 10) also took an important lesson away from his 2007 defeat for city council into the next campaign in which he was involved. Remember that part of the mudslinging in his campaign centered on religion and his opponent's supporters' claim he was an atheist and not "churched." Such a charge was important in his opponent's effort to discourage African American voters from voting for him. In the broadest form, the lesson he learned concerns the importance of understanding the cultural values of the voter group you are soliciting. More simply put, the lesson is "know your voters' values and speak their values." In its most applied, streetwise, or rawest vernacular, the lesson from his 2007 defeat that he'll take into future elections was: Never let your candidate be "out-churched."

Examples of the never-ending process of learning appear in the other campaign chronicles too, but we think you get the point.

Bottom line: In the school of campaigning there's no graduation—it's a continuing education.

Get off the Couch and into the Game

You've started your education in campaigns by reading this book. But you only really learn about campaigns and get the full impact of that continuing education by doing campaigns. Again we ask the question, Where do you go from here? Our answer: into a campaign.

You may already be a political animal. That's a good thing. You may see politics and campaigns as sport. That's fine too. But we're not interested in creating and informing mere campaign couch potatoes or Wednesday morning political quarterbacks analyzing the tapes of the Tuesday Election Day games. All sports, including politics and campaigns, are more fun when they're played. Playing a sport allows you to learn more about it and how the game is actually played. Campaigns are no different. That's why in presenting these campaign chronicles to you, we also have wanted to challenge you, whoever you are—College Democrat or Young Republican, liberal or conservative, Libertarian or Green, feminist or traditionalist, cynic or optimist—to get involved and strive for a higher level of civic engagement. We challenge you to find the interest and motivation to participate in election campaigns beyond your civic responsibility to vote. But we want you prepared for that involvement—for what is to come when you do get involved, how to do what is asked and sometimes not asked of you, and why so many of us who engage in campaigns both love it and hate it at the same time. We want you involved, but with your eyes wide open.

Bottom line: We want you bitten by the Campaign Junkie Bug.

The CJ Bug's bite can be life-altering, a chronic feeling of both pleasure and pain, and an itch constantly needing to be scratched. And therein lies the need for one more brief campaign chronicle.

Yes, Sleezer Is His Real Name

One of us (Bowers) regularly teaches a course in campaigns and elections, normally in even-numbered years to coincide with state and national elections. In 2006 a young fresh-faced student named Jesse Sleezer enrolled in Bowers's class. At the time, young Mr. Sleezer's ambition was to go to law school. He hadn't been bitten by the CJ Bug yet. (For now, we'll hold off with the obvious jokes about the name Sleezer being appropriate for either a lawyer or a politician. Jesse has heard all of them.) But after a semester of reading about campaign strategies, class discussions with local political and campaign notables, a variety of campaign war stories, and Bowers's use of the class to assist him in calculating his 2007 run for the Rochester, New York, City Council, the CJ Bug bit Jesse and the itch was bad.

That summer, rather than go home, Jesse took a job painting dorm rooms at the college for eight dollars an hour and spent his time off working as the student volunteer director for Bowers's city council campaign. As is often the case in campaigns, the position title was more glorious than the actual tasks that went with it. More often than not, it meant that Jesse was his professor's walking companion, canvassing door-to-door, passing out campaign literature, and generally helping Bowers stay motivated to keep walking. Between May and September 2007, Jesse walked most of the district (one-quarter of the city) twice and some neighborhoods three times. He walked in all kinds of weather, from 100-degree humid summer days to rainy, cool, early September evenings. Oh, yes, weekends too!

Over the course of their canvassing, Jesse consumed several pints of locally made Gitano's tangerine Italian ice (the "official ice" of the campaign) and ate a good number of Sam's Masterpiece subs drenched in Boss Sauce. Along the way, he walked through dilapidated neighborhoods with high levels of concentrated poverty. He walked through drug deals. He walked through crime-infested areas where residents warned him to leave before nightfall because they were concerned about his safety. In one relatively well-maintained neighborhood, Jesse was even playfully pelted with apples after some young kids around nine or ten years old asked him if he could catch an apple and he naïvely answered yes. Apple after apple was tossed at him as Bowers, another volunteer, and Jesse walked down the street. The kids only targeted Jesse, leaving the candidate and the young woman canvasser, who also was a former student, alone. After all, Jesse was the one who agreed to catch an apple.

Heat, rain, apples, drug sales, crime, and dilapidated neighborhoods! Jesse took it all in stride. He wasn't from Rochester. He couldn't vote for his professor. He wasn't even getting any college internship credit for his efforts! So why did he keep at it? He stayed at it because he had to scratch the itch. And the scratching felt good. The toxin from the CJ Bug bite was now in his bloodstream, and it made him want to do and learn more. And he did.

Because he got involved, showed up consistently, and demonstrated a good instinct for politics, Jesse was brought into the inner circle of friends and campaign advisers for Bowers's city council run. He attended strategy meetings and eventually assisted in the overall planning of the campaign. And by the end of the campaign, the itch from the CJ Bug bite was so bad that he no longer wanted to be a lawyer—at least not right away. The world of politics, campaigns, and elections had to come first. And so it did. Graduating a semester early, and with some assistance from Bowers and contacts he made through his professor's council campaign, Jesse Sleezer was able to land himself a job in the communications office of the county executive for Monroe County, New York—first as a paid intern and then as a full-time staff person. Along the way, he also became head of the Monroe County Young Republicans. His days are now filled with government, and his nights and weekends, particularly during an election year, are filled with campaigns and all that goes with them, from petitioning to coordinating what candidates do. In 2010 he moved up a notch, coordinating a Republican candidate's campaign for the New York State Assembly against a long-standing Democratic incumbent.

And law school? It remains on hold.

All of this came about for a simple reason: Jesse was bitten by the CJ Bug and got involved. First, he was bitten in a class very much like the one in which you are sitting. Then he was bitten again when he got involved. He learned well the key lessons that come from being inside campaigns. And his education continues.

Have You Been Bitten by the Bug?
Will You Scratch the Itch?

Like Jesse, everyone who contributed to *Inside Political Campaigns* has been bitten by the CJ Bug. Some of us have scratched the itch for many years, often starting right where you are now—where Jesse was just a few years ago—as a college student. All were bitten because, in one way or another, they became involved in campaigns. Only you know if the Campaign Junkie Bug has bitten you. We hope it has because then you're more likely to get involved in campaigns and elections. And that's exactly what we want you to do. As we stated earlier, we're not interested in creating and informing campaign couch potatoes. We want you to be in the game. We want you interested and motivated to participate in election campaigns beyond just voting. But we want you doing campaigns with your eyes wide open. So once again we ask the question: Where do you go from here?

A Note to the Instructor

Depending on how you teach this course, you may choose to use these chronicles in a different order than the one presented in the table of contents. You might find it more useful to order them by the political office that's featured in the chapter. Or you might want to look at them by type of election. There are many great ways to use these stories, so feel free to experiment! Here are some alternative chapter arrangements:

By Office

Local Office

Chapter 3: City council, mayoral, local ballot initiatives
Chapter 8: County district attorney
Chapter 10: City council
Chapter 12: Mayoral

State Office

Chapter 7: State legislative
Chapter 11: Gubernatorial

Congressional

Chapter 5: US House of Representatives
Chapter 9: US House of Representatives

Presidential

Chapter 4: Presidential primary
Chapter 6: Presidential general election

Across Offices

Chapter 2: State legislative, congressional, and others

By Type of Election

Primaries

Local: Chapter 10 (city council), Chapter 12 (mayoral)
State legislative: Chapter 7
Presidential: Chapter 4

General Elections

Local: Chapter 2 (mayoral, city council, ballot initiatives), Chapter 8 (county district attorney)
Gubernatorial: Chapter 11
Congressional: Chapter 5 (US House of Representatives), Chapter 9 (US House of Representatives)
Presidential: Chapter 6

Across Types of Elections

Chapter 2

Further Reading and Viewing

Nonfiction: Academic and Practitioner

Altschuler, Bruce E. 1996. *Running in Place: A Campaign Journal.* Chicago: Nelson-Hall.

Brady, John. 1997. *Bad Boy: The Life and Politics of Lee Atwater.* Reading, MA: Addison-Wesley.

Burton, Michael John, and Daniel M. Shea. 2003. *Campaign Mode: Strategic Vision in Congressional Elections.* Lanham, MD: Rowman and Littlefield.

Craig, Stephen C., and David B. Hill. 2010. *The Electoral Challenge: Theory Meets Practice,* 2nd ed. Washington, DC: CQ Press.

Faucheux, Ronald A. 2002. *Running for Office: The Strategies, Techniques, and Messages Modern Political Candidates Need to Win Elections.* New York: M. Evans.

Fenno, Richard F., Jr. 1992. *When Incumbency Fails.* Washington, DC: CQ Press.

Gaddie, Ronald Keith. 2004. *Born to Run: Origins of the Political Career.* Lanham, MD: Rowman and Littlefield.

Garrett, R. Sam. 2009. *Campaign Crises: Detours on the Road to Congress.* Boulder, CO: Lynne Rienner.

Herrnson, Paul S. 2000. *Congressional Elections: Campaigning at Home and in Washington,* 3rd ed. Washington, DC: CQ Press.

Lentz, Jacob. 2002. *Electing Jesse Ventura: A Third-Party Success Story.* Boulder, CO: Lynne Rienner.

Medvic, Stephen K. 2010. *Campaigns and Elections: Players and Processes.* Boston: MA: Wadsworth Cengage Learning.

Moncreif, Gary F., Peverill Squire, and Malcolm Jewell. 2001. *Who Runs for the Legislatures?* Upper Saddle River, NJ: Prentice-Hall.

Morton, Rebecca B. 2006. *Analyzing Elections.* New York: W. W. Norton.

Semiatin, Robert J. 2005. *Campaigns in the Twenty-First Century.* New York: McGraw-Hill.

———. 2008. *Campaigns on the Cutting Edge.* Washington, DC: CQ Press.

Shaw, Catherine. 2010. *The Campaign Manager: Running and Winning Local Elections,* 4th ed. Boulder, CO: Westview Press.

Shrum, Robert. 2007. *No Excuses: Confessions of a Serial Campaigner*. New York: Simon and Schuster.

Sidlow, Edward I. 2004. *Challenging the Incumbent: An Underdog's Undertaking*. Washington, DC: CQ Press.

Stonecash, Jeffery M. 2008. *Political Polling: Strategic Information in Campaigns*, 2nd ed. Lanham, MD: Rowman and Littlefield.

Swint, Kerwin. 2008. *Mudslingers: The Twenty-Five Dirtiest Political Campaigns of All Time*. New York: Union Square Press.

Watson, Robert P., and Colton C. Campbell. 2003. *Campaigns and Elections: Issues, Concepts, Cases*. Boulder, CO: Lynne Rienner.

Fiction

Anonymous. 1996. *Primary Colors*. New York: Random House.

Brown, Douglas D. 2007. *Ascension: A Novel of Politics*. Bloomington, IN: iUniverse.

Folman, Bill. 2008. *The Scandal Plan: or How to Win the Presidency by Cheating on Your Wife*. New York: William Morrow.

Gorman, Ed. 2008. *Sleeping Dogs*. New York: St. Martin's Press.

———. 2010. *Stranglehold*. New York: St. Martin's Press.

Leher, Jim. 2000. *Last Debate: A Novel of Politics and Journalism*. New York: Public Affairs.

Lundeen, Richard. 2000. *The Madhouse Candidate*. Bloomington, IN: iUniverse.

Mizner, David. 2004. *Political Animal*. New York: Soho Press.

———. 2007. *Hartsburg, USA*. New York: Bloomsbury.

Documentaries

By the People: The Election of Barack Obama. 2009. Directed by Alicia Sams and Amy Rice. Sony Pictures. Culver City, CA.

Chisholm '72: Unbought and Unbossed. 2004. Directed by Shola Lynch. 20th Century Fox Home Entertainment. Beverly Hills, CA.

Our Brand Is Crisis. 2005. Directed by Rachael Boyton. Koch-Lorber. Washington, NY.

See How They Run. 2003. Directed by Emily Morse. Chick Flick Production, Art, and Design. Los Angeles, CA.

Streetfight. 2005. Directed by Marshall Curry. Marshall Curry Production. Broooklyn, NY.

The War Room. 2004. Directed by Chris Hegedus and Da PenneBaker. Universal Studios. Universal City, CA.

Commercial Films

Bob Roberts. 1992. Directed by Tim Robbins. Polygram Film.

The Candidate. 1972. Directed by Michael Ritchie. Warner Home Video. Burbank, CA.

Election. 1999. Directed by Alexander Payne. Paramount Home Video. Hollywood, CA.

Primary Colors. 1998. Directed by Mike Nichols. Universal Home Video. Universal City, CA.

You're Not Elected, Charlie Brown. 1972. Directed by Bill Melendez. Warner Home Video. Burbank, CA.

The Contributors

Kevin Anderson earned a Ph.D. in political science from the University of Missouri and is currently assistant professor of political science at Eastern Illinois University. He teaches courses in American government, African American politics, and classical, modern, and American political thought and is completing work on his first book.

James R. Bowers is professor of political science at St. John Fisher College in Rochester, New York, where he regularly teaches a course on campaigns and elections. He is a longtime political analyst and commentator for Rochester-area media organizations. In 2001 he was elected to the Rochester City School Board (a citywide office) and served one term, declining to seek reelection in 2005. Since his 2007 primary defeat for Rochester City Council, he has remained active in local politics, advising other reform-oriented candidates. *Inside Political Campaigns* is his sixth book. It is his second book with this publisher, the other being *Governing Middle-Size Cities: Studies in Mayoral Leadership,* published in 2000 and coedited with Wilbur Rich.

Stephen Daniels is a research professor at the American Bar Foundation in Chicago, Illinois, and an adjunct professor of political science at Northwestern University. He holds a Ph.D. in political science from the University of Wisconsin–Madison. His research focuses on law and public policy and the various aspects of the US civil justice system. He has written on trial courts, juries, plaintiffs' lawyers, and the politics of civil justice reform—including the areas of medical malpractice, products liability, and punitive damages. He is coauthor (with Joanne Martin) of *Civil Juries and the Politics of Reform,* and author or coauthor of numerous articles in law reviews (e.g., *Texas Law Review, Minnesota Law Review, Vanderbilt Law Review*) and social science journals (e.g.,

Law and Society Review, Law and Policy, Justice System Journal) focusing on law and public policy.

Vladimir Gutman is a 2008 graduate of Northwestern University, where he received a B.A. in political science (with honors). While an undergraduate, he worked as a research assistant at the American Bar Foundation in Chicago, in addition to working in fund-raising for Hillary Clinton's presidential campaign. After graduation, he took a position as deputy Midwest political director for the American Israel Public Affairs Committee (AIPAC). In July 2009, he became the northeastern Ohio finance director for Fisher for Ohio. Lee Fisher is the Ohio lieutenant governor and the Democratic candidate in the US Senate election in 2010.

Richard J. (Rick) Hardy is professor and chair of the Department of Political Science at Western Illinois University. He earned his B.A. from Western Illinois University, his M.A. from the University of North Dakota, and his Ph.D. from the University of Iowa. He has served on the faculties of Northern State University, Duke University, and the University of Missouri–Columbia and has taught courses in American politics, constitutional law, civil rights, the Supreme Court, federalism, state government, policy evaluation methods, and civic leadership. He has received over fifty significant teaching and civic leadership awards and has published or edited seven books.

Jordan McNamara received his B.A. in political science from St. John Fisher College in December 2008. While at Fisher, he took several courses pertaining to campaigns and elections and wrote his senior seminar paper on the presence of the Bradley effect on Barack Obama's 2008 New Hampshire Democratic primary defeat. He is currently a law student at Ohio Northern University College of Law in Ada, Ohio.

Michael Munger is chair of the Department of Political Science at Duke (a position he has held since 2000) and holds teaching appointments in the Department of Economics, the Department of Political Science, and the Sanford School of Public Policy. His current research focuses on both strategic and practical sides of campaign finance and electoral politics in the United States.

Chapman Rackaway is associate professor of political science at Fort Hayes State University (FHSU). He received his Ph.D. in political science from the University of Missouri. Prior to coming to FHSU, he served as department chair of the Political Science Department at Linn State Technical College from 1998 to 2001. His specializations are campaign management, elections, and political parties. He also is the adviser for political science majors at FHSU who are concentrating in the political management track, a unique undergraduate concentration in campaign management offered by the FHSU Department of Political Science.

Tari Renner is currently the department chair and professor of political science at Illinois Wesleyan University. Renner received his M.A. and Ph.D. from American University in Washington, D.C. He has worked for the FBI and the EPA and served as the director of survey research for the International City/County Management Association. He is the author of numerous journal articles on local government policymaking and American electoral politics and voting behavior. He was elected to the McLean County Board in 1998 and was re-elected in 2002 and 2006.

Michael Smith is assistant professor of political science at Emporia State University. He is the author of *Bringing Representation Home,* which examines state representatives' "home styles." He is also the author of several journal articles. He currently chairs the Faith and Democracy Task Force of More-Squared, the Kansas City affiliate of the Gamaliel Foundation. He is also active in local electoral politics.

Aaron Wicks earned a B.A. in government from Georgetown University in 1995 and a Ph.D. in political science from the University of Rochester in 2001. His research has focused on congressional leadership and legislative behavior. A lifelong resident of the Rochester, New York, area, Wicks has managed campaigns for local and state office and has provided political analysis on local radio programs. He currently copublishes a political news and commentary website dedicated to Rochester and New York state politics, called the Smugtown Beacon (www.SmugtownBeacon.com).

Index

About the Book

This guided tour of the inner workings of the election campaign process de-mystifies the often murky world of professional politics.

Offering a unique blend of theory and practice, *Inside Political Campaigns* draws on the experiences of political scientists who have played such key roles as campaign managers, consultants, media advisers, and even candidates. First-hand accounts of races run at the local, state, and national levels reveal the many complex facets of the modern electoral process. Highlighting lessons learned, the authors provide a unique introduction to both the study and the execution of political campaigns.

James R. Bowers is professor of political science at St. John Fisher College. His publications include *Governing Middle-Sized Cities: Studies in Mayoral Leadership* (coedited with Wilbur C. Rich). **Stephen Daniels** is research professor at the American Bar Foundation. He is coauthor (with James R. Bowers) of *Hypotheticals: Supreme Court Decision-Making and Constitutional Interpretation.*